Farmhouse & Country Plans

300
Fresh Designs
From Classic to Modern

HOME PLANNERS

Published by Home Planners, LLC

Wholly owned by Hanley-Wood, LLC

Editorial and Corporate Offices:

3275 West Ina Road, Suite 110

Tucson, Arizona 85741

Distribution Center:

29333 Lorie Lane

Wixom, Michigan 48393

Patricia Joseph, President

Jan Prideaux, Editor-In-Chief

Marian E. Haggard, Editor

Chester E. Hawkins, Graphic Designer

Tera Morriss, Graphic Production Artist

Photo Credits:

Front Cover: Plan HPT100159 MWS Photography, Scott Moore
Built by Michael Bates Homes, Knoxville, TN

Title Page: Plan HPT100010 Riley & Riley Photography, Inc.

Back Cover: Plan HPT100011 Raef Grohne Photography

10 9 8 7 6 5 4 3 2

Printed in the United States of America

Library of Congress Catalog Card Number: 00-107971

ISBN softcover: 1-881955-77-X

Table of Contents

The Plans

SITTING ON THE PORCH IN THE SUMMERTIME WITH A GLASS OF ICED TEA...

Family gatherings in the living room or country kitchen. The sound of a screen door slamming as a child runs outside to play. These are just a few things that come to mind when people talk about farmhouses.

But not all farmhouses are the same. In this collection, Home Planners presents eight variations on a theme, showcasing a variety of homes from Classic Farmhouses to Victorian-influenced abodes, from Plantation homes to petite cottages, and from European-inspired houses to the more recent Contemporary. Each variation is subtly different.

Usually tall and upright the Classic Farmhouse begins with a covered front porch or wrapping porch. This home is almost always two stories, or at least 1½ stories. This style has a straight-gabled roof that is commonly steeply pitched. Other exterior details include a prominent chimney at one or both ends of the home and paned, shuttered windows in a symmetrical fenestration.

Plains or Prairie-type farmhouses are recognizable by their low-slung, ground-hugging appearance (to shrug off prairie winds). Sometimes they're two stories, but most often 1½ stories. They almost always have a covered front porch that wraps around at least three sides to shield the house from the sun. The roof is the most obvious design element, with the entire structure of the home dominated by a roof that is double-pitched from gable to porch covering. Looking somewhat like a large hat, these roofs function as sun-deflectors in areas of the country known for warm, dry summer seasons.

Today's Plantation-style Farmhouse resembles the Prairie Farmhouse with its double-pitched, sprawling roofline; however, it is taller and more upright overall. The porches are grand, wrapping structures that are often raised to lift the house out of wet or soggy ground. The homes may be either 1½ or two stories, though most common examples are 1½ stories. Windows are strongly symmetrical and the second-story windows are dormers that protrude from the roof.

The Victorian Farmhouse today presents many of the same properties as the Classic Farmhouse—tall, upright proportions with wood siding and covered porches. However, the Victorian era influenced these rural homes by enhancing the plainness of Farmhouse style with detailing. Such detailing includes spindled railings and friezes, spiderweb decoration at gables, shingle scallops and cornice and dentil ornamentation.

European-inspired Farmhouses represent an adaptation of homes found in the countrysides of France, Germany and Holland. In general, these homes have a classic, upright two-story stature. They can be characterized most easily by their roof types. While most are straight and gabled, they may vary to hipped versions in the French style or gambreled (or double-pitched) in the Flemish and Dutch tradition. Special details in the windows include metal-clad French bows and dormers, Dutch dormers protruding from the roof, Greek stone or brick arches over windows and doors, and the classic Palladian-style window grouping.

Country Capes and Cottages are simple, economical homes with a New England Colonial heritage. They have roots in the down-to-earth shelters constructed by the early settlers which featured a basic, boxy design. The modern versions are also constructed in a simple box-like fashion, usually with horizontal siding and a steeply pitched gabled roof. The Country Cape may be updated with projecting dormers on the second floor and sun rooms to the rear. Many of these homes are designed to "grow" by the addition of winged appendages.

Though not formally a style of Farmhouse, the brick or stone exterior is a popular choice for just about any variation. Because of their solid-looking appearance, brick and stone are used as a statement of permanence, antiquity and heritage. One or both may serve as an accent or embellishment to other exterior sidings. These materials are easy to care for and retain their good looks and durability for may years.

In the Contemporary Farmhouse, design takes a classic 1½- or two-story farmhouse structure and modifies it with more rounded, open or vaulted forms. Wood, stone and glass are the major components of the style and afford it a modern look and ambience. The open floor plans usually contained in these homes allow for easy traffic patterns and great indoor/outdoor livability.

Filled with the spirit of the country life, this book brings together a combination of the "tried-and-true" styles with entirely new and exciting forms. Enjoy.

Featured Favorites

This home, as shown in the photograph, may differ from the actual blueprints. For more detailed information, please check the floor plans carefully.

Photo by Carl Socolow

SECOND FLOOR

FIRST FLOOR

QUOTE ONE®

Cost to build? See page 310 to order complete cost estimate to build this house in your area!

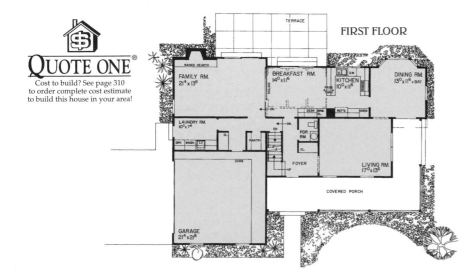

PLAN HPT100002

Here's a great farmhouse adaptation with all the most up-to-date features. The quiet corner living room opens to the sizable dining room. This room will enjoy plenty of natural light from the delightful bay window overlooking the rear yard and is conveniently located near the efficient U-shaped kitchen. The kitchen features many built-ins and a pass-through to the beam-ceilinged nook. Sliding glass doors to the terrace are found in both the family room and the nook. A clothes closet and a large walk-in pantry flank the service entrance to the garage. Pursue recreational activities and hobbies in the basement area. Four bedrooms and two baths are located on the second floor. The owners bedroom furnishes a dressing room and double vanities.

Total: 2,335 sq. ft.
First Floor: 1,366 sq. ft.
Second Floor: 969 sq. ft.
Bonus Room: 969 sq. ft.
Width: 59'-6" **Depth:** 46'-0"

L D

*This home, as shown in the photograph, may differ from the actual blueprints.
For more detailed information, please check the floor plans carefully.*

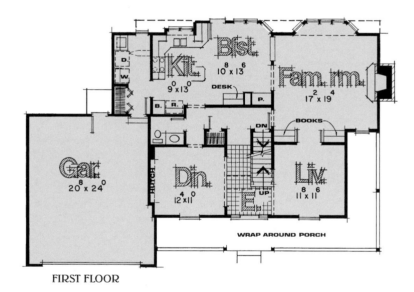

FIRST FLOOR

SECOND FLOOR

DESIGN BY
©**Design Basics, Inc.**

PLAN HPT100003

Total: 2,360 sq. ft.
First Floor: 1,188 sq. ft.
Second Floor: 1,172 sq. ft.
Width: 58'-0" **Depth:** 40'-0"

Beginning with the interest of a wraparound porch, there's a feeling of country charm in this two-story plan. Formal dining and living rooms, visible from the entry, offer ample space for gracious entertaining. The large family room is truly a place of warmth and welcome with its gorgeous bay window, fireplace and French doors to the living room. The kitchen, with an island counter, pantry and desk, makes cooking a delight. Upstairs, the secondary bedrooms share an efficient compartmented bath. The expansive owners suite possesses its own luxury bath with a double vanity, whirlpool tub, walk-in closet and dressing area.

This home, as shown in the photograph, may differ from the actual blueprints.
For more detailed information, please check the floor plans carefully.

Photo by Rafe Grohne Photography

DESIGN BY
©**Select Home Designs**

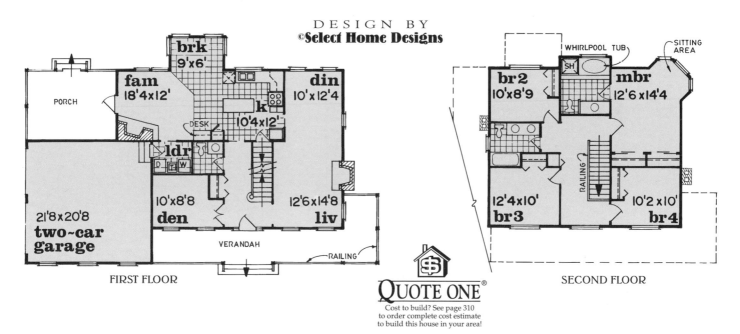

FIRST FLOOR

PORCH

fam
18'4x12'

brk
9'x6'

din
10'x12'4

k
10'4x12'

DESK

ldr
D W

two-car garage
21'8 x 20'8

den
10'8'8

liv
12'6x14'8

VERANDAH

RAILING

SECOND FLOOR

br2
10'x8'9

WHIRLPOOL TUB
SH

mbr
12'6x14'4

SITTING AREA

RAILING

br3
12'4x10'

br4
10'2 x10'

Quote One®
Cost to build? See page 310
to order complete cost estimate
to build this house in your area!

A covered railed veranda and shuttered windows decorate this deluxe farmhouse. Flanking the foyer are a den with a double-door entry and the living room/dining room combination with a fireplace. Enter the L-shaped kitchen from either the central hall or from an entry at the dining room. An island work counter and planning desk add to the kitchen's efficiency. A light-filled breakfast room serves casual meals. Sleeping quarters occupy the second floor. The owners bedroom presents two separate closets, a sitting area and a whirlpool tub. Three additional bedrooms have generous closet space and share a full hall bath.

PLAN HPT100004

Total: 2,094 sq. ft.
First Floor: 1,098 sq. ft.
Second Floor: 996 sq. ft.
Width: 62'-6" **Depth:** 40'-0"

DESIGN BY
©**Select Home Designs**

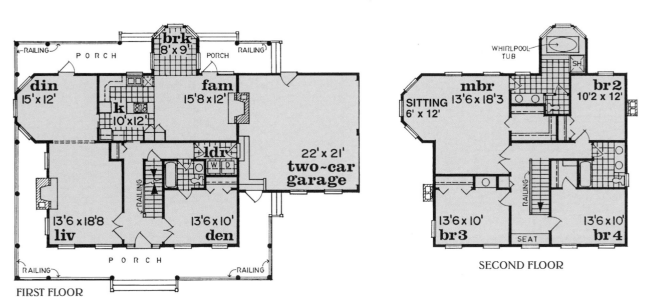

FIRST FLOOR

SECOND FLOOR

PLAN HPT100005

Total: 2,582 sq. ft.
First Floor: 1,291 sq. ft.
Second Floor: 1,291 sq. ft.
Width: 64'-6" **Depth:** 47'-0"

Traditional with an essence of farmhouse flavor, this four-bedroom home begins with a wraparound covered porch. The floor plan revolves around a central hall with a formal living room and dining room on the left and a private den on the right. The casual family room sits to the rear and is open to the bayed breakfast room and the L-shaped kitchen with an island work center. Hearths warm both the family room and the living room. Doors in the family room and the bayed dining room open to two rear porches. The owners suite on the second level has a bayed sitting room and a bath with a whirlpool tub and separate shower. Three family bedrooms share a full bath. Note the window seat on the landing.

FIRST FLOOR

MSTR. BATH
10 FT CLG

PORCH

MASTER BEDROOM
16'-4"x19'-0"
10 FT CLG

LIVING ROOM
17'-8"x16'-8"
10 FT CLG

DINING
15'-6"x12'-2"
10 FT CLG

KITCHEN
21'-4"x13'-0"
10 FT CLG

PAN

FAMILY ROOM
18'-6"x15'-2"
10 FT CLG

BREAKFAST
12'-8"x11'-6"
10 FT CLG

GARAGE
21'-6"x36'-6"

UTL.
10 FT CLG

PORCH

FOYER
2 STORY CLG

PWD.

BATH 2

BEDROOM 2
13'-4"x13'-4"
10 FT CLG

PORCH
10'-6" CLG

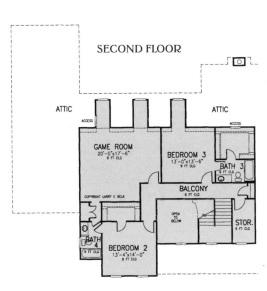

SECOND FLOOR

ATTIC

ATTIC

GAME ROOM
20'-0"x17'-6"
8 FT CLG

BEDROOM 3
13'-0"x13'-6"
9 FT CLG

BATH 3
9 FT CLG

BALCONY
9 FT CLG

COPYRIGHT LARRY E. BELK

OPEN TO BELOW

STOR.
9 FT CLG

BATH 4
9 FT CLG

BEDROOM 2
13'-4"x14'-0"
9 FT CLG

DESIGN BY
©**Larry E. Belk Designs**

Brick and fieldstone adorn this two-story, four-bedroom home. A wraparound covered porch offers shelter from the elements and ushers you into a two-story foyer. Arches and columns separate the formal living and dining rooms while the kitchen presents interesting angles and opens to the spacious family room via a snack bar. Note the direct access to the rear covered porch from the living room as well as from the family room. A secondary bedroom resides on the first floor and could be used as a guest suite or a cozy den. The owners suite is sure to please with its many amenities. Upstairs, two family bedrooms are complete with private baths and large walk-in closets. A game room finishes this floor.

PLAN HPT100006

Total: 4,250 sq. ft.
First Floor: 2,931 sq. ft.
Second Floor: 1,319 sq. ft.
Width: 103'-7" **Depth:** 63'-9"

Photo by Bob Greenspan

PLAN HPT100007

The decorative pillars and the wrap-around porch are just the beginning of this comfortable home. Inside, an angled, U-shaped stairway leads to the sleeping zone on the second-floor. On the first floor, French doors lead to a bay-windowed den that shares a see-through fireplace with the two-story family room. The large island kitchen includes a writing desk, corner sink, breakfast nook and access to the laundry room, powder room and two-car garage. Upstairs, the owners suite is a real treat with its French-door access, vaulted ceiling and luxurious bath. Two other bedrooms and a full bath complete the second floor.

Total: 2,287 sq. ft.
First Floor: 1,371 sq. ft.
Second Floor: 916 sq. ft.
Width: 43'-0" **Depth:** 69'-0"

QUOTE ONE®
Cost to build? See page 310
to order complete cost estimate
to build this house in your area!

SECOND FLOOR

BR. 3
10/6 X 13/0

PLANT SHELF

FAMILY BELOW

LINEN

DN.

BR. 2
12/4 X 11/0

VAULTED
MASTER
12/0 X 15/0 +

FIRST FLOOR

GARAGE
21/4 X 20/0

W. D.

NOOK
10/6 X 13/0
(9' CLG.)

REF.

10/6 X 13/0

FAMILY
15/0 X 16/4 +
(9' CLG.)

DESK

DINING
12/0 X 10/0
(9' CLG.)

UP

FOYER

LIVING
14/0 X 11/0 +/-
(9' CLG.)

DEN
14/0 X 10/0 +
(9' CLG.)

DESIGN BY
©Alan Mascord Design Associates, Inc.

SECOND FLOOR

3,90 X 4,30
13'-0" X 14'-4"

3,30 3,00
11'-0" X 10'-0"

3,60 X 3,30
12'-0" X 11'-0"

5,60 X 3,90
18'-8" X 13'-0"

4,00 X 3,30
13'-4" X 11'-0"

4,00 X 4,20
13'-4" X 14'-0"

3,60 X 4,00
12'-0" X 13'-4"

6,40 X 6,80
21'-4" X 22'-8"

FIRST FLOOR

DESIGN BY
©**Drummond Designs, Inc.**

PLAN HPT100008

Two covered porches will entice you outside, while inside a special sun room on the first floor brings the outdoors in. The foyer opens on the right to a comfortable family room that may be used as a home office. On the left, the living area is warmed by the sun room and a cozy, corner fireplace. A formal dining area lies adjacent to an efficient kitchen with a central island and breakfast nook overlooking the back porch. The second level holds two bedrooms served by a full bath. A spacious owners suite with a walk-in closet and luxurious bath completes the second floor. This home is designed with a basement foundation.

Total: 2,089 sq. ft.
First Floor: 1,146 sq. ft.
Second Floor: 943 sq. ft.
Bonus Room: 419 sq. ft.
Width: 56'-0" **Depth:** 38'-0"

*This home, as shown in the photograph, may differ from the actual blueprints.
For more detailed information, please check the floor plans carefully.*

FIRST FLOOR

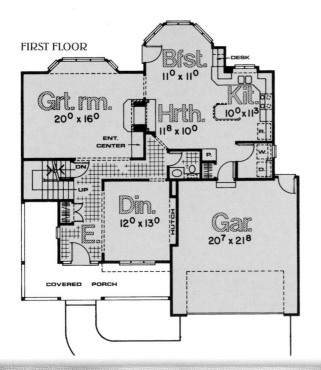

Bfst.
11⁰ x 11⁰

DESK

Grt. rm.
20⁰ x 16⁰

Kit.
10⁰ x 11³

Hrth.
11⁸ x 10⁰

ENT. CENTER

Din.
12⁰ x 13⁰

Gar.
20⁷ x 21⁸

COVERED PORCH

SECOND FLOOR

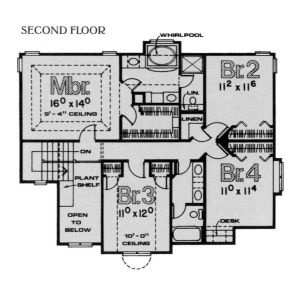

WHIRLPOOL

Mbr.
16⁰ x 14⁰
9'-4" CEILING

Br 2
11² x 11⁶

LIN.

LINEN

DN

PLANT SHELF

Br 3
11⁰ x 12⁰
10'-0" CEILING

Br 4
11⁰ x 11⁴

OPEN TO BELOW

DESK

DESIGN BY
©**Design Basics, Inc.**

PLAN HPT100009

Total: 2,270 sq. ft.
First Floor: 1,150 sq. ft.
Second Floor: 1,120 sq. ft.
Width: 46'-0" **Depth:** 48'-0"

Lap siding, special windows and a covered porch enhance the elevation of this popular style. The spacious two-story entry surveys the formal dining room with hutch space. An entertainment center, through-fireplace and bayed windows add appeal to the great room. Families will love the spacious kitchen with its breakfast and hearth rooms. Comfortable secondary bedrooms and a sumptuous owners suite feature privacy by design. Bedroom 3 is highlighted by a half-round window, volume ceiling and double closets, while Bedroom 4 features a built-in desk. The owners suite provides a vaulted ceiling, large walk-in closet, His and Hers vanities, and an oval whirlpool tub.

This home, as shown in the photograph, may differ from the actual blueprints.
For more detailed information, please check the floor plans carefully.

Photo by Riley & Riley Photography, Inc.

FIRST FLOOR

PORCH

MASTER BD. RM.
15-6 x 14-0

walk-in closet

FAMILY RM.
18-8 x 23-2
(two story ceiling)
fireplace
balcony above

BRKFST.
13-4 x 13-8

pd. rm.
cl

storage

lin.

master bath

walk-in closet

LIVING RM.
13-4 x 13-6

FOYER
8-8 x 10-2

cl

KIT.
13-4 x 12-0

pan.

up

DINING
13-4 x 13-6

UTIL.
6-10 x 10-0
w
d

up

GARAGE
21-8 x 28-4

PORCH

© 1996 Donald A. Gardner Architects, Inc.

SECOND FLOOR

family room below

railing

LOFT/ STUDY
8-8 x 10-2

BED RM.
13-4 x 11-10

attic storage

cl cl

lin.

skylights

walk-in closet

bath

shelves

walk-in closet

bath

down

down

down

BONUS RM.
21-8 x 16-5

BED RM.
13-4 x 12-2

railing

balcony

BED RM.
13-4 x 13-6

DESIGN BY
Donald A. Gardner Architects, Inc.

This beautiful farmhouse with its prominent twin gables and bays adds just the right amount of country style. The owners suite is quietly tucked away downstairs with no rooms directly above. The family cook will love the spacious U-shaped kitchen and adjoining bayed breakfast nook. A bonus room is easily accessible from the back stairs or from the second floor, where three large bedrooms share two full baths. Storage space abounds with walk-ins, half-shelves and linen closets. A curved balcony borders a versatile loft/study, which overlooks the stunning two-story family room.

PLAN HPT100010

Total: 3,163 sq. ft.
First Floor: 2,086 sq. ft.
Second Floor: 1,077 sq. ft.
Bonus Room: 403 sq. ft.
Width: 81'-10" **Depth:** 51'-8"

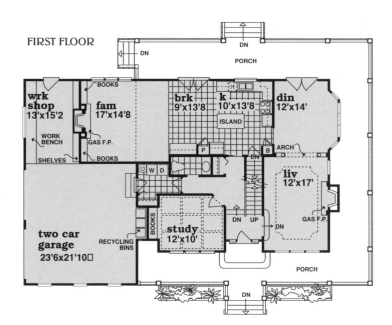

FIRST FLOOR

SECOND FLOOR

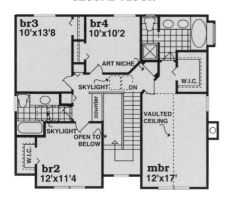

D E S I G N   B Y
©**Select Home Designs**

PLAN HPT100011

Total: 2,462 sq. ft.
First Floor: 1,333 sq. ft.
Second Floor: 1,129 sq. ft.
Width: 69'-8" **Depth:** 49'-0"

A large wraparound porch graces the exterior of this home and gives it great outdoor livability. The raised foyer spills into a hearth-warmed living room and to the bay-windowed dining room beyond. French doors open from the breakfast and dining rooms to the spacious porch. Built-ins surround another hearth in the family room. The front study is adorned by a beamed ceiling and also features built-ins. Three bedrooms and an owners suite are found on the second floor. The owners suite features a walk-in closet and a private bath. Don't miss the workshop area in the garage.

This home, as shown in the photograph, may differ from the actual blueprints. For more detailed information, please check the floor plans carefully.

Photo by Dave Dawson

DECK

SUN ROOM
12'-0" X 9'-0"

MASTER BATH

DECK

DESIGN BY
©Stephen Fuller, Inc.

KITCHEN
12'-0" X 16'-0"

BREAKFAST
12'-0" X 12'-0"

GREAT ROOM
17'-3" X 16'-0"

W.I.C.

MASTER SUITE
14'-0" X 16'-0"

LAUNDRY

PANTRY

DN.

2-CAR GARAGE
21'-6" X 21'-0"

DINING ROOM
13'-0" X 16'-6"

FOYER

UP

OPTION ROOM
LIVING
STUDY
GUEST BED
12'-0" X 13'-0"

COVERED PORCH

FIRST FLOOR

1/2 VAULT
OPEN TO BELOW

W.I.C.

BATH

BEDROOM NO. 4
14'-0" X 13'-0"

W.I.C.

W.I.C.

BEDROOM NO. 3
13'-0" X 13'-0"

DN.

OPEN TO
BELOW

BEDROOM NO. 2
13'-0" X 16'-9"

W.I.C.

BATH

UNFINISHED
STORAGE

SECOND FLOOR

QUOTE ONE®
Cost to build? See page 310
to order complete cost estimate
to build this house in your area!

The covered front porch of this home warmly welcomes family and visitors. To the right of the foyer is a versatile option room. On the other side is the formal dining room, located just across from the open great room—which also opens into the breakfast room. The kitchen includes a cooking island/breakfast bar. Adjacent to the breakfast room is the sun room. At the rear of the main level, the owners suite features a lavish bath loaded with amenities. Just off the bedroom is a private deck. Three additional bedrooms and two baths occupy the second level. This home is designed with a walkout basement foundation.

PLAN HPT100012

Total: 3,434 sq. ft.
First Floor: 2,199 sq. ft.
Second Floor: 1,235 sq. ft.
Bonus Room: 150 sq. ft.
Width: 62'-6" **Depth:** 54'-3"

PLAN HPT100013

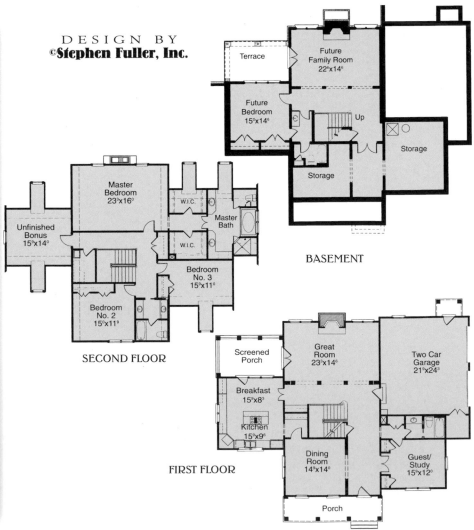

Only a sloping pediment above double front windows adorns this simple, country-style house, where a side-entry garage looks like a rambling addition. The wide porch signals a welcome that continues throughout the house. A front study doubles as a guest room with an adjacent full bath. A large dining room is ideal for entertaining and a sun-filled breakfast room off a spacious kitchen provides comfortable space for casual family meals. The open, contemporary interior plan flows from a stair hall at the heart of the house. On the private second floor, the owners bedroom includes a luxurious bath; two other bedrooms share a bath that includes dual vanities. An extra room over the kitchen makes a perfect children's play area. This home is designed with a walkout basement foundation.

Total: 3,232 sq. ft.
First Floor: 1,634 sq. ft.
Second Floor: 1,598 sq. ft.
Bonus Room: 273 sq. ft.
Width: 62'-0" **Depth:** 54'-9"

DESIGN BY
©**Stephen Fuller, Inc.**

BASEMENT

SECOND FLOOR

FIRST FLOOR

This home, as shown in the photograph, may differ from the actual blueprints. For more detailed information, please check the floor plans carefully.

Photo courtesy of American Home Gallery

QUOTE ONE®

Cost to build? See page 310 to order complete cost estimate to build this house in your area!

FIRST FLOOR

SECOND FLOOR

DESIGN BY
©**Stephen Fuller, Inc.**

The covered front stoop of this two-story, traditionally styled home gives way to the foyer and formal areas inside. A cozy living room with a fireplace sits on the right, and an elongated dining room is on the left. For fine family living, a great room and a kitchen/breakfast area account for the rear of the first-floor plan. A guest room with a nearby full bath finishes off the accommodations. Upstairs, four bedrooms include an owners suite fit for royalty. A bonus room rests near Bedroom 2 and would make a great office or additional bedroom. This home is designed with a walkout basement foundation.

PLAN HPT100014

Total: 3,285 sq. ft.
First Floor: 1,700 sq. ft.
Second Floor: 1,585 sq. ft.
Bonus Room: 176 sq. ft.
Width: 60'-0" **Depth:** 47'-6"

This home, as shown in the photograph, may differ from the actual blueprints. For more detailed information, please check the floor plans carefully.

DESIGN BY
©Stephen Fuller, Inc.

FIRST FLOOR

DECK

BREAKFAST
10'-6" X 11'-0"

KITCHEN
10'-4" X 15'-8"

GREAT ROOM
17'-10" X 16'-10"

MASTER BEDROOM
13'-4" X 18'-2"

MASTER BATH
12'-4" X 13'-6"

FOYER

DINING ROOM
12'-0" X 12'-3"

STUDY
11'-4" X 13'-5"

PORCH

LAUNDRY
10'-8" X 6'-0"

TWO CAR GARAGE
20'-4" X 24'-6"

SECOND FLOOR

BEDROOM NO. 2
10'-8" X 14'-0"

BEDROOM NO. 3
12'-0" X 12'-0"

BATH

BATH

BEDROOM NO. 4
11'-0" X 22'-0"

QUOTE ONE®
Cost to build? See page 310
to order complete cost estimate
to build this house in your area!

PLAN HPT100015

Total: 2,898 sq. ft.
First Floor: 1,944 sq. ft.
Second Floor: 954 sq. ft.
Width: 51'-6" **Depth:** 73'-0"

This gracious home combines warm informal materials with a modern, livable floor plan to create a true Southern classic. The dining room, study and great room work together to create one large, exciting space. Just beyond the open rail, the breakfast room is lined with windows. Plenty of counter space and storage make the kitchen truly usable. The owners suite, with its tray ceiling and decorative wall niche, is a welcome retreat. Upstairs, two additional bedrooms each have their own vanity within a shared bath, while the third bedroom or guest room includes its own bath and walk-in closet. This home is designed with a walkout basement foundation.

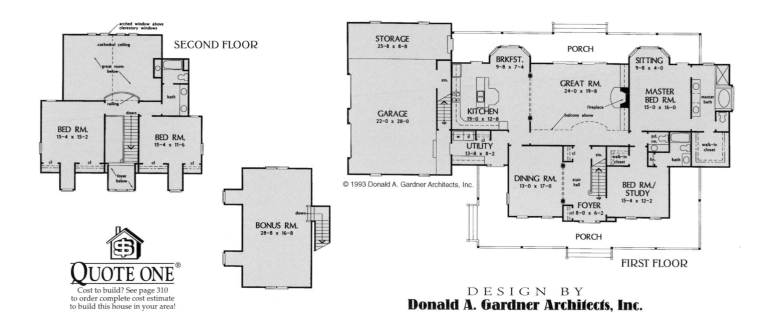

SECOND FLOOR

arched window above
clerestory windows

cathedral ceiling

great room
below

railing

great room below

bath

BED RM.
15-4 x 15-2

down

BED RM.
15-4 x 11-6

foyer
below

BONUS RM.
28-8 x 16-8

down

QUOTE ONE®
Cost to build? See page 310
to order complete cost estimate
to build this house in your area!

STORAGE
25-8 x 8-8

PORCH

BRKFST.
9-8 x 7-4

SITTING
9-8 x 4-0

GREAT RM.
24-0 x 19-8

MASTER
BED RM.
15-0 x 16-0

master
bath

GARAGE
22-0 x 28-0

KITCHEN
19-0 x 12-8

fireplace

balcony above

walk-in
closet

UTILITY
13-8 x 8-2

pd.
rm.

walk-in
closet

bath

lin.

DINING RM.
13-0 x 17-0

stair
hall

BED RM./
STUDY
15-4 x 12-2

FOYER
8-0 x 6-2

up

PORCH

FIRST FLOOR

© 1993 Donald A. Gardner Architects, Inc.

DESIGN BY
Donald A. Gardner Architects, Inc.

This gracious farmhouse with its wraparound porch offers a touch of symmetry in a well-defined, open plan. A Palladian clerestory window gives an abundance of natural light to the foyer. The vaulted great room furthers this feeling of airiness with a second-floor balcony above and two sets of sliding glass doors. The country kitchen, with an island countertop, the bayed breakfast nook and the dining room all enjoy nine-foot ceilings. Upstairs, each family bedroom has two closets. A full bath with a double-bowl vanity rests to one side of the hall. For privacy, the owners suite occupies the right side of the first floor. With a sitting room and all the amenities of a spa-style bath, this room won't fail to please.

PLAN HPT100016

Total: 3,037 sq. ft.
First Floor: 2,316 sq. ft.
Second Floor: 721 sq. ft.
Bonus Room: 545 sq. ft.
Width: 95'-4" **Depth:** 54'-10"

19

This home, as shown in the photograph, may differ from the actual blueprints. For more detailed information, please check the floor plans carefully.

PLAN HPT100017

The welcoming charm of this country farmhouse is expressed by its many windows and its covered, wraparound porch. A two-story entrance foyer is enhanced by a Palladian window in a clerestory dormer above to allow natural lighting. A first-floor owners suite allows privacy and accessibility. The owners bath includes a whirlpool tub, separate shower and double-bowl vanity along with a walk-in closet. The first floor features nine-foot ceilings throughout with the exception of the kitchen area, which features an eight-foot ceiling. The second floor provides two additional bedrooms, a full bath and plenty of storage space. A bonus room provides room to grow.

Total: 1,898 sq. ft.
First Floor: 1,356 sq. ft.
Second Floor: 542 sq. ft.
Bonus Room: 393 sq. ft.
Width: 59'-0" **Depth:** 64'-0"

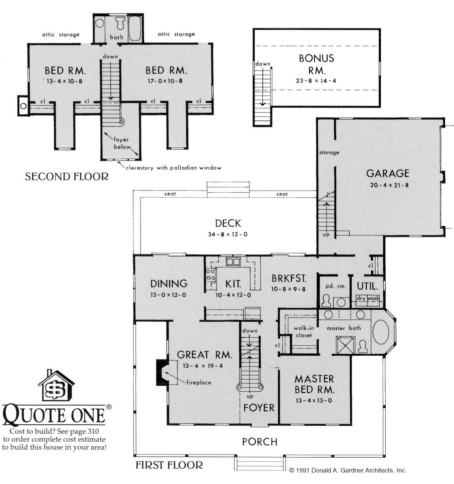

QUOTE ONE®
Cost to build? See page 310 to order complete cost estimate to build this house in your area!

SECOND FLOOR

FIRST FLOOR

© 1991 Donald A. Gardner Architects, Inc.

DESIGN BY
Donald A. Gardner Architects, Inc.

DESIGN BY
©**Michael E. Nelson,
Nelson Design Group, LLC**

SECOND FLOOR

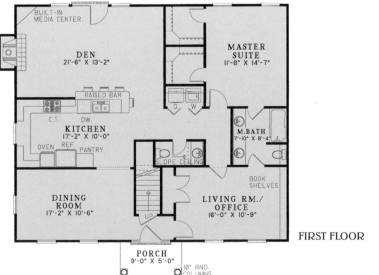

FIRST FLOOR

PLAN HPT100018

Traditional country dormers are dressed up with a Greek Revival porch on this two-story home. The formal areas are placed to the front of this design, with the dining area to left of the entry, and the living room/office—with built-in shelves!—to the right. Informal eating will be a breeze at the raised snack bar in the U-shaped kitchen. A warming fireplace and a built-in media center enhance the den, which accesses the rear yard. Privacy is the hallmark of the stunning owners suite, located on the first floor. Upstairs, walk-in closets adorn the two family bedrooms—which share a full bath. Please specify basement, crawlspace or slab foundation when ordering.

Total: 2,044 sq. ft.
First Floor: 1,400 sq. ft.
Second Floor: 644 sq. ft.
Width: 42'-4" **Depth:** 40'-0"

Photo by Stephanie Nelson

This home, as shown in the photograph, may differ from the actual blueprints.
For more detailed information, please check the floor plans carefully.

PLAN HPT100019

Four graceful columns support a long covered porch, topped by three attractive dormers. The two-story foyer is flanked by a formal dining room and a cozy study—or make it a guest suite with the full bath nearby. The island kitchen is sure to please with a walk-in pantry and easy access to the breakfast area. A spacious great room has a fireplace and a balcony overlook from the second floor. The owners suite boasts two walk-in closets, a whirlpool tub and a separate shower. Upstairs, three bedrooms—all with window seats—share a full hall bath. Please specify basement, crawlspace or slab foundation when ordering.

Total: 2,698 sq. ft.
First Floor: 1,813 sq. ft.
Second Floor: 885 sq. ft.
Width: 70'-2" **Depth:** 51'-4"

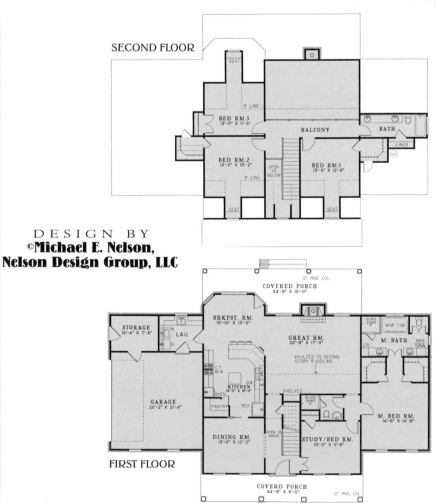

DESIGN BY
©**Michael E. Nelson,**
Nelson Design Group, LLC

This home, as shown in the photograph, may differ from the actual blueprints. For more detailed information, please check the floor plans carefully.

Photo by Riley & Riley Photography, Inc.

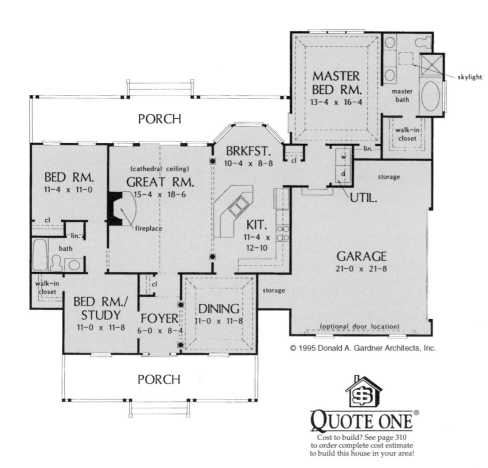

PORCH

BED RM.
11-4 x 11-0

(cathedral ceiling)
GREAT RM.
15-4 x 18-6

fireplace

cl

lin.

bath

walk-in closet

BED RM./
STUDY
11-0 x 11-8

FOYER
6-0 x 8-4

DINING
11-0 x 11-8

PORCH

MASTER
BED RM.
13-4 x 16-4

master bath

skylight

walk-in closet

lin.

BRKFST.
10-4 x 8-8

cl

w d

storage

UTIL.

KIT.
11-4 x 12-10

GARAGE
21-0 x 21-8

storage

(optional door location)

© 1995 Donald A. Gardner Architects, Inc.

Quote One®
Cost to build? See page 310
to order complete cost estimate
to build this house in your area!

DESIGN BY
Donald A. Gardner Architects, Inc.

PLAN HPT100020

This country home has a big heart in a cozy package. Special touches—interior columns, a bay window and dormers—add elegance. The central great room features a cathedral ceiling and a fireplace. A clerestory window splashes the room with natural light. The open kitchen easily services the breakfast area and the nearby dining room. The private owners suite, with a tray ceiling and a walk-in closet, boasts amenities found in much larger homes. The bath features skylights over the whirlpool tub. Two additional bedrooms share a bath. The front bedroom features a walk-in closet and would make a nice study with an optional foyer entrance.

Square Footage: 1,632
Width: 62'-4" **Depth:** 55'-2"

Photo by Riley & Riley Photography, Inc.

This home, as shown in the photograph, may differ from the actual blueprints. For more detailed information, please check the floor plans carefully.

PLAN HPT100021

The charm of this home is evident at first glance, but you'll especially appreciate its qualities the moment you step inside. The vaulted foyer ushers guests to the formal dining room and leads back to casual living space. A magnificent great room beckons with a cathedral ceiling and an extended-hearth fireplace, while sliding glass doors, framed by tall windows, provide access to the rear covered porch. The gourmet kitchen with an island counter enjoys sunlight from the nearby breakfast bay, and leads to a hall with rear-porch access. A first-floor owners suite features a tray ceiling and a skylit bath with a garden tub and a U-shaped walk-in closet. A sizable skylit bonus room above the garage awaits future development.

Square Footage: 1,832
Bonus Room: 425 sq. ft.
Width: 65'-4" **Depth:** 62'-0"

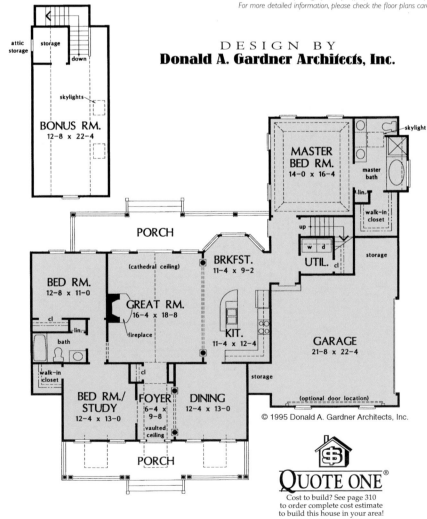

DESIGN BY
Donald A. Gardner Architects, Inc.

© 1995 Donald A. Gardner Architects, Inc.

Quote One®
Cost to build? See page 310
to order complete cost estimate
to build this house in your area!

This home, as shown in the photograph, may differ from the actual blueprints.
For more detailed information, please check the floor plans carefully.

Photo courtesy of Chatham Home Planning, Inc.

FIRST FLOOR

Deck   Breakfast

Dining
13' x 12'

Living
13' x 20'

Bedroom
12' x 15'

Porch

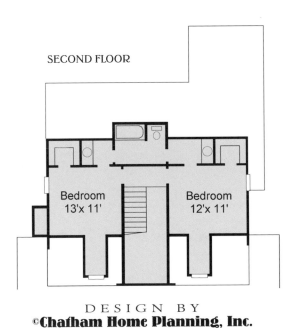

SECOND FLOOR

Bedroom
13' x 11'

Bedroom
12' x 11'

DESIGN BY
©Chatham Home Planning, Inc.

A relaxing full front porch rich with columns and an entry door with a transom and side-lights create the beginning of this heartwarming home. The entry leads to the formal dining area conveniently accessible to the galley kitchen through a butler's pantry. A break-fast nook, with access to the side yard, has a full view of the rear yard. Two doors that access the back deck frame the warming fireplace in the living room. The owners suite completes the first floor, with a luxurious bath and roomy walk-in closet. Away from the secluded owners suite, two family bedrooms with separate dressing rooms share a bath on the second level. Please specify crawlspace or slab foundation when ordering.

PLAN HPT100022

Total: 1,819 sq. ft.
First Floor: 1,242 sq. ft.
Second Floor: 577 sq. ft.
Width: 43'-0" **Depth:** 47'-0"

PLAN HPT100023

Comforting country charm is assured with this affordable three-bedroom home. Sit and watch the sunset on this relaxing front porch, or go inside for intimate conversation by the fireplace in the great room. A bay window in the dining area will adorn any meal with sun or moonlight. A spacious owners bedroom has a large walk-in closet and a full bath. Two secondary bedrooms share a full bath with the main living areas. A bonus room upstairs allows room for expansion later. Please specify basement, crawlspace or slab foundation when ordering.

Square Footage: 1,656
Bonus Room: 427 sq. ft.
Width: 52'-8" **Depth:** 54'-6"

DESIGN BY
©**Larry James & Associates, Inc.**

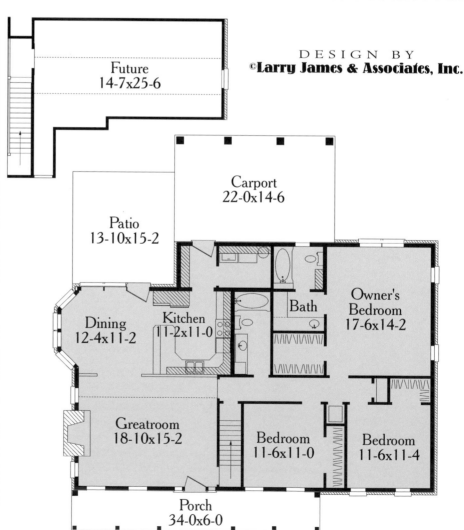

Future
14-7x25-6

Carport
22-0x14-6

Patio
13-10x15-2

Owner's
Bedroom
17-6x14-2

Bath

Dining
12-4x11-2

Kitchen
11-2x11-0

Greatroom
18-10x15-2

Bedroom
11-6x11-0

Bedroom
11-6x11-4

Porch
34-0x6-0

Porch

Keeping Room
10⁹x12⁰

Breakfast
10⁰x10⁹

Great Room
18⁹x21⁹

Master Bedroom
17⁶x16⁰

Kitchen
18⁶x10⁰

Bedroom No. 2
12⁰x13⁰

Dining Room
13³x13⁹

Foyer

Dn

Two Car Garage
21³x21³

Porch

Bedroom No. 3
12⁰x13³

DESIGN BY
©Stephen Fuller, Inc.

PLAN HPT100024

Country details brighten the exterior of this one-story design and grace it with a warmth and charm that says home. The floor plan includes a formal dining room and an all-purpose great room that opens to the kitchen and the keeping room. A bayed breakfast room is completely enclosed in glass. An owners suite—to the rear of the plan for privacy—holds access to the rear covered porch and sports an extra large walk-in closet and detailed bath. The family bedrooms share a full bath but each has its own lavatory. A two-car, side-load garage holds extra room for storage. This home is designed with a walkout basement foundation.

Square Footage: 2,796
Width: 70'-9" **Depth:** 66'-6"

27

PLAN HPT100025

Here's a country home that offers lots of down-home appeal but steps out with upscale style within. The grand foyer leads to a spacious great room with an extended-hearth fireplace and access to the rear covered porch. Open planning allows the windowed breakfast nook to enjoy the glow of the fireplace, while the secluded formal dining room has its own hearth. The owners suite offers private access to the rear covered porch, and a spacious bath that boasts two walk-in closets, twin vanities and a windowed, whirlpool tub. Two upstairs bedrooms share a full bath in the balcony hall, which leads to a bonus room with a walk-in closet.

Total: 2,887 sq. ft.
First Floor: 1,993 sq. ft.
Second Floor: 894 sq. ft.
Bonus Room: 176 sq. ft.
Width: 55'-0" **Depth:** 78'-6"

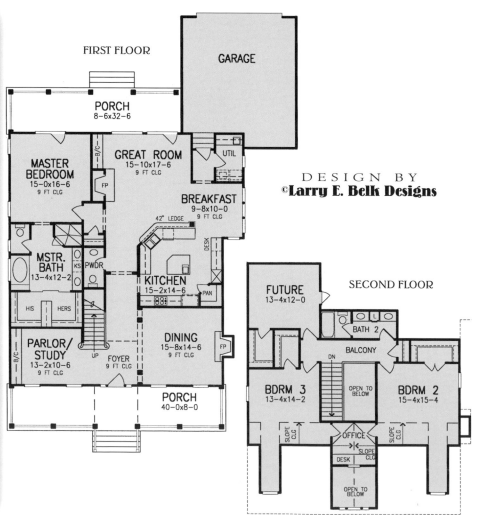

DESIGN BY
©**Larry E. Belk Designs**

28

This home, as shown in the photograph, may differ from the actual blueprints. For more detailed information, please check the floor plans carefully.

Photo by Riley & Riley Photography, Inc.

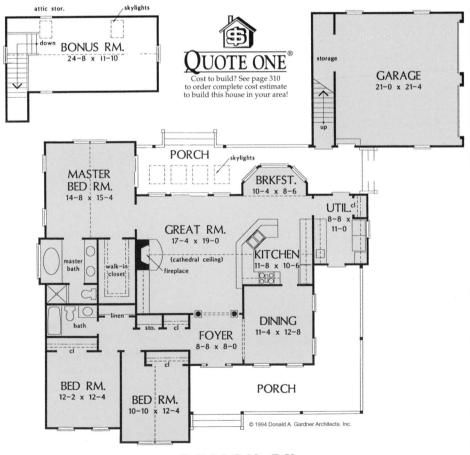

attic stor.   skylights

BONUS RM.
24-8 x 11-10

down

Quote One®

Cost to build? See page 310 to order complete cost estimate to build this house in your area!

storage

GARAGE
21-0 x 21-4

up

PORCH   skylights

MASTER BED RM.
14-8 x 15-4

BRKFST.
10-4 x 8-6

UTIL. cl
8-8 x 11-0

master bath

walk-in closet

GREAT RM.
17-4 x 19-0

(cathedral ceiling)

fireplace

KITCHEN
11-8 x 10-6

linen

bath

cl

BED RM.
12-2 x 12-4

sto.   cl

FOYER
8-8 x 8-0

DINING
11-4 x 12-8

cl

BED RM.
10-10 x 12-4

PORCH

© 1994 Donald A. Gardner Architects, Inc.

DESIGN BY
Donald A. Gardner Architects, Inc.

PLAN HPT100026

Dormers, arched windows and covered porches lend this home its country appeal. Inside, the foyer opens to the dining room on the right and leads through a columned entrance to the great room warmed by a fireplace. Access is provided to the covered, skylit rear porch for outdoor livability. The open kitchen easily serves the great room, the bayed breakfast area and the dining room. A cathedral ceiling graces the owners bedroom, which includes a walk-in closet and a private bath with a dual vanity and whirlpool tub. Two additional bedrooms share a full bath. A detached garage with a skylit bonus room connects to the covered rear porch.

Square Footage: 1,815
Bonus Room: 336 sq. ft.
Width: 70'-8"   **Depth:** 70'-2"

29

This home, as shown in the photograph, may differ from the actual blueprints.
For more detailed information, please check the floor plans carefully.

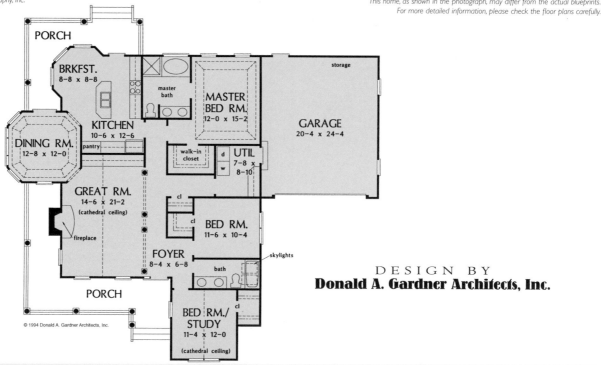

DESIGN BY
Donald A. Gardner Architects, Inc.

PLAN HPT100027

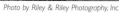

Square Footage: 1,737
Width: 65'-10" **Depth:** 59'-8"

Inviting porches are just the beginning of this lovely country home. To the left of the foyer, a columned entry supplies a classic touch to the spacious great room, which features a cathedral ceiling, built-in bookshelves and a fireplace that invites you to share its warmth. An octagonal dining room with a tray ceiling provides a perfect setting for formal occasions. The adjacent kitchen is designed to easily serve both formal and informal areas. It includes an island and a built-in pantry, with the sunny breakfast area just a step away. The owners bedroom is located in the rear of the plan—separated from the two family bedrooms—and offers privacy and comfort.

This home, as shown in the photograph, may differ from the actual blueprints.
For more detailed information, please check the floor plans carefully.

Photo by Andrew D. Lautman

DESIGN BY
©Home Planners

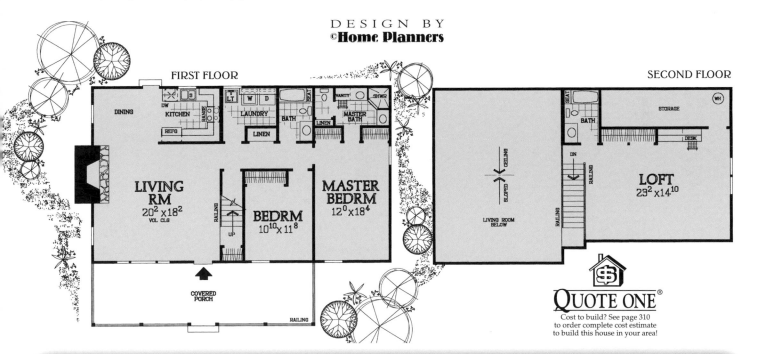

FIRST FLOOR

DINING

KITCHEN

DW

RANGE

REFG

LAUNDRY

LT W D

LINEN

BATH

LINEN

SEAT

VANITY

MASTER BATH

SHWR

LIVING RM
20²x18²
VOL CLG

RAILING

UP

BEDRM
10¹⁰x11⁸

MASTER BEDRM
12⁰x18⁴

COVERED PORCH

RAILING

SECOND FLOOR

SLOPED CEILING

LIVING ROOM BELOW

DN

RAILING

SEAT

BATH

STORAGE

DESK

WH

LOFT
23²x14¹⁰

QUOTE ONE®
Cost to build? See page 310
to order complete cost estimate
to build this house in your area!

Split-log siding and a rustic balustrade create country charm with this farmhouse-style retreat. An open living area features a natural stone fireplace and a cathedral ceiling with exposed rough-sawn beam and brackets. A generous kitchen and dining area complement the living room and share the warmth of its fireplace. An owners suite with a complete bath, and a nearby family bedroom with a hall bath complete the main floor. Upstairs, a spacious loft affords extra sleeping space—or provides a hobby/recreation area—and includes a full bath.

PLAN HPT100028

Total: 1,846 sq. ft.
First Floor: 1,356 sq. ft.
Second Floor: 490 sq. ft.
Width: 50'-7" **Depth:** 38'-0"

L·D

This home, as shown in the photograph, may differ from the actual blueprints. For more detailed information, please check the floor plans carefully.

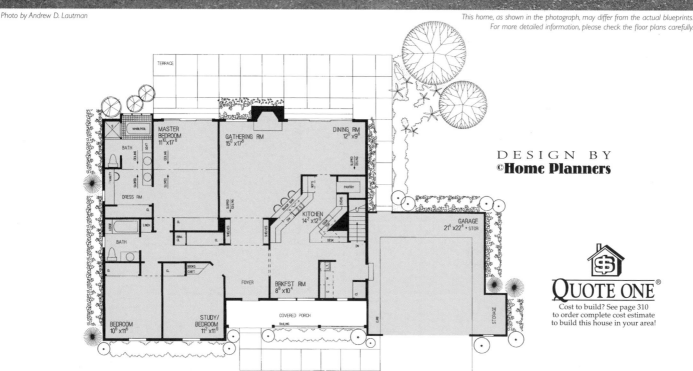

DESIGN BY
©**Home Planners**

QUOTE ONE®
Cost to build? See page 310
to order complete cost estimate
to build this house in your area!

PLAN HPT100029

Square Footage: 1,830
Width: 75'-0" **Depth:** 43'-5"

L·D

This charming one-story traditional home greets visitors with a covered porch. A uniquely shaped galley-style kitchen shares a snack bar with the spacious gathering room where a fireplace is the focal point. The dining room offers sliding glass doors to the rear terrace as does the owners suite. This bedroom area also includes a luxury bath with a whirlpool tub and separate dressing room. Two additional bedrooms, one that could double as a study, are located at the front of the home. The two-car garage features a large storage area and can be reached through the service entrance or from the rear terrace.

Classic Farmhouses

FIRST FLOOR

DESIGN BY
©**Home Design Services, Inc.**

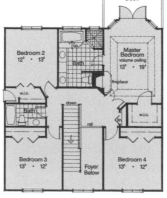

SECOND FLOOR

PLAN HPT100030

A wraparound porch, shutters, and sidelights by the double-door entrance lend this four-bedroom home comfort and charm. Inside, the foyer leads to the formal dining room on the left, and the living room to the right. Double doors connect the living room to the great room, sure to be a favorite with its warming fireplace and numerous windows. The U-shaped kitchen features a pass-through window to the rear covered porch—great for entertaining outside. Light pours in from the breakfast-nook bay windows. The second floor holds an owners suite adorned with a tray ceiling, a bay window with access to the private deck, a cozy fireplace, a roomy walk-in closet and a lavish bath. Bedrooms 2, 3, and 4 upstairs share a full bath.

Total: 2,594 sq. ft.
First Floor: 1,267 sq. ft.
Second Floor: 1,327 sq. ft.
Width: 58'-8"   **Depth:** 38'-0"

FIRST FLOOR

SECOND FLOOR

DESIGN BY
©**Home Planners**

QUOTE ONE®
Cost to build? See page 310
to order complete cost estimate
to build this house in your area!

PLAN HPT100031

Total: 2,580 sq. ft.
First Floor: 1,427 sq. ft.
Second Floor: 1,153 sq. ft.
Width: 70'-0" **Depth:** 34'-0"

L·D

This Early American home offers plenty of modern comfort with the covered front porch with pillars and rails, the double chimneys and spacious rooms. A step-down family room features a fireplace, as does the formal living room. The country kitchen offers plenty of counter space and storage with an added broom room and storage closet. Upstairs, three family bedrooms share a full hall bath. The owners suite is complete with a dual vanity and a compartmented bath with a dressing room and a walk-in closet. Special features of this home include a laundry/sewing room with freezer and washer/dryer space, a large rear terrace and an entry-hall powder room.

FIRST FLOOR

SECOND FLOOR

Quote One®
Cost to build? See page 310
to order complete cost estimate
to build this house in your area!

DESIGN BY
©Design Basics, Inc.

Here's the luxury you've been looking for—from the wraparound covered front porch to the bright sun room off the breakfast room. A sunken family room with a fireplace serves everyday casual gatherings while the more formal living and dining rooms are reserved for special entertaining situations. The kitchen provides a central island with a snack bar and is located most conveniently for serving and cleaning up. The breakfast area and adjacent sun room are sure to let in the sunshine for a pleasant breakfast. Upstairs, the lovely owners suite contains French doors into the bath and a whirlpool tub with a dramatic bay window. A double vanity in the shared bath serves the three family bedrooms.

PLAN HPT100032

Total: 2,594 sq. ft.
First Floor: 1,322 sq. ft.
Second Floor: 1,272 sq. ft.
Width: 56'-0" **Depth:** 48'-0"

PLAN HPT100033

French doors to the kitchen and a U-shaped stairway highlight the entry of this traditional country elevation. Large cased openings define both the great room and the dining room without restricting any space. The U-shaped kitchen and the adjoining breakfast area provide functional access to the utility room, garage, powder room and the side and rear yards. A workbench and extra storage space are available in the garage. Upstairs, secondary bedrooms share a generous compartmented bath that includes two sinks. The stately owners suite features dual walk-in closets, a nine-foot box ceiling and a whirlpool tub. This design embraces the classic features of the farmhouses from the past.

Total: 1,700 sq. ft.
First Floor: 904 sq. ft.
Second Floor: 796 sq. ft.
Width: 46'-0" **Depth:** 41'-4"

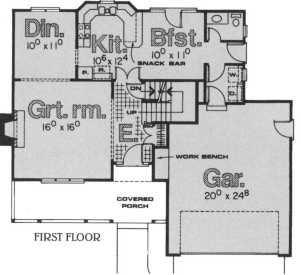

FIRST FLOOR

DESIGN BY
©**Design Basics, Inc.**

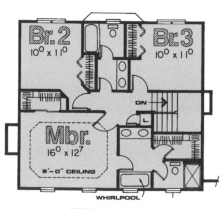

SECOND FLOOR

36

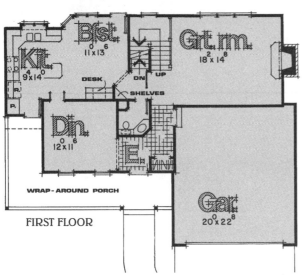

Bfst. 11x13

Kit. 9x14

Grt. rm. 18x14

DESK

SHELVES

UP

DN

Dn. 12x11

Gar. 20x22

WRAP-AROUND PORCH

FIRST FLOOR

DESIGN BY
©**Design Basics, Inc.**

Br. 12x10

Mbr. 15x13

DN

Br. 11x11

Br. 11x11

LIN.

WHIRL POOL

SECOND FLOOR

PLAN HPT100034

If you've ever dreamed of living in the country, you'll love the wrapping porch on this four-bedroom, two-story home. Comfortable living begins in the great room with windows, a fireplace and nearby staircase. Just off the entry, a formal dining room was designed to make entertaining a pleasure. The large kitchen includes a pantry, island counter, roll-top desk and lazy Susan. Don't miss the bright dinette. Upstairs, secondary bedrooms share a centrally located bath that includes a double vanity. Double doors access the deluxe owners bedroom. In the owners bath, special features include the whirlpool tub, transom window and sloped ceiling. The utility room is favorable for its convenient location near the bedrooms.

Total: 2,090 sq. ft.
First Floor: 927 sq. ft.
Second Floor: 1,163 sq. ft.
Width: 48'-0" **Depth:** 38'-0"

37

PLAN HPT100035

This masterfully affordable farmhouse manages to include all the basics—then adds a little more. Note the wrap-around covered porch, the large family room with a raised-hearth fireplace and wet bar, the spacious kitchen with an island cooktop, the formal dining room and the rear terrace. Upstairs, the plan is as flexible as they come: three or four bedrooms (the fourth could easily be a study or playroom) and plenty of unfinished attic space just waiting to be transformed into living space. This area would make a fine sewing room, home office or children's playroom. Special amenities make this home a standout from others in its class. Don't miss the built-ins such as the sliding glass doors, the terrace, and the wealth of closets and storage space.

Total: 2,615 sq. ft.
First Floor: 1,644 sq. ft.
Second Floor: 971 sq. ft.
Bonus Room: 971 sq. ft.
Width: 59'-8" **Depth:** 56'-0"

OPTIONAL ATTIC

SECOND FLOOR

Quote One®
Cost to build? See page 310
to order complete cost estimate
to build this house in your area!

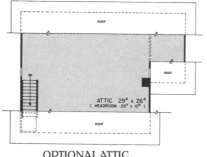

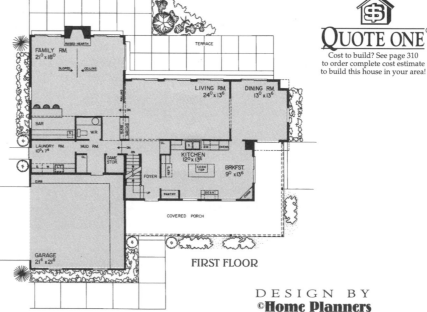

FIRST FLOOR

DESIGN BY
©**Home Planners**

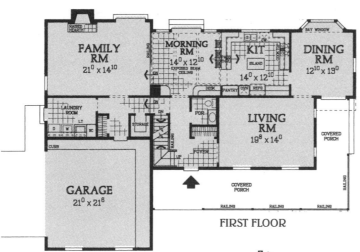

FIRST FLOOR

FAMILY RM
21⁰ x 14¹⁰

MORNING RM
14⁰ x 12¹⁰

KIT
14⁰ x 12¹⁰

DINING RM
12¹⁰ x 13⁰

LAUNDRY ROOM

LIVING RM
19⁸ x 14⁰

COVERED PORCH

FOYER

GARAGE
21⁰ x 21⁶

COVERED PORCH

Quote One®

Cost to build? See page 310
to order complete cost estimate
to build this house in your area!

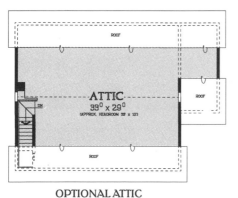

ATTIC
39⁰ x 29⁰
(APPROX. HEADROOM 39' x 12')

OPTIONAL ATTIC

DESIGN BY
©**Home Planners**

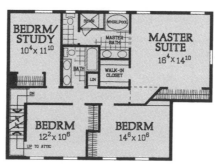

BEDRM/STUDY
10⁴ x 11¹⁰

MASTER BATH

MASTER SUITE
18⁴ x 14¹⁰

WALK-IN CLOSET

BEDRM
12² x 10⁸

BEDRM
14⁶ x 10⁶

SECOND FLOOR

PLAN **HPT100036**

Horizontal clapboard siding, varying roof planes and finely detailed window treatments set a delightful tone for this farmhouse favorite. A tiled foyer leads past a convenient powder room to a spacious central morning room with an exposed beam ceiling and a wide door to the entertainment terrace. The U-shaped island kitchen serves the formal dining room, which enjoys a bay window and leads to an expansive living room. A family room with a raised hearth is located to the rear of the two-car garage. Upstairs, a gallery hall connects the owners suite, three family bedrooms and a hall bath. The vast attic provides storage space.

Total: 2,707 sq. ft.
First Floor: 1,595 sq. ft.
Second Floor: 1,112 sq. ft.
Width: 63'-6" **Depth:** 48'-0"

L·D

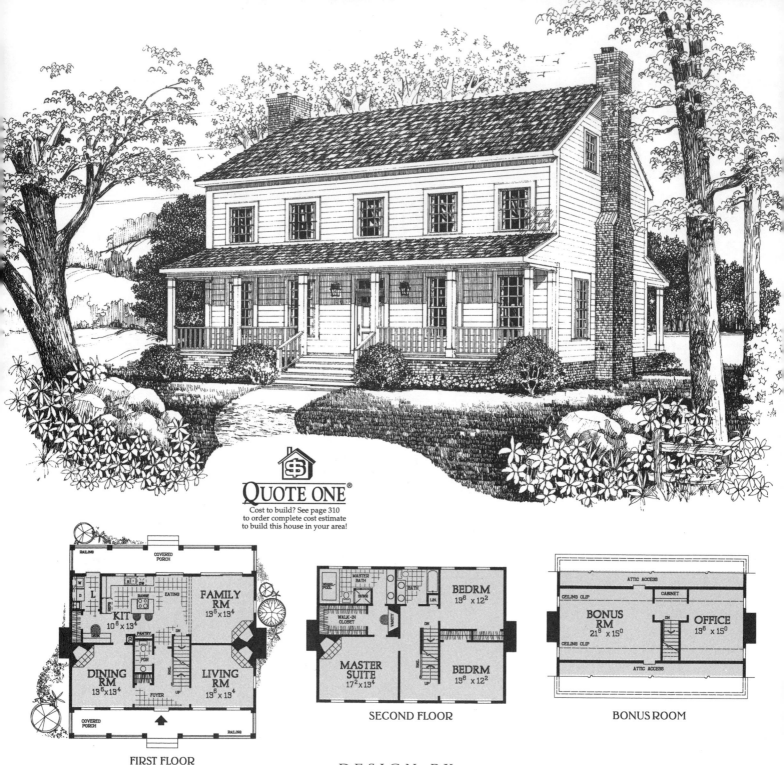

Quote One®

Cost to build? See page 310
to order complete cost estimate
to build this house in your area!

FIRST FLOOR

SECOND FLOOR

BONUS ROOM

DESIGN BY
©**Home Planners**

PLAN HPT100037

Total: 2,203 sq. ft.
First Floor: 1,120 sq. ft.
Second Floor: 1,083 sq. ft.
Bonus Space: 597 sq. ft.
Width: 40'-0" **Depth:** 40'-0"

Sweeping front and rear raised covered porches, delicately detailed railings and an abundance of fireplaces give this farmhouse its character. Designed to accommodate a relatively narrow building site, the efficient floor plan delivers outstanding livability for the active family. Both the formal living and dining rooms have corner fireplaces, as does the family room. The large tiled country kitchen furnishes an abundance of work space, a planning desk and easy access to the utility room. On the second floor, the charming owners retreat contains yet another fireplace. An expansive bathing and dressing suite includes a huge walk-in closet, whirlpool tub, double sinks and separate vanity.

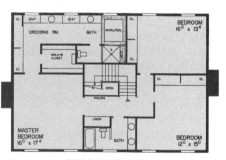

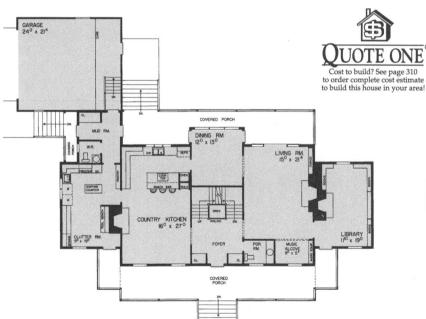

FIRST FLOOR

SECOND FLOOR

DESIGN BY
©Home Planners

QUOTE ONE®
Cost to build? See page 310
to order complete cost estimate
to build this house in your area!

This two-story design faithfully recalls the 18th-Century homestead of Secretary of Foreign Affairs John Jay. First-floor livability includes a grand living room with a fireplace and a music alcove. Adjacent to the living room, the library features a second fireplace; the third fireplace resides in the splendid country kitchen with a cooktop island and snack bar. Providing convenience, an enormous utility room provides a sorting counter. The owners suite consists of a whirlpool tub and a shower, a spacious dressing area, vanity seating and double sinks. Each of the family bedrooms contains a double closet; a full bath with dual sinks is shared by the two additional bedrooms.

PLAN HPT100038

Total: 3,412 sq. ft.
First Floor: 2,026 sq. ft.
Second Floor: 1,386 sq. ft.
Width: 84'-0" **Depth:** 65'-8"

L

PLAN HPT100039

From its covered front porch to its covered rear porch, this farmhouse is a real charmer. The formal dining room is filled with light from a bay window and directly accesses the efficient kitchen. A matching bay is found in the cozy breakfast room. The large great room is graced with a warming fireplace and even more windows. An L-shaped staircase leads up to the sleeping zone containing two family bedrooms that share a full bath. Within the owners suite, a private bath is filled with an array of luxuries. A bonus room extending over the garage can be developed into a game room, a fourth bedroom or a study at a later date.

Total: 1,792 sq. ft.
First Floor: 959 sq. ft.
Second Floor: 833 sq. ft.
Bonus Room: 344 sq. ft.
Width: 52'-6" **Depth:** 42'-8"

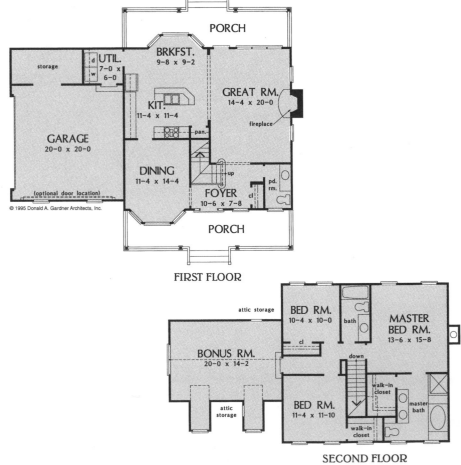

FIRST FLOOR

SECOND FLOOR

DESIGN BY
Donald A. Gardner Architects, Inc.

42

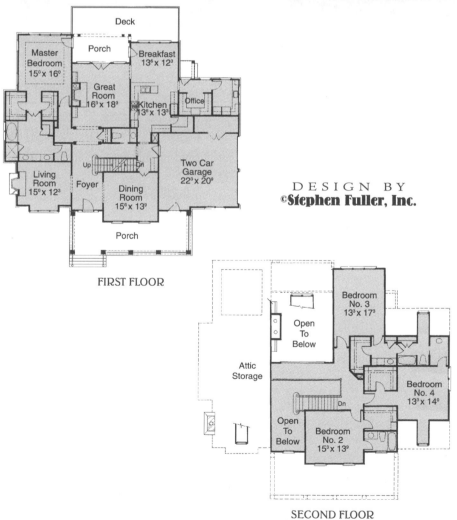

FIRST FLOOR

DESIGN BY
©Stephen Fuller, Inc.

SECOND FLOOR

PLAN HPT100040

This Colonial farmhouse inspires a sense of history, but is built to be cherished for generations to come. Inside, a two-story foyer opens to a quiet living room with a focal-point fireplace. The L-shaped kitchen overlooks a bright breakfast area with triple-window views and access to the covered rear porch and deck. A cathedral ceiling soars above the great room, which enjoys a warming hearth. The owners suite with an oversized private bath nestles to the rear of the plan. A balcony hall on the second floor joins three family bedrooms—Bedroom 2 includes a private bath, while Bedrooms 3 and 4 share a full bath. This home is designed with a walkout basement foundation.

Total: 3,743 sq. ft.
First Floor: 2,421 sq. ft.
Second Floor: 1,322 sq. ft.
Width: 66'-9" **Depth:** 63'-0"

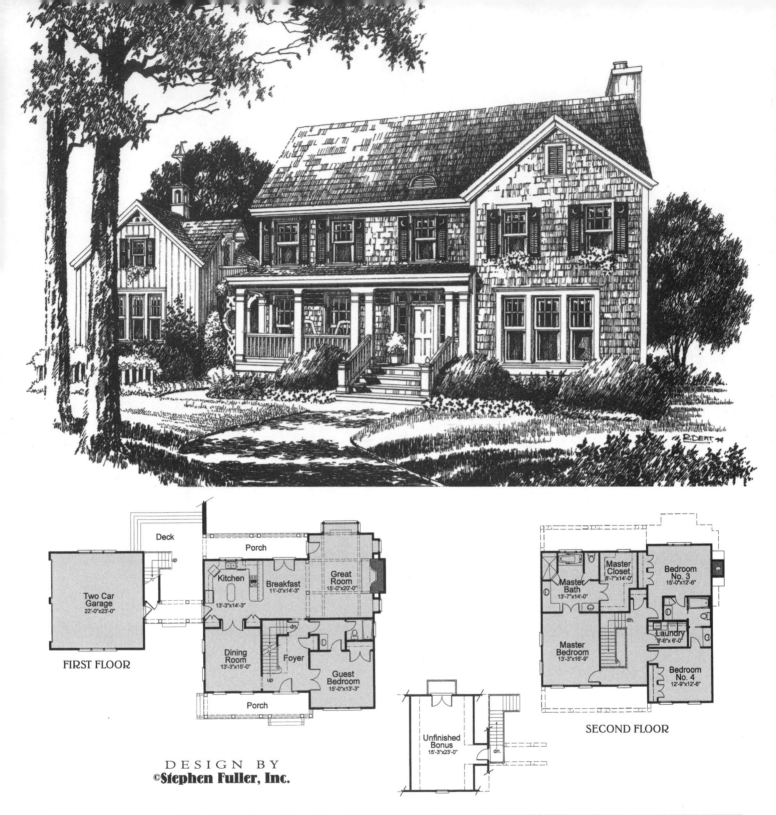

FIRST FLOOR

Two Car
Garage
22'-0"x23'-0"

Deck

Porch

Kitchen
13'-3"x14'-3"

Breakfast
11'-0"x14'-3"

Great
Room
15'-0"x20'-0"

Dining
Room
13'-3"x15'-0"

Foyer

Guest
Bedroom
15'-0"x13'-3"

Porch

DESIGN BY
©Stephen Fuller, Inc.

Unfinished
Bonus
15'-3"x23'-0"

SECOND FLOOR

Master
Bath
13'-7"x14'-0"

Master
Closet
8'-7"x14'-0"

Bedroom
No. 3
15'-0"x12'-6"

Master
Bedroom
13'-3"x16'-9"

Laundry
9'-8"x 6'-0"

Bedroom
No. 4
12'-9"x12'-6"

PLAN HPT100041

Total: 2,902 sq. ft.
First Floor: 1,578 sq. ft.
Second Floor: 1,324 sq. ft.
Bonus Room: 352 sq. ft.
Width: 76'-0" **Depth:** 77'-9"

Shingles, shutters and vertical siding lend country cottage appeal to this home. The foyer leads to family living space, featuring a great room with a spider-beam ceiling, a bumped-out bay window and a focal-point fireplace. Also near the foyer, the guest bedroom enjoys a compartmented vanity and a full bath. Double doors join the formal dining room to the efficient U-shaped kitchen with an island workstation. The breakfast nook has French doors opening to the rear covered porch—perfect for an indoor/outdoor tea party. Upstairs, an L-shaped hall connects the owners suite and the two family bedrooms that share a full compartmented bath. This home is designed with a basement foundation.

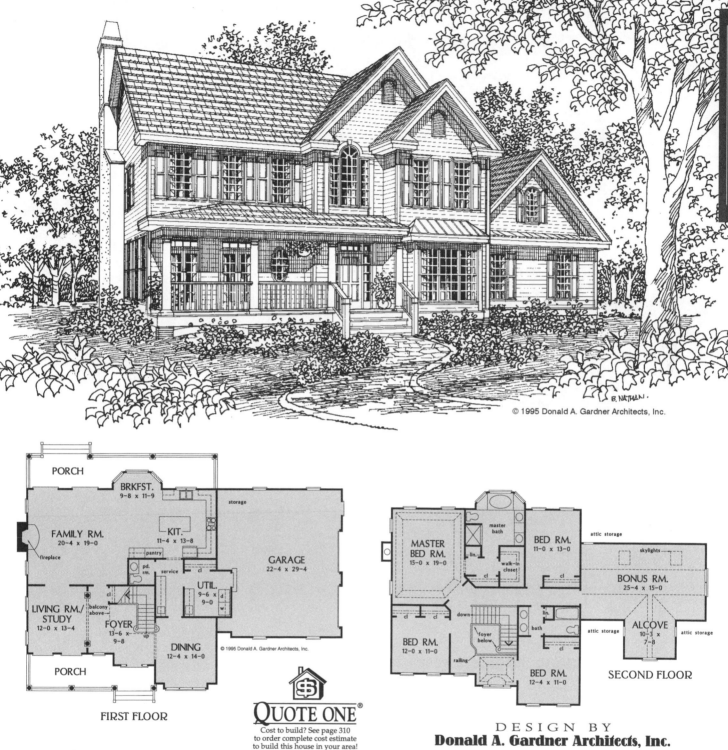

© 1995 Donald A. Gardner Architects, Inc.

FIRST FLOOR

PORCH

BRKFST.
9-8 x 11-9

storage

FAMILY RM.
20-4 x 19-0

KIT.
11-4 x 13-8

fireplace

pantry

GARAGE
22-4 x 29-4

pd. rm.

service

cl

LIVING RM./
STUDY
12-0 x 13-4

balcony above

cl

UTIL.
9-6 x 9-0

d w

FOYER
13-6 x 9-8

up

DINING
12-4 x 14-0

PORCH

© 1995 Donald A. Gardner Architects, Inc.

SECOND FLOOR

master bath

MASTER
BED RM.
15-0 x 19-0

lin.

walk-in closet

cl

BED RM.
11-0 x 13-0

attic storage

skylights

cl

BONUS RM.
25-4 x 15-0

cl

cl

down

lin.

bath

BED RM.
12-0 x 11-0

foyer below

cl

attic storage

ALCOVE
10-3 x 7-8

attic storage

railing

BED RM.
12-4 x 11-0

Quote One®
Cost to build? See page 310
to order complete cost estimate
to build this house in your area!

DESIGN BY
Donald A. Gardner Architects, Inc.

With two covered porches to encourage outdoor living, multi-pane windows and an open layout, this farmhouse has plenty to offer. Columns define the living room/study area. A fireplace accents the family room, which accesses the rear porch. An adjacent sunny bayed breakfast room is convenient to the oversized island kitchen. Between the kitchen and dining room, an efficient service area allows meals to be easily served in the dining room. Four bedrooms upstairs include a deluxe owners suite with a lush bath, walk-in closet and linen closet. Three family bedrooms have plenty of storage space and share a full hall bath. The bonus room has an alcove and still plenty of attic storage remains!

PLAN HPT100042

Total: 2,832 sq. ft.
First Floor: 1,483 sq. ft.
Second Floor: 1,349 sq. ft.
Bonus Room: 486 sq. ft.
Width: 66'-10" **Depth:** 47'-8"

FIRST FLOOR

SECOND FLOOR

DESIGN BY
©**Stephen Fuller, Inc.**

PLAN HPT100043

Total: 3,159 sq. ft.

First Floor: 1,613 sq. ft.

Second Floor: 1,546 sq. ft.

Width: 69'-0" **Depth:** 57'-0"

This new design wears the ageless appeal of classic country style, but gives it a fresh face. A low-pitched roof complements the columns and balusters of the front covered porch and creates a sense of shelter. Formal areas are secluded to one side of the plan, while the family room, gourmet kitchen and sunny breakfast area enjoy open interior space and views to the rear property. A plush owners suite on the second floor boasts a windowed whirlpool tub and twin lavatories. Each of two family bedrooms enjoys private access to a shared bath, while a fourth bedroom offers its own full bath. This home is designed with a walkout basement foundation.

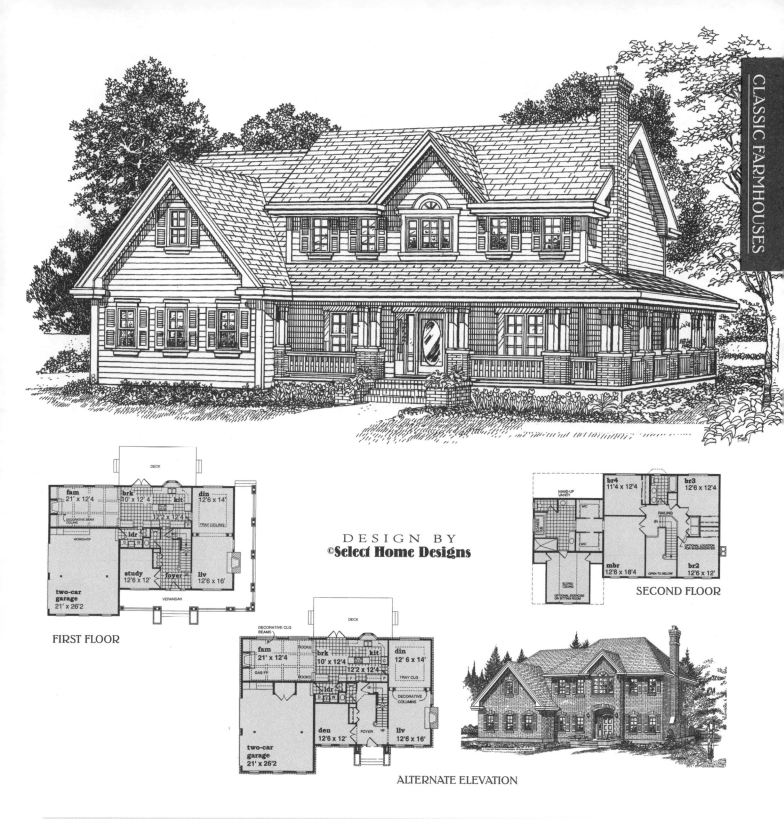

DESIGN BY
©Select Home Designs

FIRST FLOOR

SECOND FLOOR

ALTERNATE ELEVATION

Choose from one of two exteriors for this grand design—a lovely wood-sided farmhouse or a stately brick traditional. Plans include details for both facades. Special moldings and trim add interest to the nine-foot ceilings on the first floor. The dining room features a tray ceiling and is separated from the hearth-warmed living room by decorative columns. A study is secluded behind double doors just off the entry. The centrally located kitchen features a large cooking island, pantry, telephone desk and ample cupboard and counter space. The private owners bedroom possesses a most exquisite bath with His and Hers walk-in closets, a soaking tub, separate shower, make-up vanity and an optional exercise/sitting room.

PLAN HPT100044

Total: 2,858 sq. ft.
First Floor: 1,439 sq. ft.
Second Floor: 1,419 sq. ft.
Bonus Room: 241 sq. ft.
Width: 63'-10" **Depth:** 40'-4"

PLAN HPT100045

Established tradition meets new style with this country exterior—an old-fashioned covered porch complements sunbursts and asymmetrical gables. The tiled entry leads to a formal dining room or parlor and to casual living space, which includes a centered fireplace and views through three windows to the rear property. An L-shaped kitchen offers a snack bar, wide wrapping counters and a breakfast area with doors to the patio. A second-floor owners suite hosts a roomy walk-in closet, windowed whirlpool tub, compartmented toilet and double-bowl vanity. A nearby secondary bedroom, with a window seat and an ample wardrobe, could be used as a study. Two additional bedrooms share a full bath.

Total: 1,771 sq. ft.
First Floor: 866 sq. ft.
Second Floor: 905 sq. ft.
Width: 39'-4" **Depth:** 46'-0"

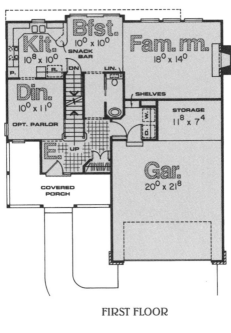

FIRST FLOOR

DESIGN BY
©Design Basics, Inc.

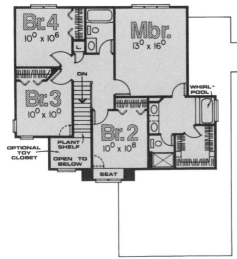

SECOND FLOOR

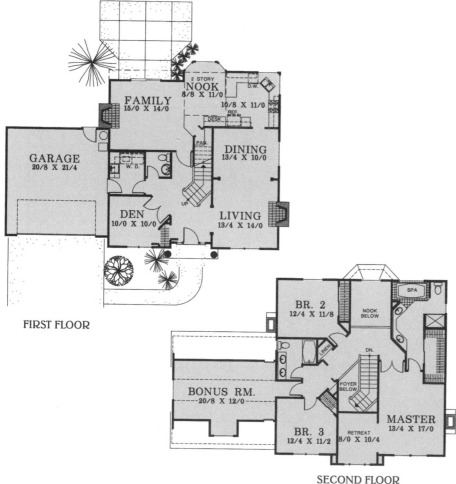

FIRST FLOOR

FAMILY
15/0 X 14/0

NOOK
8/8 X 11/0

2 STORY

10/8 X 11/0

DESK

GARAGE
20/8 X 21/4

DINING
13/4 X 10/0

PAN.

W. D.

UP

DEN
10/0 X 10/0

LIVING
13/4 X 14/0

SECOND FLOOR

BR. 2
12/4 X 11/8

NOOK
BELOW

SPA

LINEN

DN.

BONUS RM.
20/8 X 12/0

FOYER
BELOW

BR. 3
12/4 X 11/2

RETREAT
8/0 X 10/4

MASTER
13/4 X 17/0

DESIGN BY
©**Alan Mascord Design Associates, Inc.**

PLAN HPT100046

This gracious home integrates timeless traditional styling with a functional, cost-effective plan. An interesting feature is the two-story nook area with a bay window, and a desk, set between the gourmet kitchen and the large family room. Warming fireplaces occupy both the family room and living area. Across from the bottom of the staircase sits a den with French doors. Rounding out the upper floor, a sumptuous owners suite makes its own private retreat over the entry with an enormous bath that contains a spa and separate shower. Two bedrooms share a full bath that includes dual sinks. A conveniently located door in the upper hallway opens to the large bonus room over the two-car garage.

Total: 2,356 sq. ft.
First Floor: 1,236 sq. ft.
Second Floor: 1,120 sq. ft.
Bonus Room: 270 sq. ft.
Width: 56'-0" **Depth:** 38'-0"

FIRST FLOOR

SECOND FLOOR

DESIGN BY
©**Design Basics, Inc.**

PLAN HPT100047

Total: 2,071 sq. ft.
First Floor: 1,096 sq. ft.
Second Floor: 975 sq. ft.
Width: 54'-0" **Depth:** 40'-8"

The term "Country Charm" perfectly describes this delightful three-bedroom home. Create a very large great room or place a strategically located wall to provide a living room toward the front. The dining room features extra hutch space. The roomy kitchen is complete with a large island counter/snack bar, a pantry and a desk. The gazebo-shaped breakfast room shares a through-fireplace with the great room. The three-bedroom second floor includes an owners suite that boasts an eye-catching arched transom window and a bath with a whirlpool tub and separate vanities with sinks. The two additional bedrooms each contain double closet doors.

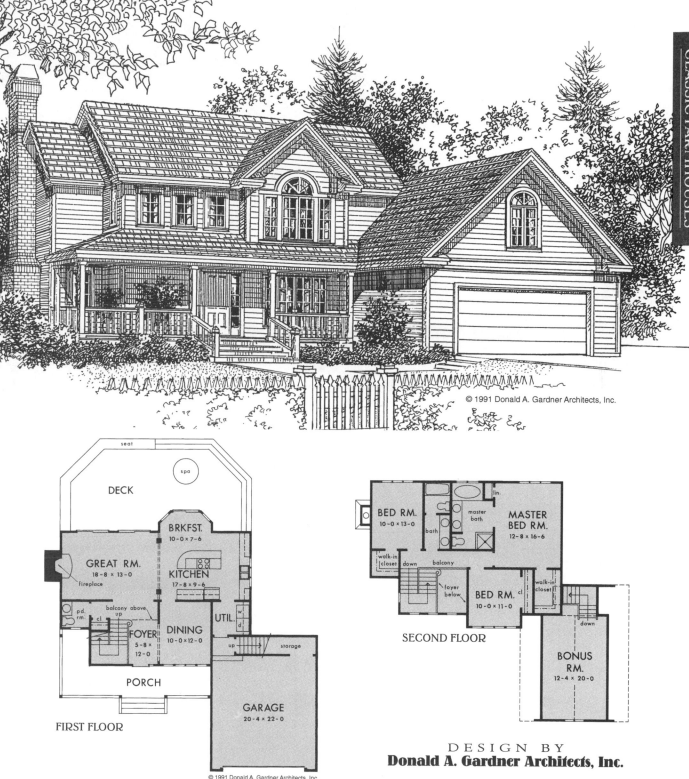

© 1991 Donald A. Gardner Architects, Inc.

DESIGN BY
Donald A. Gardner Architects, Inc.

© 1991 Donald A. Gardner Architects, Inc.

Curve-top windows and an inviting covered porch offer an irresistible appeal for this three-bedroom plan. A two-story foyer provides a spacious feeling to this well-organized open layout. Round columns between the great room and the kitchen add to the impressive quality of the plan. Inside the kitchen, plenty of counter space makes gourmet cooking enjoyable; the breakfast area has a bay window. An expansive deck with a seat and spa promotes casual outdoor living to its fullest. The owners suite with a walk-in closet and private bath resides on the second floor along with two additional bedrooms and a full bath. The bonus room over the garage offers room for expansion.

PLAN HPT100048

Total: 1,783 sq. ft.
First Floor: 943 sq. ft.
Second Floor: 840 sq. ft.
Bonus Room: 323 sq. ft.
Width: 53'-4" **Depth:** 64'-4"

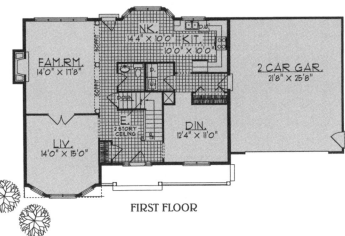

FIRST FLOOR

DESIGN BY
©Ahmann Design, Inc.

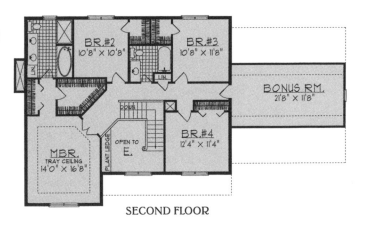

SECOND FLOOR

PLAN HPT100049

Total: 2,370 sq. ft.
First Floor: 1,228 sq. ft.
Second Floor: 1,142 sq. ft.
Bonus Room: 253 sq. ft.
Width: 62'-0" **Depth:** 36'-0"

This four-bedroom, two-story home has much to offer. The front covered porch is perfect for reading the evening paper. Inside, the large kitchen furnishes everything the family cook needs. The bay nook's sliding glass doors open to the backyard. The family room has a fireplace and large rear-facing windows. Off the foyer, the formal living room has French doors, which can be closed for privacy. The formal dining room is off the foyer to the right and provides a perfect setting for holiday gatherings. Upstairs, the owners bedroom boasts a tray ceiling, two closets and a private bath. The private bath includes a spa tub, separate shower and double vanity. Bedrooms 2, 3 and 4 share a full bath.

VERANDA

MASTER BEDROOM
11⁰ X 15⁰

WHIRLPOOL

GREAT RM
13⁶ X 15⁴

KITCHEN

BATH

SNACK BAR

DN

UP

PANTRY

LAUNDRY

W. D.

DINING ROOM
11⁰ X 11⁰

FOYER

LIVING ROOM
12⁰ X 13⁴

GARAGE
23⁰ X 24⁶

VERANDA

RAILING

FIRST FLOOR

QUOTE ONE®
Cost to build? See page 310
to order complete cost estimate
to build this house in your area!

OPEN BELOW

BEDROOM
11⁰ X 13⁰

STORAGE

BATH

DN

LINEN

BEDROOM
12⁸ X 12⁰

DESK

BEDROOM
12⁰ X 14⁴

SECOND FLOOR

DESIGN BY
©**Home Planners**

Horizontal siding with corner boards, muntin windows and a raised veranda enhance the appeal of this country home. Twin carriage lamps flank the sheltered entrance. Inside, the central foyer delights with its two sets of columns at the openings to the formal living and dining rooms. In the L-shaped kitchen, an adjacent snack bar offers everyday ease. Open to the kitchen, the great room boasts a centered fireplace, a high ceiling and access to the veranda. Sleeping accommodations start off with the owners bedroom; a connecting bath with a whirlpool tub will be a favorite spot. Upstairs, three bedrooms share a full bath that includes twin lavatories. The storage room is also added to the second floor.

PLAN HPT100050

Total: 2,208 sq. ft.
First Floor: 1,395 sq. ft.
Second Floor: 813 sq. ft.
Width: 53'-8" **Depth:** 57'-0"

PLAN HPT100051

This traditional siding-and-brick home has its focus on the family. A charming covered porch welcomes guests, while inside, a formal dining area and the great room with a fireplace are perfect for entertaining. A large efficient kitchen with an easy-access island and bayed breakfast area are handy for those easy meals. Three family bedrooms, two of which have walk-in closets, share a compartmented bath that includes dual sinks. The comfortable owners suite opens with French doors, and the private bath gratifies with a whirlpool tub, separate shower and double sinks. A loft area, located near the stairs, makes a popular family retreat. A powder room sits just beyond the entry to the two-car garage.

Total: 2,105 sq. ft.
First Floor: 1,006 sq. ft.
Second Floor: 1,099 sq. ft.
Width: 47'-0" **Depth:** 43'-0"

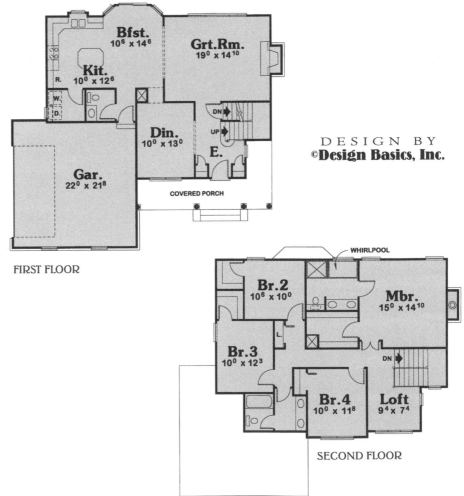

FIRST FLOOR

SECOND FLOOR

DESIGN BY
©**Design Basics, Inc.**

FIRST FLOOR

Bfst.
12⁴x10⁸

Grt. rm.
18⁰x16⁰
SLOPED CEILING

Mbr.
15⁰x13⁰
10'-0"CLG.

SNACK BAR

Kit.
12⁴x10⁸

Din.
12⁰x13⁰

SHELVES

Gar.
20⁷x24⁷

COVERED PORCH

HUTCH

W/P

SECOND FLOOR

LIN.

Br.3
12⁴x10¹

Br.2
12⁰x11³

DESIGN BY
©**Design Basics, Inc.**

PLAN HPT100052

This handsome exterior will surely make for plenty of pleasing home-comings. Step up from a long walkway onto the covered porch and into the wonderful interior: to the left, enter the dining room enhanced with hutch space and a tray ceiling. Straight ahead, the inviting great room provides a hearth and sloped ceiling. To the left, a bayed breakfast room and a roomy kitchen with a snack bar await your enjoyment. The owners bedroom complements the first floor with all the necessary amenities: a double vanity, separate shower, angled whirlpool tub and compartmented bath. Two additional family bedrooms and a full bath make up the second floor. The two-car garage enters through the utility room and has a side door and shelves for extra storage.

Total: 1,778 sq. ft.
First Floor: 1,348 sq. ft.
Second Floor: 430 sq. ft.
Width: 54'-0" **Depth:** 48'-8"

PLAN HPT100053

This traditional elevation combines aesthetics and economy. Symmetrical coat closets and cased openings frame the entry's view of the great room. Inside the great room, a fireplace is surrounded by mitered windows. The bayed breakfast room includes backyard access and a staircase to the second level. The luxurious owners suite contains a built-in dresser between His and Hers walk-in closets. A roomy, compartmented dressing area with a whirlpool tub sets the tone in the owners bath. A bookshelf resides near the entrance of the full hall bath. Bedrooms 2 and 3 each hold double-door closets and muntin windows. The two-car garage is highlighted by extra storage space.

Total: 1,745 sq. ft.
First Floor: 852 sq. ft.
Second Floor: 893 sq. ft.
Width: 44'-8" **Depth:** 40'-0"

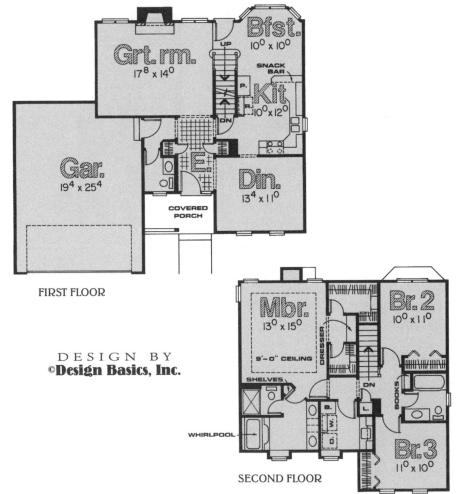

DESIGN BY
©**Design Basics, Inc.**

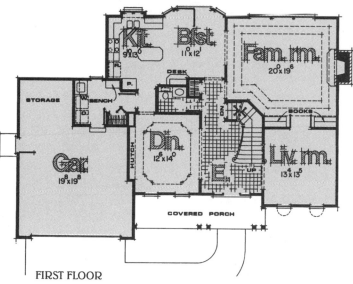

FIRST FLOOR

DESIGN BY
©**Design Basics, Inc.**

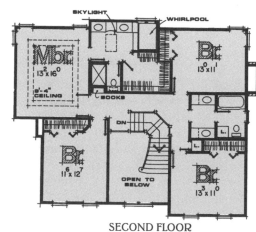

SECOND FLOOR

PLAN HPT100054

Amenities for casual family living and entertaining abound in this attractive farmhouse. A charming, covered front porch makes for an inviting exterior. Inside, the two-story entry with a flared staircase opens to the formal dining and living rooms. A tray ceiling and a hutch complement the dining room. French doors connect the living room with the more informal family room for expanded entertaining space. A spacious kitchen handily serves both the family and dining rooms. Also note the bay-windowed breakfast area. Upstairs, the owners suite provides a skylit bath with a whirlpool tub and a large walk-in closet. A compartmented bath and two vanities with sinks make sharing a bath between the three additional bedrooms less burdensome.

Total: 2,557 sq. ft.
First Floor: 1,386 sq. ft.
Second Floor: 1,171 sq. ft.
Width: 58'-0" **Depth:** 41'-4"

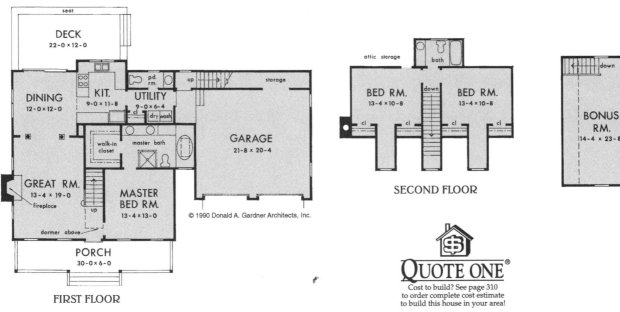

DECK
22-0 × 12-0

DINING
12-0 × 12-0

KIT.
9-0 × 11-8

UTILITY
9-0 × 6-4

storage

dry wash

walk-in closet

master bath

GARAGE
21-8 × 20-4

GREAT RM.
13-4 × 19-0
fireplace

MASTER BED RM.
13-4 × 13-0

dormer above

© 1990 Donald A. Gardner Architects, Inc.

PORCH
30-0 × 6-0

FIRST FLOOR

attic storage

bath

BED RM.
13-4 × 10-8

BED RM.
13-4 × 10-8

SECOND FLOOR

BONUS RM.
14-4 × 23-8

QUOTE ONE®
Cost to build? See page 310
to order complete cost estimate
to build this house in your area!

DESIGN BY
Donald A. Gardner Architects, Inc.

PLAN HPT100055

Total: 1,557 sq. ft.
First Floor: 1,057 sq. ft.
Second Floor: 500 sq. ft.
Bonus Room: 342 sq. ft.
Width: 59'-4" **Depth:** 50'-0"

This cozy country cottage is perfect for the economically conscious family. Its entrance foyer is highlighted by a clerestory dormer above for natural light. Columns accent the great room (with a fireplace) and the dining room. The owners suite is conveniently located on the first level for privacy and accessibility. The owners bath boasts a skylight, huge walk-in closet, garden tub, separate shower and dual sinks. Second-level bedrooms share a full bath, and each bedroom has a dormer and two closets. The bonus room may be finished above the garage. The two-car garage is complete with a storage area.

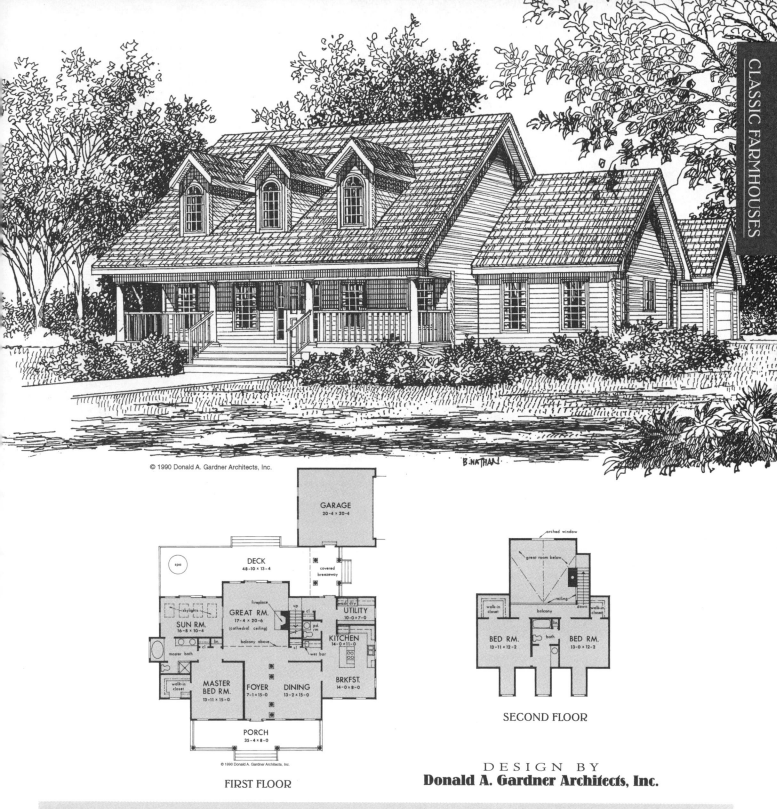

© 1990 Donald A. Gardner Architects, Inc.

B. NATHAN

GARAGE
20-4 x 20-4

DECK
48-10 x 13-4

spa

covered breezeway

up

wash dry

GREAT RM.
17-4 x 20-6
(cathedral ceiling)

fireplace

SUN RM.
16-8 x 10-4

skylights

balcony above

lin
cl

master bath

cl

walk-in closet

UTILITY
10-0 x 7-0

pd. rm.

KITCHEN
14-0 x 11-0

wet bar

MASTER BED RM.
13-11 x 15-0

FOYER
7-1 x 15-0

DINING
13-2 x 15-0

BRKFST.
14-0 x 8-0

PORCH
35-4 x 8-0

© 1990 Donald A. Gardner Architects, Inc.

FIRST FLOOR

arched window

great room below

railing

down

walk-in closet

walk-in closet

balcony

bath

BED RM.
13-11 x 12-2

BED RM.
13-0 x 12-2

SECOND FLOOR

DESIGN BY
Donald A. Gardner Architects, Inc.

This three-bedroom country home features large, round columns and dormers. Circle-head windows illuminate the floor plan inside. Columns define the foyer and the dining room. In the spacious great room, a fireplace and an arched window lend an air of comfort. Reach the rear deck from both the great room and the skylit sun room. The first-floor owners bedroom enjoys its own access to the sun room and features a bath with a bumped-out garden tub. The kitchen contains a cooktop island and a breakfast area. Upstairs, two bedrooms accommodate family and guests alike with walk-in closets and private access to a shared bath. The spa and covered breezeway on the rear deck are definitely a treat.

PLAN HPT100056

Total: 2,587 sq. ft.
First Floor: 1,852 sq. ft.
Second Floor: 735 sq. ft.
Width: 60'-0" **Depth:** 74'-8"

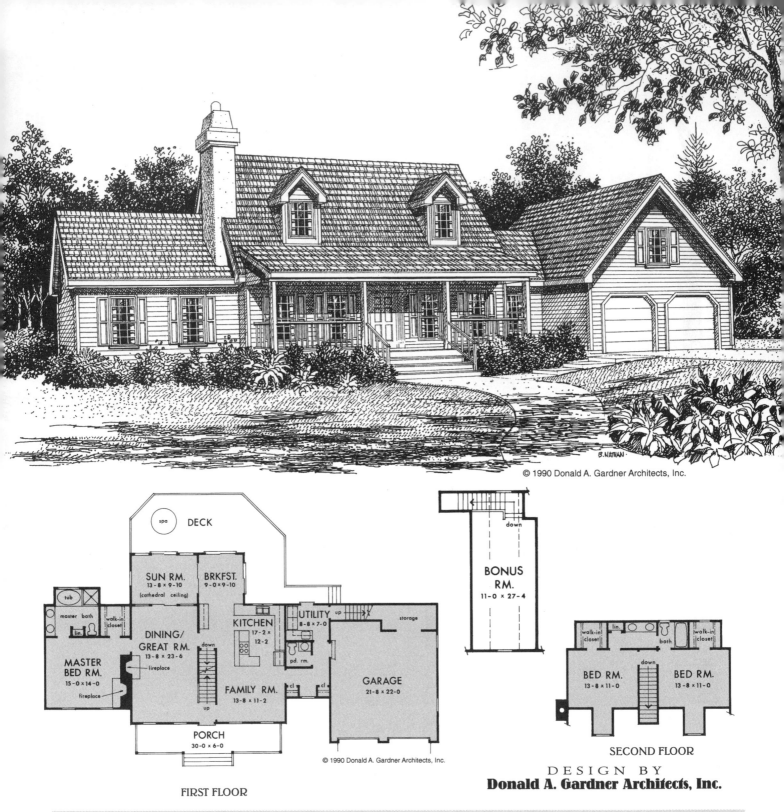

© 1990 Donald A. Gardner Architects, Inc.

FIRST FLOOR

DECK

SUN RM.
13-8 x 9-10
(cathedral ceiling)

BRKFST.
9-0 x 9-10

spa

tub

master bath

walk-in closet

lin.

DINING/
GREAT RM.
13-8 x 23-6

KITCHEN
17-2 x
12-2

UTILITY
8-8 x 7-0

storage

up

MASTER
BED RM.
15-0 x 14-0

fireplace

down

pd. rm.

GARAGE
21-8 x 22-0

fireplace

FAMILY RM.
13-8 x 11-2

cl.

cl

up

PORCH
30-0 x 6-0

© 1990 Donald A. Gardner Architects, Inc.

BONUS
RM.
11-0 x 27-4

down

SECOND FLOOR

walk-in closet

lin.

bath

walk-in closet

BED RM.
13-8 x 11-0

BED RM.
13-8 x 11-0

down

DESIGN BY
Donald A. Gardner Architects, Inc.

PLAN HPT100057

Total: 2,130 sq. ft.
First Floor: 1,581 sq. ft.
Second Floor: 549 sq. ft.
Bonus Room: 334 sq. ft.
Width: 80'-4" **Depth:** 52'-4"

Great flexibility is available in this plan—the great room/dining room can be reworked into one large great room with the dining room relocated to the family room. A sun room with a cathedral ceiling and sliding glass door to the deck is accessible from both the breakfast and dining rooms. A large kitchen boasts a convenient cooking island. The owners bedroom features a fireplace, walk-in closet and spacious private bath. Two second-level bedrooms are equal in size and share a full bath that includes a double-bowl vanity. Both bedrooms have a dormer window and a walk-in closet. A large bonus room over the garage is accessible from the utility room below.

© 1984 Donald A. Gardner Architects, Inc.

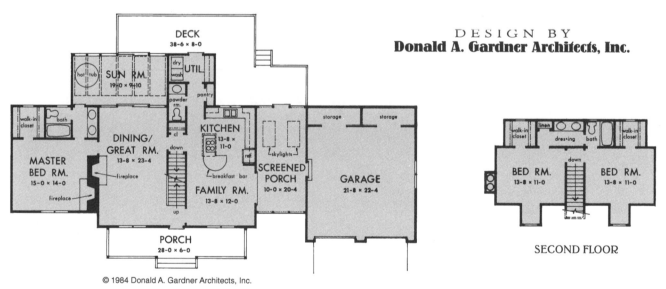

DECK
38-6 × 8-0

SUN RM.
19-0 × 9-10

hot tub

dry
wash

UTIL.

powder
rm.

pantry

walk-in
closet

bath

DINING/
GREAT RM.
13-8 × 23-4

cl

KITCHEN
13-8 ×
11-0

down

MASTER
BED RM.
15-0 × 14-0

fireplace

breakfast bar

ref.

skylights

storage

storage

fireplace

FAMILY RM.
13-8 × 12-0

SCREENED
PORCH
10-0 × 20-4

GARAGE
21-8 × 22-4

up

PORCH
28-0 × 6-0

© 1984 Donald A. Gardner Architects, Inc.

FIRST FLOOR

D E S I G N   B Y
Donald A. Gardner Architects, Inc.

walk-in
closet

linen

dressing

bath

walk-in
closet

BED RM.
13-8 × 11-0

down

BED RM.
13-8 × 11-0

SECOND FLOOR

Two covered porches, sunny dormers and multi-pane windows combine to give this three-bedroom home plenty of curb appeal. Directly to the left of the foyer, the spacious great room offers a cathedral ceiling, a fireplace and doors to the rear porch; to the immediate right is the family room. The spacious kitchen is thoughtfully set through a small walkway near the dining/great room. Access the highlighted screened porch from the kitchen or garage. A second fireplace resides in the owners suite, also complemented with a tray ceiling, walk-in closet and compartmented bath. On the second floor, the sleeping zone is split by the staircase; each bedroom contains a walk-in closet and access to the full bath.

PLAN HPT100058

Total: 1,913 sq. ft.
First Floor: 1,377 sq. ft.
Second Floor: 536 sq. ft.
Width: 81'-8" **Depth:** 40'-8"

PLAN HPT100059

Arches in the foyer of this traditional home echo the porch theme and lead to an open great room with sliding doors to the rear yard. The kitchen overlooks the great room and furnishes a walk-in pantry and breakfast nook. Just off the kitchen, a private study or guest suite provides a hall bath and door to the veranda. The owners suite enjoys a spacious bath and two walk-in closets. Three family bedrooms on the second floor share a hall bath, and two of the three access the rear balcony. A computer loft has built-ins for books and software. Please specify basement or slab foundation when ordering.

Total: 2,527 sq. ft.
First Floor: 1,676 sq. ft.
Second Floor: 851 sq. ft.
Width: 55'-0" **Depth:** 50'-0"

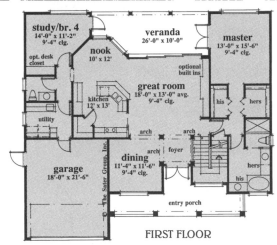

FIRST FLOOR

DESIGN BY
©**The Sater Design Collection**

SECOND FLOOR

62

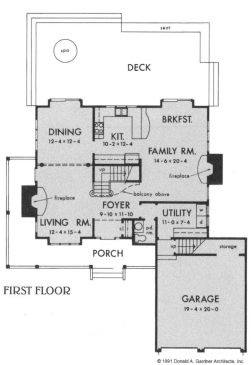

DECK

DINING
12-4 × 12-4

KIT.
10-2 × 12-4

BRKFST.

FAMILY RM.
14-6 × 20-4

fireplace

up

balcony above

FOYER
9-10 × 11-10

fireplace

LIVING RM.
12-4 × 15-4

UTILITY
11-0 × 7-4

PORCH

up

storage

GARAGE
19-4 × 20-0

FIRST FLOOR

© 1991 Donald A. Gardner Architects, Inc.

DESIGN BY
Donald A. Gardner Architects, Inc.

master bath

BED RM.
11-8 × 10-0

BED RM.
11-0 × 10-0

walk-in closet

MASTER BED RM.
12-4 × 15-4

BED RM.
11-0 × 12-0

balcony

foyer below

bath

walk-in closet

SECOND FLOOR

down

BONUS RM.
11-0 × 20-4

The beauty of the exterior of this four-bedroom plan is enhanced by the use of arched windows, gabled dormers and a wraparound front porch with a railing. Both the living and family rooms have fireplaces. The U-shaped kitchen is centrally located between the breakfast area and dining room for maximum efficiency. A large rear deck enhances outdoor living with a seat and spa. An owners suite with two walk-in closets and a bath full of amenities shares the second floor with three additional bedrooms. Across the balcony, a full bath with double sinks is available. A bonus room provides extra space above the garage.

PLAN HPT100060

Total: 2,218 sq. ft.
First Floor: 1,165 sq. ft.
Second Floor: 1,053 sq. ft.
Bonus Room: 300 sq. ft.
Width: 53'-0" **Depth:** 70'-8"

PLAN HPT100061

With an interior designed as one large open space, this home combines elegance with convenience, for the utmost in comfortable living. The great room, with a fireplace and built-ins, opens to the well-planned kitchen, which leads to the formal dining room through a butler's pantry. To the rear of the plan, the guest suite enjoys private access to a small side porch and a full bath. Upstairs, the owners bedroom provides a private suite with a garden tub, separate shower and many other amenities. Three additional bedrooms share the large central bath and linen closet. Closets with two double doors are found in the three additional bedrooms. This home is designed with a basement foundation.

Total: 2,972 sq. ft.
First Floor: 1,726 sq. ft.
Second Floor: 1,246 sq. ft.
Width: 71'-0" **Depth:** 48'-3"

DESIGN BY
©Stephen Fuller, Inc.

FIRST FLOOR

SECOND FLOOR

Plains or Prairie-Type Farmhouses

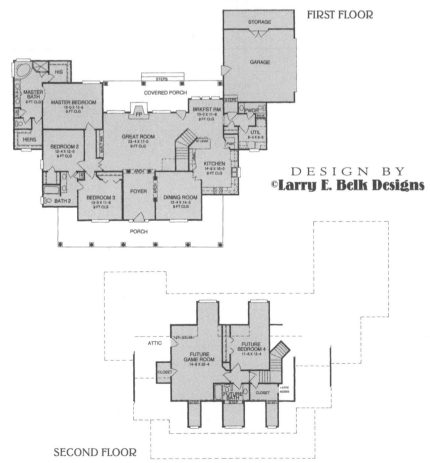

FIRST FLOOR

DESIGN BY
©**Larry E. Belk Designs**

SECOND FLOOR

PLAN HPT100062

Designed to meet the needs of today's lifestyles, this historical elevation is a familiar one. Inside, the large great room is designed with entertaining in mind. The nearby kitchen boasts all the latest features, including a snack bar, extensive pantry and breakfast room. The bedroom wing features a luxurious owners suite with a lush bath and twin walk-in closets. Two additional bedrooms are comfortably sized, and each has its own access to a private bath. The upper level can be finished later and is designed to add a bedroom, a full bath and a large game room with a closet. Please specify crawlspace or slab foundation when ordering.

Square Footage: 2,465
Bonus Space: 788 sq. ft.
Width: 85'-8" Depth: 70'-7"

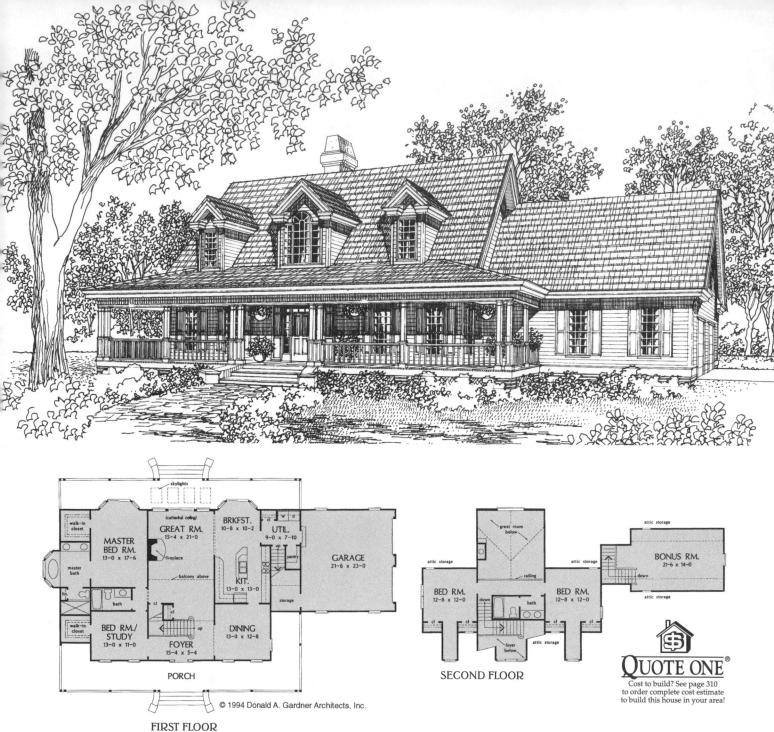

FIRST FLOOR

© 1994 Donald A. Gardner Architects, Inc.

SECOND FLOOR

Quote One®
Cost to build? See page 310
to order complete cost estimate
to build this house in your area!

DESIGN BY
Donald A. Gardner Architects, Inc.

PLAN HPT100063

Total: 2,435 sq. ft.
First Floor: 1,841 sq. ft.
Second Floor: 594 sq. ft.
Bonus Room: 391 sq. ft.
Width: 82'-2" **Depth:** 48'-10"

Spaciousness and lots of amenities earmark this design as a family favorite. The front wraparound porch leads to the foyer where a bedroom/study, with a walk-in closet, and the dining room open. The central great room presents a warming fireplace, a cathedral ceiling and access to the rear porch. The kitchen with an island and the bayed breakfast area are nearby. In the owners bedroom suite, a private bath with a bumped-out tub and a double-sink vanity are extra enhancements. Upstairs, two bedrooms flank a full bath; each bedroom has twin closets. The balcony with a railing looks over the great room. A bonus room over the garage allows for future expansion.

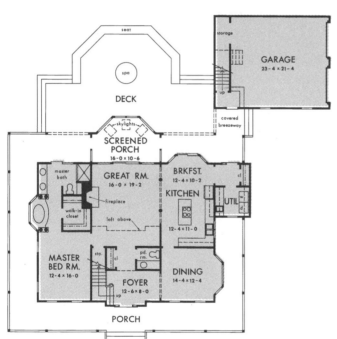

FIRST FLOOR

© 1992 Donald A. Gardner Architects, Inc.

Cost to build? See page 310
to order complete cost estimate
to build this house in your area!

BONUS RM.
27-0 × 12-0

SECOND FLOOR

DESIGN BY
Donald A. Gardner Architects, Inc.

This beautiful farmhouse boasts all the extras a three-bedroom design could offer. Clerestory windows with arched tops enhance the exterior at the front and back as well as allow natural light to penetrate into the foyer and the great room. A kitchen with an island counter and a breakfast area is open to the spacious great room through a cased opening with a colonnade. The exquisite owners suite has a generous bedroom, a large walk-in closet and a dramatically designed owners bath providing emphasis on the whirlpool tub flanked by double columns. Access the rear deck from the screened porch, the owners bath and the breakfast area. Two family bedrooms share a full bath on the second level.

PLAN HPT100064

Total: 2,161 sq. ft.
First Floor: 1,526 sq. ft.
Second Floor: 635 sq. ft.
Bonus Room: 355 sq. ft.
Width: 76'-4" **Depth:** 74'-2"

PLAN HPT100065

A charming array of arches and the keystone entryway draws you into an elegant home designed for comfort. The foyer divides the study and dining area. In the great room, French doors stand on each side of a gracious hearth. Meal preparations are a cinch with a cooktop island; the breakfast area adds to the spacious kitchen. In the owners bedroom, highlights include three mitered windows and a large private bath with dual sinks, a garden tub, separate shower and His and Hers closets. Upstairs, a full hall bath is shared between two bedrooms. Two rooms at each end of the hall are added for future expansion. Please specify basement, crawlspace or slab foundation when ordering.

Total: 2,344 sq. ft.
First Floor: 1,791 sq. ft.
Second Floor: 553 sq. ft.
Bonus Space: 284 sq. ft.
Width: 64'-4" **Depth:** 66'-1"

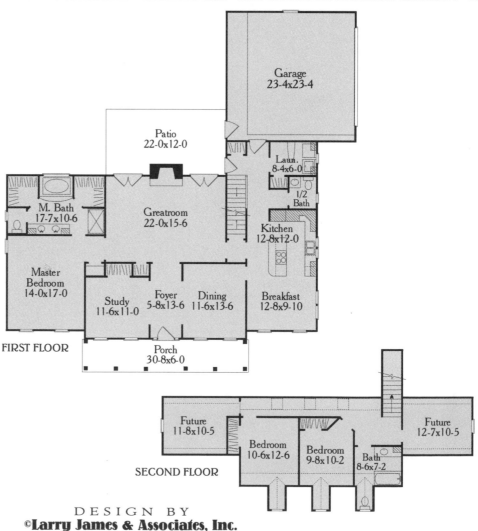

Garage
23-4x23-4

Patio
22-0x12-0

Laun.
8-4x6-0

1/2
Bath

M. Bath
17-7x10-6

Greatroom
22-0x15-6

Kitchen
12-8x12-0

Master
Bedroom
14-0x17-0

Study
11-6x11-0

Foyer
5-8x13-6

Dining
11-6x13-6

Breakfast
12-8x9-10

FIRST FLOOR

Porch
30-8x6-0

Future
11-8x10-5

Bedroom
10-6x12-6

Bedroom
9-8x10-2

Bath
8-6x7-2

Future
12-7x10-5

SECOND FLOOR

DESIGN BY
©**Larry James & Associates, Inc.**

68

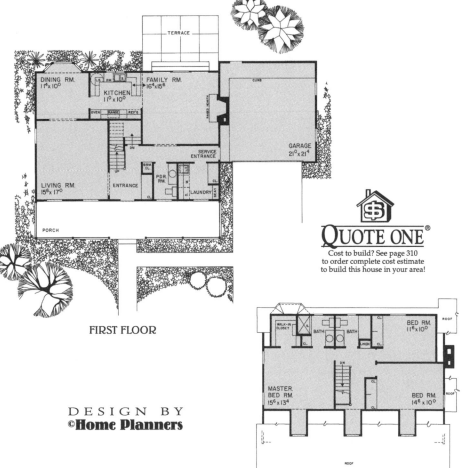

FIRST FLOOR

QUOTE ONE®

Cost to build? See page 310
to order complete cost estimate
to build this house in your area!

DESIGN BY
©**Home Planners**

SECOND FLOOR

PLAN HPT100066

This board-and-batten farmhouse design carries down-home country charm with a dash of uptown New England flavor. Warm weather will invite friends and family out to the large, front covered porch to enjoy the outdoors. Just off the front entrance, a spacious living room opens to the formal dining room, which enjoys a bay window and easy service from the U-shaped kitchen. The family room offers casual living space warmed by a raised-hearth fireplace and extended by double-door access to the rear terrace. The second floor houses two family bedrooms that share a full bath, and a generous owners suite with a walk-in closet and a private bath.

Total: 2,008 sq. ft.
First Floor: 1,134 sq. ft.
Second Floor: 874 sq. ft.
Width: 61'-4" **Depth:** 38'-0"

L·D

PLAN HPT100067

Double columns attract attention while supporting the wraparound porch of this easy farm home. A cozy living room with a hearth connects to the bayed breakfast area and vast kitchen with a snack bar. The owners bedroom may be entered through the front entry positioned near the bottom of the staircase, or by a rear entrance, leading into the owners bath. Inside the owners bedroom, a bay window provides a grand view of the outdoors. At the top of the staircase are a linen closet and a full hall bath. To the right is Bedroom 2, and to the left is a comfy study or playroom and Bedroom 3, which includes double closets.

Total: 1,673 sq. ft.
First Floor: 979 sq. ft.
Second Floor: 694 sq. ft.
Width: 52'-0" **Depth:** 63'-4"

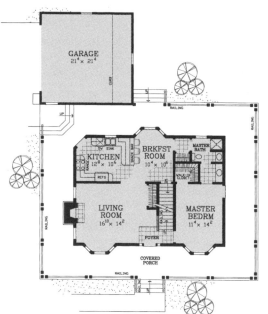

FIRST FLOOR

QUOTE ONE®
Cost to build? See page 310
to order complete cost estimate
to build this house in your area!

DESIGN BY
©**Home Planners**

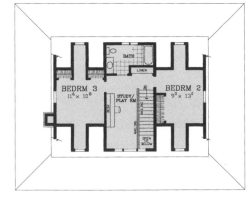

SECOND FLOOR

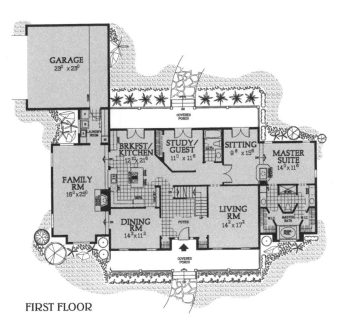

FIRST FLOOR

GARAGE
29⁰ x 29⁰

LAUNDRY ROOM

COVERED PORCH

BRKFST/ KITCHEN
12¹⁰ x 21⁶

STUDY/ GUEST
11⁰ x 11⁶

SITTING
9⁸ x 15⁶

BATH

MASTER SUITE
14⁰ x 11⁶

FAMILY RM
16⁰ x 25⁰

W.I.C.

MASTER BATH

W.I.C.

DINING RM
14² x 11²

FOYER

LIVING RM
14² x 17²

COVERED PORCH

D E S I G N   B Y
©**Home Planners**

QUOTE ONE®

Cost to build? See page 310
to order complete cost estimate
to build this house in your area!

SECOND FLOOR

BEDRM
11¹⁰ x 17⁰

RAILING

OPEN TO FOYER

BATH

BEDRM
11¹⁰ x 17⁰

PLAN HPT100068

Dormered windows, a covered porch and symmetrical balustrades provide a warm country welcome. Inside, formal living and dining rooms flank the foyer. To the left of the dining room, and down a step, rests a spacious family room with a raised-hearth fireplace. The nearby breakfast/kitchen area features an island cooktop, a pantry and a planning desk. French doors in the breakfast area, the study (or optional guest room) and the sitting area of the owners suite provide access to the rear porch. A lavish owners bath is complete with a whirlpool tub and separate His and Hers dressing areas. The second floor contains two family bedrooms and a full bath with separate vanities.

Total: 3,112 sq. ft.
First Floor: 2,300 sq. ft.
Second Floor: 812 sq. ft.
Width: 83'-0" **Depth:** 69'-6"

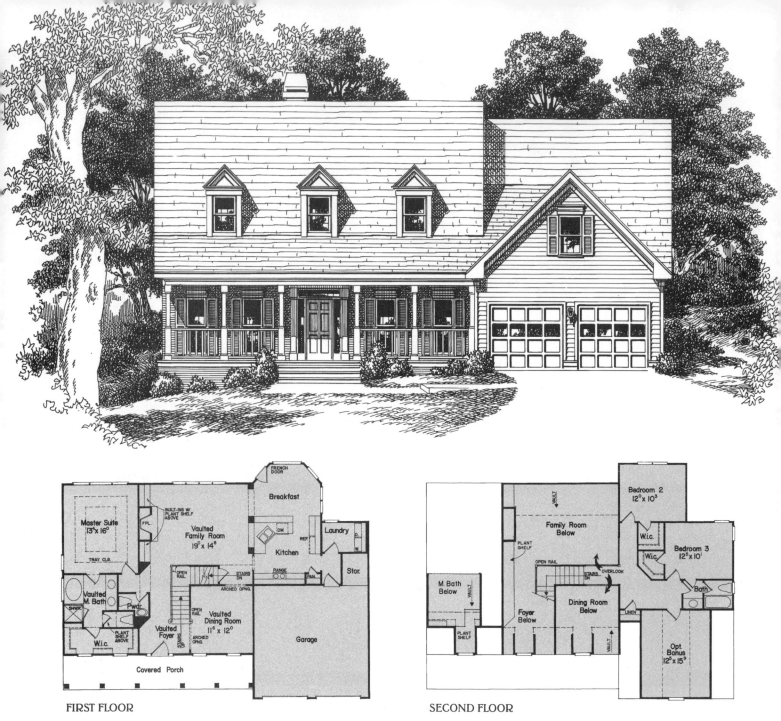

FIRST FLOOR

SECOND FLOOR

DESIGN BY
©Frank Betz Associates, Inc.

PLAN HPT100069

Total: 1,916 sq. ft.
First Floor: 1,414 sq. ft.
Second Floor: 502 sq. ft.
Bonus Room: 208 sq. ft.
Width: 56'-0" **Depth:** 42'-6"

The sunny breakfast room of this quaint country home is the perfect place to start your day. The breakfast room and adjacent kitchen lead to a vaulted family room with scenic views and a fireplace flanked by built-in cabinets and plant shelves. The dining room is conveniently close to the kitchen but with enough separation to cut down on disruptive cooking and cleanup noises. A luxurious owners suite with a vaulted bath and an enormous walk-in closet sits on the first floor. Two family bedrooms with walk-in closets share a full bath upstairs. An optional bonus room can be developed as another bedroom or as an office, study or game room.

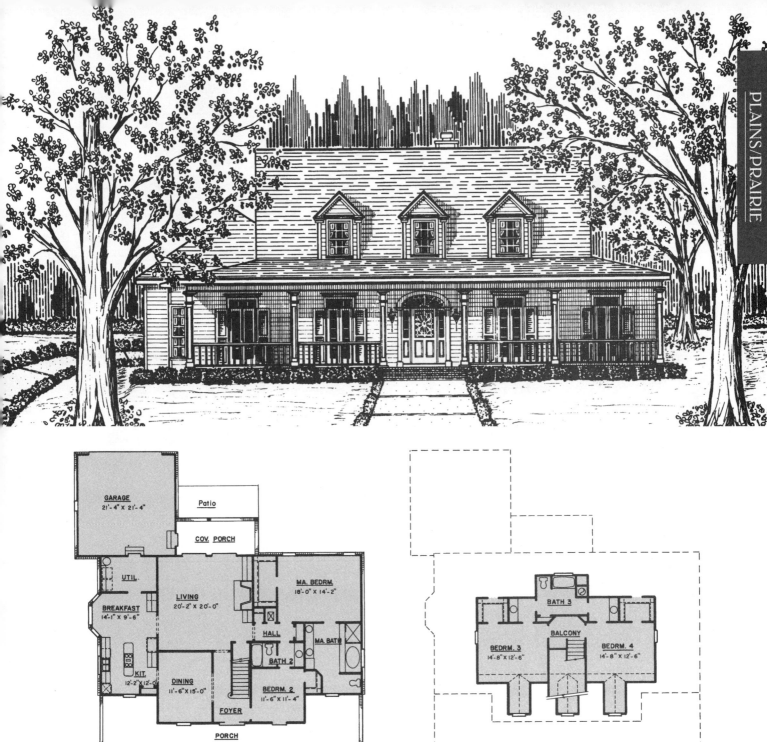

GARAGE
21'-4" X 21'-4"

Patio

COV. PORCH

UTIL.

BREAKFAST
14'-1" X 9'-6"

LIVING
20'-2' X 20'-0"

MA. BEDRM.
18'-0" X 14'-2"

HALL

MA. BATH

KIT.
12'-2"X12'-0"

BATH 2

DINING
11'-6" X 15'-0"

BEDRM. 2
11'-6" X 11'-4"

FOYER

PORCH

FIRST FLOOR

BATH 3

BEDRM. 3
14'-8" X 12'-6"

BALCONY

BEDRM. 4
14'-8" X 12'-6"

SECOND FLOOR

DESIGN BY
©**Chatham Home Planning, Inc.**

Graceful French doors and tall, shuttered windows combine with a sprawling country front porch to give this charming home its unique appeal. Nine-foot ceilings expand the main floor. Walk through the elegant foyer to a grand living area, with a centered fireplace and built-in bookcase. This living space opens to the rear covered porch. The private owners suite with a walk-in closet features a luxurious bath with a separate shower and compartmented toilet. A guest room (or make it a study) also has access to a full bath. Just off the formal dining area, the gourmet kitchen revolves around an island cooktop counter. Please specify crawlspace or slab foundation when ordering.

PLAN HPT100070

Total: 2,665 sq. ft.
First Floor: 1,916 sq. ft.
Second Floor: 749 sq. ft.
Width: 63'-0" **Depth:** 63'-9"

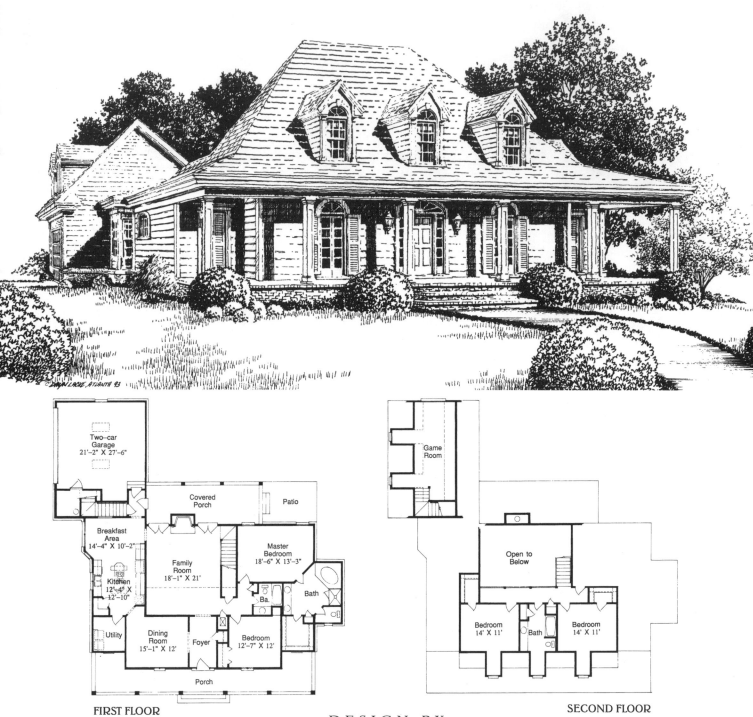

FIRST FLOOR

DESIGN BY
©Chatham Home Planning, Inc.

SECOND FLOOR

PLAN HPT100071

Total: 2,664 sq. ft.
First Floor: 1,977 sq. ft.
Second Floor: 687 sq. ft.
Width: 69'-6" **Depth:** 69'-9"

The game room above the garage of this four-bedroom, 1½-story Southern traditional home provides a separate entrance and could make a convenient home office. The wrap-around porch adds charm and function to the exterior. A formal dining room and a large family room with a fireplace and double doors to the rear covered porch are accessed from the foyer. The owners suite features a large offset bath with a corner tub, and across the hall is a second bedroom that could easily double as a study. Two additional bedrooms and a full bath reside on the second level. Please specify crawlspace or slab foundation when ordering.

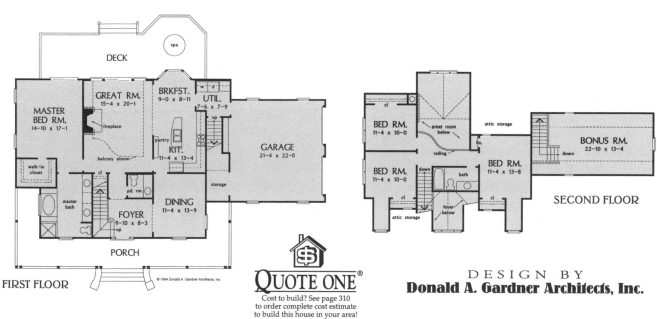

DECK
spa

GREAT RM.
15-4 x 20-1

BRKFST.
9-0 x 8-11

UTIL.
7-6 x 7-9

w d

MASTER
BED RM.
14-10 x 17-1

fireplace

balcony above

pantry

KIT.
11-4 x 13-4

up

GARAGE
21-4 x 22-0

walk-in
closet

storage

master
bath

cl

pd. rm.

DINING
11-4 x 13-9

FOYER
9-10 x 8-3

up

PORCH

© 1994 Donald A. Gardner Architects, Inc.

FIRST FLOOR

BED RM.
11-4 x 10-0

cl

great room
below

attic storage

lin.

BONUS RM.
22-10 x 13-4

down

railing

BED RM.
11-4 x 10-0

down

bath

BED RM.
11-4 x 13-8

SECOND FLOOR

attic storage

cl

foyer
below

cl

QUOTE ONE®

Cost to build? See page 310
to order complete cost estimate
to build this house in your area!

DESIGN BY
Donald A. Gardner Architects, Inc.

The warm, down-home appeal of this country house is as apparent inside as it is out. A wraparound front porch and a rear deck with a spa provide plenty of space to enjoy the surrounding scenery. Inside, a two-story foyer and a great room with a hearth give the home an open feel. The great room leads to the breakfast area and the efficient kitchen with an island work area and a large pantry. The owners bedroom is situated on the left side of the house for privacy. It features deck access, a large walk-in closet and a bath that includes dual vanities, a whirlpool tub and a separate shower. Three additional bedrooms, a full bath and bonus space are located upstairs.

PLAN HPT100072

Total: 2,164 sq. ft.
First Floor: 1,499 sq. ft.
Second Floor: 665 sq. ft.
Bonus Room: 380 sq. ft.
Width: 69'-8" **Depth:** 40'-6"

PLAN HPT100073

Symmetrical gables and clapboard siding lend a Midwestern style to this prairies-and-plains farmhouse. A spacious foyer opens to a formal dining room on the left and a living room on the right. The foyer leads straight ahead to a casual living area with a tiled-hearth fireplace and a breakfast bay. The U-shaped kitchen enjoys an easy-care ceramic tile floor and a walk-in pantry. The second-floor sleeping quarters include a generous owners suite that offers a window-seat dormer and a private bath with a whirlpool tub, walk-in closet, twin vanities and linen storage. Three family bedrooms share a full bath that includes a linen closet. A central hall leads to additional storage and a laundry.

Total: 2,407 sq. ft.
First Floor: 1,216 sq. ft.
Second Floor: 1,191 sq. ft.
Width: 56'-0"   **Depth:** 42'-0"

L·D

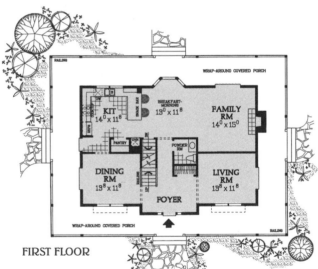

FIRST FLOOR

DESIGN BY
©**Home Planners**

Quote One®
Cost to build? See page 310
to order complete cost estimate
to build this house in your area!

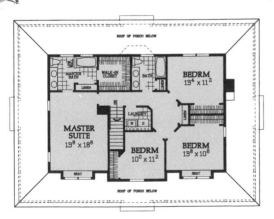

SECOND FLOOR

76

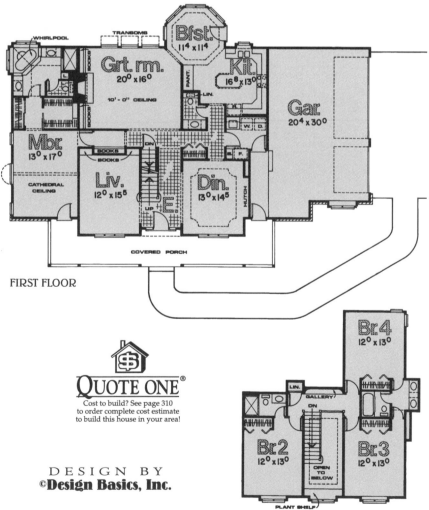

FIRST FLOOR

WHIRLPOOL

TRANSOMS

Bfst.
11⁴ x 11⁴

Grt. rm.
20⁰ x 16⁰

10' - 0" CEILING

Kit.
16⁸ x 13⁰

PANT.

LIN.

Gar.
20⁴ x 30⁰

W. D.

Mbr.
13⁰ x 17⁰

BOOKS

CATHEDRAL CEILING

BOOKS

BOOKS

DN

Liv.
12⁰ x 15⁵

UP

Din.
13⁰ x 14⁵

HUTCH

COVERED PORCH

QUOTE ONE®

Cost to build? See page 310
to order complete cost estimate
to build this house in your area!

DESIGN BY
©**Design Basics, Inc.**

Br. 4
12⁰ x 13⁰

LIN.

GALLERY

DN

Br. 2
12⁰ x 13⁰

Br. 3
12⁰ x 13⁰

OPEN TO BELOW

PLANT SHELF

SECOND FLOOR

PLAN HPT100074

Oval windows and an appealing covered porch lend character to this home. Inside, a volume entry views the formal living and dining rooms. Three large windows and a raised-hearth fireplace flanked by bookcases highlight a volume great room. An island kitchen with a huge pantry and two lazy Susans serves a captivating gazebo dinette. In the owners suite, a cathedral ceiling, corner whirlpool tub that separates two vanities, and roomy dressing room are sure to please. A gallery wall for displaying family mementos and prized heirlooms graces the upstairs corridor. Each secondary bedroom conveniently accesses the bathrooms. This home's charm and blend of popular amenities will fit your lifestyle!

Total: 2,695 sq. ft.
First Floor: 1,881 sq. ft.
Second Floor: 814 sq. ft.
Width: 72'-0" **Depth:** 45'-4"

PLAN HPT100075

Although this home would work well on a narrow lot, it would fit just as comfortably on a lot surrounded by land available for a garden or for the kids to have plenty of running room. The front covered porch leads to a vaulted foyer and a formal dining room with a tray ceiling. A vaulted great room with a fireplace and rear-yard access will be ideal for family gatherings. The owners suite is located on the first floor for privacy and features a vaulted bath with a walk-in closet, oversized tub and separate shower. Two bedrooms and a full bath are available upstairs, as well as an optional bonus room that can be developed later as needed. Please specify basement or crawlspace foundation when ordering.

Total: 1,500 sq. ft.
First Floor: 1,065 sq. ft.
Second Floor: 435 sq. ft.
Bonus Room: 175 sq. ft.
Width: 50'-0" **Depth:** 37'-4"

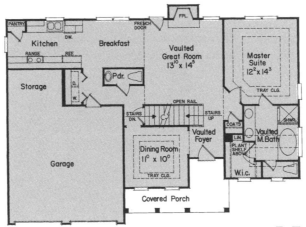

FIRST FLOOR

DESIGN BY
©Frank Betz Associates, Inc.

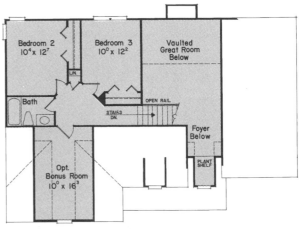

SECOND FLOOR

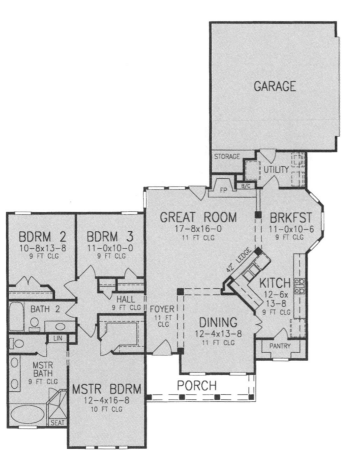

PLAN HPT102001

Twin dormers perch above a welcoming covered front porch in this three-bedroom home. Inside, a formal dining room on the right is defined by pillars, while the spacious great room lies directly ahead. This room is enhanced by a fireplace, plenty of windows, access to the rear yard, and a forty-two-inch ledge looking into the angular kitchen. Nearby, a bayed breakfast room awaits casual mealtimes. The sleeping zone consists of two family bedrooms sharing a full hall bath and a luxurious master bedroom suite with a huge walk-in closet and a sumptuous private bath. Please specify crawlspace or slab foundation when ordering.

Square Footage: 1,654
Width: 54'-10" **Depth:** 69'-10"

DESIGN BY
©**Larry E. Belk Designs**

FIRST FLOOR

SECOND FLOOR

GREAT RM.
14/2 X 23/0

DINING
11/6 X 14/6

11/0 X 13/8

PANTRY

REF

UP

GARAGE
20/8 X 21/0

D W

MASTER
14/2 X 12/0

BR. 2
11/6 X 10/10

LINEN

DN

FOYER
BELOW

DN

BR. 3
11/0 X 11/10

BONUS RM.
18/6 X 15/0

DESIGN BY
©Alan Mascord Design Associates, Inc.

PLAN HPT100077

Total: 1,902 sq. ft.
First Floor: 1,032 sq. ft.
Second Floor: 870 sq. ft.
Bonus Room: 306 sq. ft.
Width: 66'-0" **Depth:** 38'-0"

A wraparound covered porch and symmetrical dormers produce an inviting appearance to this farmhouse. Inside, the two-story foyer leads directly to the large great room graced by a fireplace and an abundance of windows. The U-shaped island kitchen is convenient to the sunny dining room with a powder room nearby. The utility room offers access to the two-car garage. Upstairs, two family bedrooms share a full hall bath and have convenient access to a large bonus room. The owners suite is full of amenities, including a walk-in closet and a pampering bath. A bonus room is also available upstairs near the hall bath.

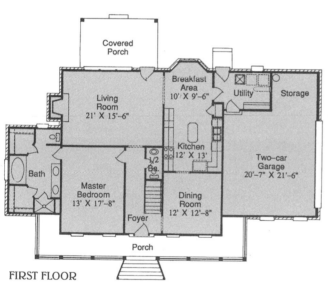

Covered
Porch

Living
Room
21' X 15'-6"

Breakfast
Area
10' X 9'-6"

Utility

Storage

Kitchen
12' X 13'

Two-car
Garage
20'-7" X 21'-6"

Bath

1/2
Ba.

Master
Bedroom
13' X 17'-8"

Dining
Room
12' X 12'-8"

Foyer

Porch

FIRST FLOOR

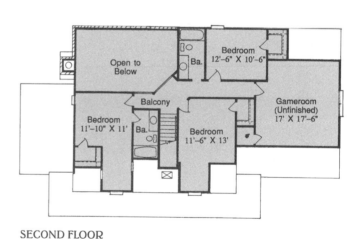

Open to
Below

Ba.

Bedroom
12'-6" X 10'-6"

Balcony

Gameroom
(Unfinished)
17' X 17'-6"

Bedroom
11'-10" X 11'

Ba.

Bedroom
11'-6" X 13'

SECOND FLOOR

DESIGN BY
©Chatham Home Planning, Inc.

This roomy country design features two covered porches and an island kitchen with a breakfast area. The long foyer leads to the living room with a fireplace and to the stunning owners suite with an oversized tub, glass shower, toilet compartment and His and Hers walk-in closets. A balcony overlooks the living area and leads to three additional bedrooms and two full baths. An unfinished game room can store all those family treasures, or finish it for added hobby, entertainment or workspace. Please specify crawlspace or slab foundation when ordering.

PLAN HPT100078

Total: 2,357 sq. ft.
First Floor: 1,492 sq. ft.
Second Floor: 865 sq. ft.
Bonus Room: 285 sq. ft.
Width: 66'-10" **Depth:** 49'-7"

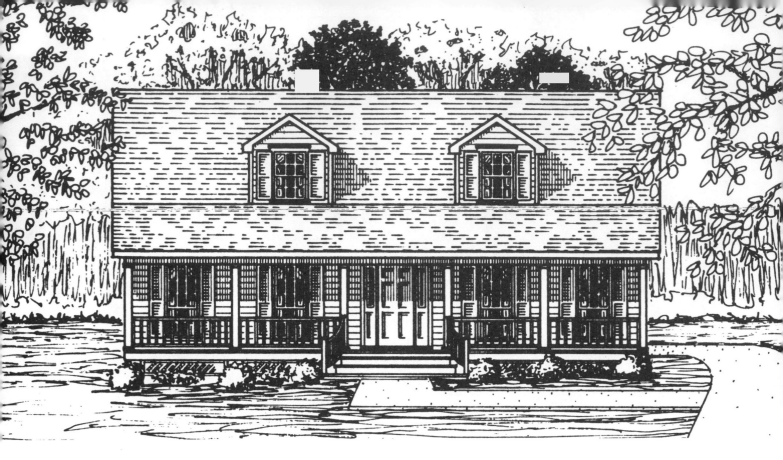

PLAN HPT100079

Old-fashioned Southern style is offset by the innovative floor plan of this charming home. Exterior details include a covered front porch accessed by a flared stairway, and a covered rear porch plus a carport and storage room. Full-height windows line the front porch, drawing natural light and generous views into the front rooms. The foyer with a nine-foot ceiling leads past the formal dining room on the right to the spacious living room with a sloped ceiling and fireplace to the rear. The large galley kitchen spans the right side of the plan, opens to the bay-windowed breakfast area to the rear and serves the dining room to the front. The left rear of the plan is entirely devoted to the owners suite with an octagonal tray ceiling, His and Hers walk-in closets, a garden tub and separate shower. Please specify crawlspace or slab foundation when ordering.

Square Footage: 1,704
Width: 47'-0" **Depth:** 66'-0"

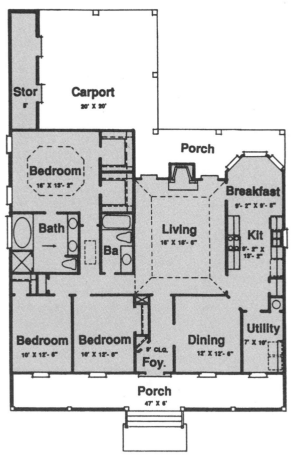

DESIGN BY
©Chatham Home Planning, Inc.

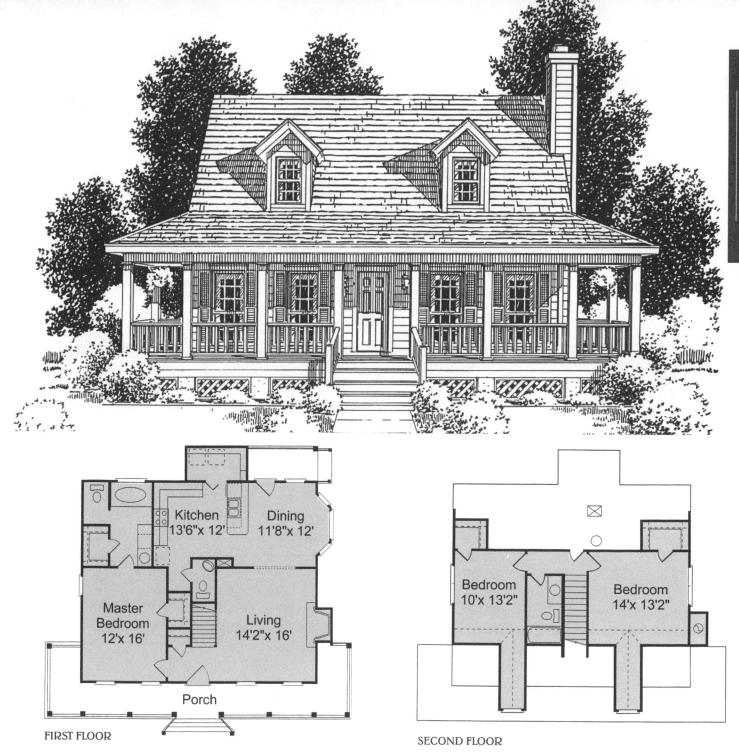

Kitchen
13'6"x 12'

Dining
11'8"x 12'

Master
Bedroom
12'x 16'

Living
14'2"x 16'

Porch

FIRST FLOOR

Bedroom
10'x 13'2"

Bedroom
14'x 13'2"

SECOND FLOOR

DESIGN BY
©Chatham Home Planning, Inc.

A deep wraparound porch trimmed with square pillars, a wood balustrade and traditional lattice adds character and interest to this Cape Cod design. Floor-to-ceiling double-hung windows with true divided lights downstairs and dormers upstairs complete the rustic look. The main floor includes a fireplace in the living room, a bay window in the dining room and an owners suite with a walk-in closet. The dining room and kitchen are divided by a peninsula with seating for informal dining. The peninsula contains the sink, in keeping with one of the latest trends in kitchen design. Upstairs, two bedrooms, each with a walk-in closet, share a full bath. Please specify crawlspace or slab foundation when ordering.

PLAN HPT100080

Total: 1,618 sq. ft.
First Floor: 1,046 sq. ft.
Second Floor: 572 sq. ft.
Width: 44'-0" **Depth:** 39'-0"

PLAN HPT100081

This splendid farmhouse begins with twin gabled dormers and an alluring wide porch for the entire family to enjoy. The thoughtfully planned great room and dining area offer copious space and share a warming fireplace. Connected to the dining room is the kitchen with ample counter space; a lovely window sink faces the rear yard. The owners bedroom is charmed with a fireplace, French doors leading to the rear porch, and a private bath designed precisely for Him and Her. On the second floor, a playroom and two bedrooms with dormers greet family members or guests. Two bedrooms share a full hall bath. Don't miss the laundry room with a folding counter adjacent to the two-car garage. Please specify basement, crawlspace or slab foundation when ordering.

Total: 2,132 sq. ft.
First Floor: 1,501 sq. ft.
Second Floor: 631 sq. ft.
Width: 76'-0"   **Depth:** 48'-4"

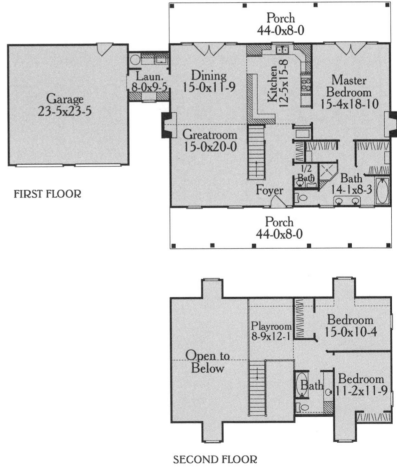

FIRST FLOOR

Garage 23-5x23-5
Laun. 8-0x9-5
Porch 44-0x8-0
Dining 15-0x11-9
Kitchen 12-5x15-8
Master Bedroom 15-4x18-10
Greatroom 15-0x20-0
1/2 Bath
Bath 14-1x8-3
Foyer
Porch 44-0x8-0

SECOND FLOOR

Playroom 8-9x12-1
Bedroom 15-0x10-4
Open to Below
Bath
Bedroom 11-2x11-9

DESIGN BY
©Larry James & Associates, Inc.

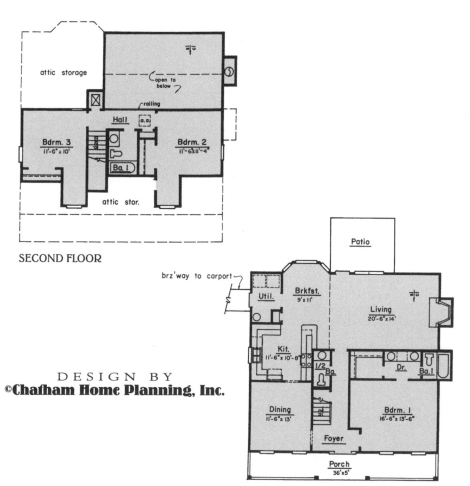

SECOND FLOOR

brz'way to carport

FIRST FLOOR

DESIGN BY
©Chatham Home Planning, Inc.

PLAN HPT100082

Nostalgic country style combined with modern livability sets this design apart from the rest. The living room, complete with a sloped ceiling and warming fireplace, opens to a bright, bay-windowed breakfast area. The nearby kitchen features wraparound cabinets and a sit-down bar. Guests will appreciate the convenient half-bath, just under the stairs. An impressive owners suite, with a separate dressing area and a dual-sink vanity, opens just off the foyer. Upstairs, a balcony hall overlooks the spacious living area and connects two family bedrooms that share a bath. Please specify crawlspace or slab foundation when ordering.

Total: 1,737 sq. ft.
First Floor: 1,238 sq. ft.
Second Floor: 499 sq. ft.
Width: 38'-4" **Depth:** 41'-0"

FIRST FLOOR

QUOTE ONE®

Cost to build? See page 310
to order complete cost estimate
to build this house in your area!

SECOND FLOOR

DESIGN BY
©**Home Planners**

PLAN HPT100083

Total: 3,096 sq. ft.
First Floor: 1,855 sq. ft.
Second Floor: 1,241 sq. ft.
Width: 82'-0" **Depth:** 50'-0"

L·D

With its classic farmhouse good looks and just-right floor plan, this country residence has it all. The wraparound covered porch at the entry gives way to a long foyer with an open staircase. To the left opens the living room with a fireplace and the formal dining room. The extensive country kitchen pampers the chef with a cooktop island and hearth. A spectacular private bath with a separate dressing room, whirlpool tub and huge walk-in closet completes the owners suite. The second floor has a total of two bedrooms, one with a walk-in closet and a full bath. A bedroom/sitting room with a built-in desk divides the two bedrooms. A full hall bath is located at the top of the staircase to the far right.

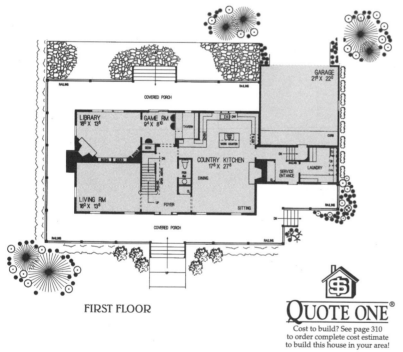

FIRST FLOOR

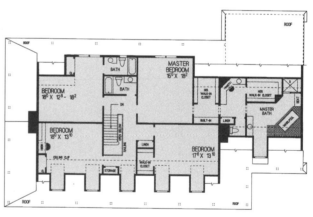

SECOND FLOOR

DESIGN BY
©Home Planners

This is the ultimate in farmhouse living with six dormer windows and a porch that stretches essentially around the entire house. Inside, the plan is open and inviting. Besides the large country kitchen with a fireplace, there is a small game room with an attached tavern, a library with built-in bookshelves and a fireplace, and a formal living room. The second floor features four bedrooms and three full baths. You'll delight in the separate His and Hers walk-in closets and the whirlpool spa in the owners bath. The service entrance contains a mudroom and a laundry area conveniently located just off the garage.

PLAN HPT100084

Total: 3,818 sq. ft.
First Floor: 1,716 sq. ft.
Second Floor: 2,102 sq. ft.
Width: 82'-0" **Depth:** 49'-8"

L·D

PLAN HPT100085

This design takes inspiration from the casual fishing cabins of the Pacific Northwest and interprets it for modern livability. It offers three options for a main entrance. One door opens to a mud porch, where a small hall leads to a galley kitchen and the vaulted great room. Two French doors on the side porch open into a dining room with bay-window seating. Another porch entrance opens directly to the great room. The great room is centered around a massive stone fireplace and is accented with a beautiful wall of windows. The secluded owners suite features a private bath with a clawfoot tub and twin pedestal sinks, as well as a separate shower and walk-in closet. Two more bedrooms share a spacious bath. Ideal for a lounge or extra sleeping space, an unfinished loft looks over the great room.

Square Footage: 2,019
Bonus Room: 384 sq. ft.
Width: 56'-0" **Depth:** 56'-3"

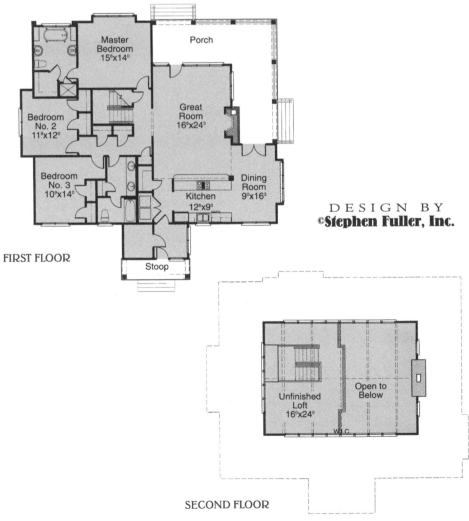

DESIGN BY
©**Stephen Fuller, Inc.**

FIRST FLOOR

CARPORT

BEDRM 2
12-0 X 11-0

BATH 2

HIDDEN CLOSET

+HINGED SHELF

MASTER BEDRM
12-0 X 14-6

MASTER BATH

SCREENED PORCH
11-0 X 11-0

PANTRY

KITCHEN
10-0 14-8

42" LEDGE

DINING RM
10-6 X 14-0

GREAT RM
20-0 X 17-6
VAULTED TO 16' CLG

FP

COVERED PORCH
38-0 X 7-0

DESIGN BY
©Larry E. Belk Designs

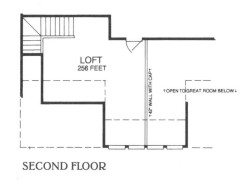

LOFT
256 FEET

+42" WALL WITH CAP†

†OPEN TO GREAT ROOM BELOW†

SECOND FLOOR

PLAN HPT100086

This rustic Craftsman-style cottage provides an open interior with good outdoor flow. The front covered porch invites casual gatherings, while inside, the dining area is set for both everyday and planned occasions; to the right a centered fireplace in the great room shares its warmth with the dining room. On the left, the kitchen connects to the dining room with a cooktop island and includes a vast pantry. A rear hall leads to the owners suite with a full private bath and a walk-in closet. Also down the hall is a secondary bedroom and a full bath. A loft upstairs can be used as a computer area or even a sitting area.

Square Footage: 1,404
Bonus Room: 256 sq. ft.
Width: 54'-7" **Depth:** 46'-6"

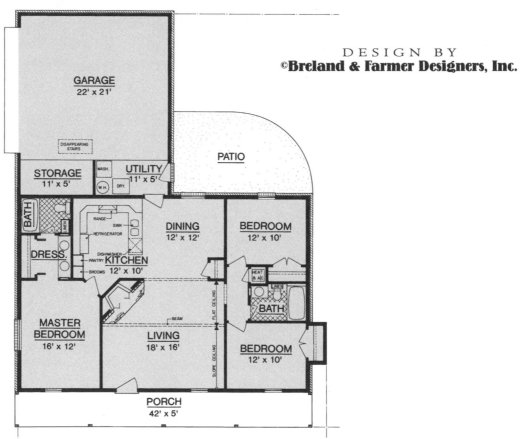

GARAGE
22' x 21'

DISAPPEARING STAIRS

DESIGN BY
©**Breland & Farmer Designers, Inc.**

PATIO

STORAGE
11' x 5'

WASH.
UTILITY
11' x 5'
W. H.   DRY.

BATH

RANGE
SINK
REFRIGERATOR

DINING
12' x 12'

BEDROOM
12' x 10'

DRESS.

DISHWASHER
PANTRY   **KITCHEN**
BROOMS   12' x 10'

HEAT & A/C

LINEN

BATH

MASTER BEDROOM
16' x 12'

BEAM
FLAT CEILING
SLOPE CEILING

LIVING
18' x 16'

BEDROOM
12' x 10'

PORCH
42' x 5'

PLAN HPT100087

Square Footage: 1,191
Width: 44'-6"   **Depth:** 59'-0"

This compact floor plan has something for the entire family. The covered front porch is a perfect place for quiet contemplation and viewing the great outdoors. Inside, the corner fireplace and pitched ceiling will make the living room a favorite gathering place. Adjacent to the living room, the dining room provides entrance to the utility room and rear patio. The owners suite is a welcoming retreat away from busy family life with its private dressing room and full bath. An efficient U-shaped kitchen is conveniently located near the garage and has a view of the formal dining area. Two family bedrooms with a shared bath complete this lovely home. Please specify crawlspace or slab foundation when ordering.

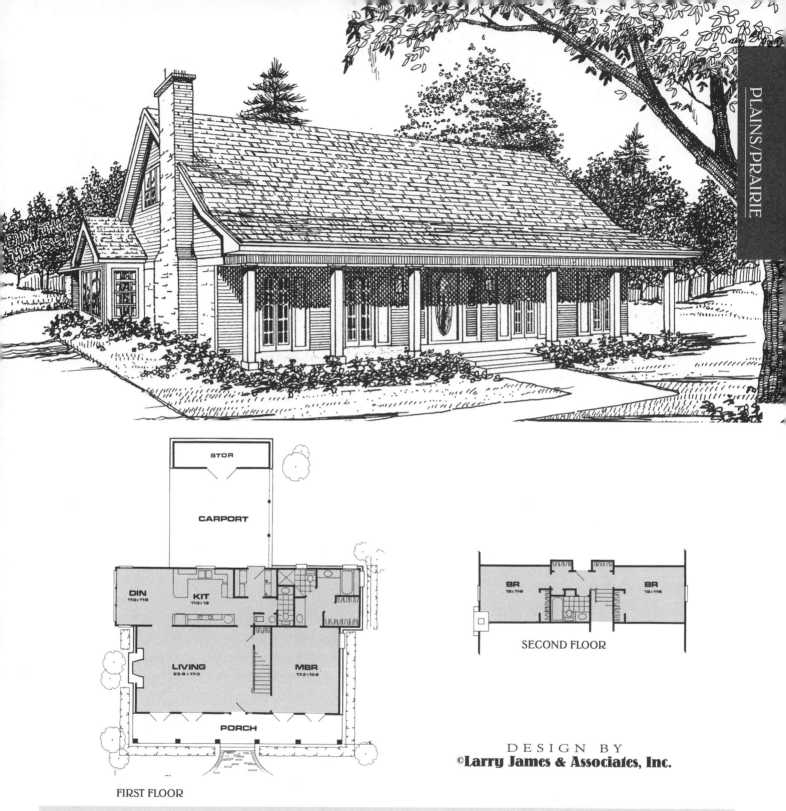

STOR

CARPORT

DIN
11-3 x 11-8

KIT
11-3 x 12

LIVING
23-6 x 17-3

MBR
17-3 x 13-9

PORCH

FIRST FLOOR

BR
12 x 11-8

BR
12 x 11-8

SECOND FLOOR

DESIGN BY
©Larry James & Associates, Inc.

This house was designed with spring days in mind, having four French doors at the front to draw in the fresh air and sunshine. To the right of the entrance is the owners bedroom and full bath including both a shower and a tub and a large walk-in closet. Sit by a warm fire in the living room, or enjoy a game of cards in the dining room. An efficient kitchen sits conveniently near the carport entrance, a laundry room and a powder room. Two bedrooms and a full bath are tucked upstairs. Please specify basement, crawlspace or slab foundation when ordering.

PLAN HPT100088

Total: 1,869 sq. ft.
First Floor: 1,369 sq. ft.
Second Floor: 500 sq. ft.
Width: 51'-0" **Depth:** 61'-6"

PLAN HPT100089

Balustrades and brackets, dual balconies and a wraparound porch create a country-style exterior reminiscent of soft summer evenings spent watching fireflies and sipping sun tea. The well-planned interior starts with a tiled foyer that opens to an expansive two-story great room filled with light from six windows, a fireplace with a tiled hearth, and a sloped ceiling. A sunny, bayed nook invites casual dining and shares its natural light with a snack counter and a well-appointed U-shaped kitchen. A spacious owners suite occupies the bay on the opposite side of the plan and offers a sumptuous bath. Upstairs, two family bedrooms, each with a private balcony and a walk-in closet, share a full bath that includes twin lavatory sinks.

Total: 1,974 sq. ft.
First Floor: 1,374 sq. ft.
Second Floor: 600 sq. ft.
Width: 51'-8" **Depth:** 50'-8"

L·D

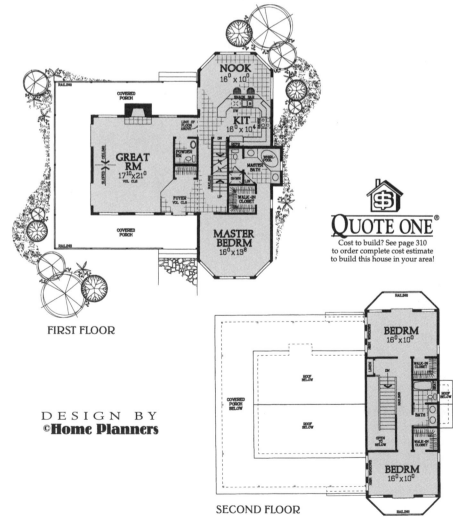

FIRST FLOOR

DESIGN BY
©**Home Planners**

Quote One®
Cost to build? See page 310
to order complete cost estimate
to build this house in your area!

SECOND FLOOR

92

Southern or Plantation-Style Farmhouses

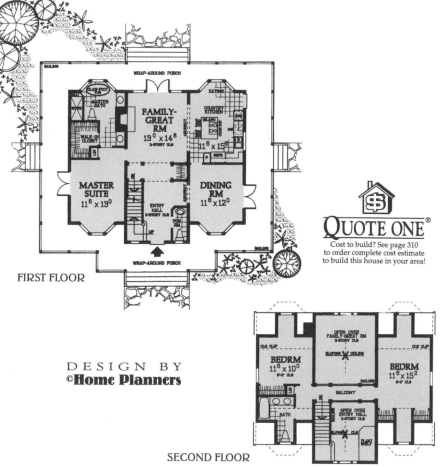

FIRST FLOOR

SECOND FLOOR

DESIGN BY
©**Home Planners**

QUOTE ONE®
Cost to build? See page 310
to order complete cost estimate
to build this house in your area!

PLAN HPT100090

There's nothing that tops gracious Southern hospitality—unless it's offered Southern farmhouse style! The entry hall opens through an archway on the right to a formal dining room. Nearby, the efficient country kitchen shares space with a bay-windowed eating area. The two-story family/great room is warmed by a fireplace in the winter and open to outdoor country comfort in the summer via double French doors. The first-floor owners suite offers a bay window and access to the porch through French doors. The second floor holds two family bedrooms that share a full bath. Plans for an optional indoor swimming pool/spa and detached garage are included.

Total: 1,771 sq. ft.
First Floor: 1,171 sq. ft.
Second Floor: 600 sq. ft.
Width: 50'-0" **Depth:** 44'-0"

L•D

PLAN HPT100091

A wraparound covered porch at the front and sides of this house and an open deck at the back provide plenty of outside living area. The spacious great room features a fireplace, cathedral ceiling and clerestory with an arched window. The island kitchen has an attached skylit breakfast room complete with a bay window. The first-floor owners bedroom contains a generous closet and a private bath with a garden tub, double-bowl vanity and shower. The second floor sports two bedrooms and a full bath with a double-bowl vanity. An elegant balcony overlooks the great room.

Total: 2,321 sq. ft.
First Floor: 1,756 sq. ft.
Second Floor: 565 sq. ft.
Width: 56'-8" **Depth:** 54'-4"

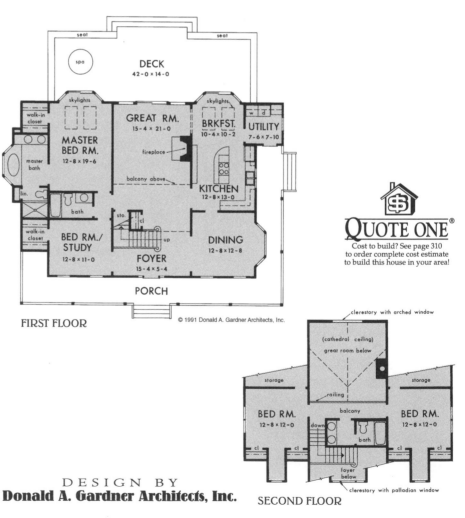

FIRST FLOOR

SECOND FLOOR

QUOTE ONE®
Cost to build? See page 310
to order complete cost estimate
to build this house in your area!

DESIGN BY
Donald A. Gardner Architects, Inc.

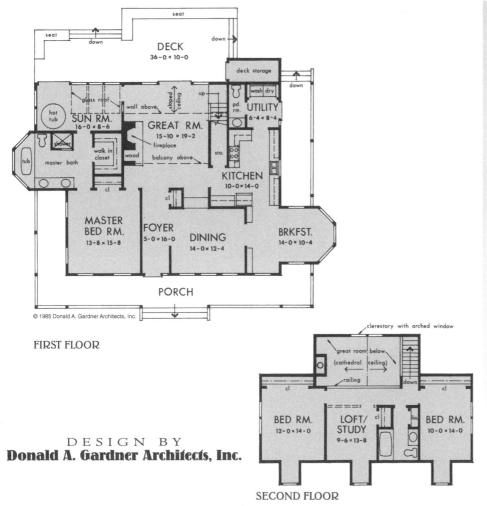

FIRST FLOOR

DECK
36-0 × 10-0

SUN RM.
16-0 × 8-6

hot tub

GREAT RM.
15-10 × 19-2
fireplace

UTILITY
6-4 × 8-4

deck storage

wash dry

pd. rm.

glass roof

wall above

sloped ceiling

up

down

balcony above

walk in closet

wood

sto.

master bath

tub

shower

KITCHEN
10-0 × 14-0

cl

MASTER BED RM.
13-8 × 15-8

FOYER
5-0 × 16-0

DINING
14-0 × 12-4

BRKFST.
14-0 × 10-4

cl

PORCH

© 1985 Donald A. Gardner Architects, Inc.

seat

down

seat

seat

down

DESIGN BY
Donald A. Gardner Architects, Inc.

SECOND FLOOR

clerestory with arched window

great room below
(cathedral ceiling)

railing

down

BED RM.
12-0 × 14-0

LOFT/STUDY
9-6 × 13-8

BED RM.
10-0 × 14-0

cl

cl

lin.

PLAN HPT100092

Outdoor living takes a beautiful turn in this lovely home. The interior is just as great—bay windows in the breakfast room and owners bath, dormers and arched rear windows, and an incredible sun room with a hot tub and glass roof. The spacious great room features a fireplace, cathedral ceiling and clerestory with arched window. The owners bath complements the owners bedroom with a garden tub, separate shower, double-bowl vanity and walk-in closet. Two bedrooms share the upper level with a study/loft overlooking the great room. This study area could be converted into a fourth bedroom.

Total: 2,452 sq. ft.
First Floor: 1,724 sq. ft.
Second Floor: 728 sq. ft.
Width: 61'-4" **Depth:** 46'-6"

PLAN HPT100093

This compact design has all the amenities available in larger plans with little wasted space. In addition, a wraparound covered porch, a front Palladian window, dormers and rear arched windows provide exciting visual elements to the exterior. The spacious great room holds a fireplace, cathedral ceiling and clerestory windows. A second-level balcony overlooks this gathering area. The kitchen is centrally located for maximum flexibility in layout and features a pass-through to the great room. Besides the generous owners suite with a full bath, there are two family bedrooms located on the second level sharing a full bath that includes a double vanity.

Total: 1,778 sq. ft.
First Floor: 1,325 sq. ft.
Second Floor: 453 sq. ft.
Width: 48'-4" **Depth:** 51'-10"

FIRST FLOOR

© 1991 Donald A. Gardner Architects, Inc.

SECOND FLOOR

QUOTE ONE®
Cost to build? See page 310 to order complete cost estimate to build this house in your area!

DESIGN BY
Donald A. Gardner Architects, Inc.

© 1990 Donald A. Gardner Architects, Inc.

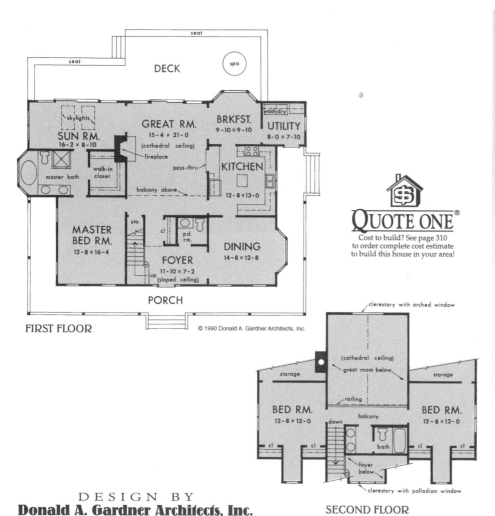

DECK

seat

seat

spa

skylights

SUN RM.
16-2 × 8-10

GREAT RM.
15-4 × 21-0
(cathedral ceiling)
fireplace

BRKFST.
9-10 × 9-10

wash dry

UTILITY
8-0 × 7-10

master bath

walk-in closet

pass-thru

KITCHEN
12-8 × 13-0

balcony above

MASTER
BED RM.
12-8 × 16-4

sto.

cl

pd. rm.

DINING
14-8 × 12-8

FOYER
11-10 × 7-2
(sloped ceiling)

up

PORCH

FIRST FLOOR

© 1990 Donald A. Gardner Architects, Inc.

clerestory with arched window

storage

(cathedral ceiling)
great room below

storage

railing

BED RM.
12-8 × 12-0

balcony

BED RM.
12-8 × 12-0

cl

cl

down

bath

cl

cl

foyer below

clerestory with palladian window

SECOND FLOOR

Quote One®

Cost to build? See page 310
to order complete cost estimate
to build this house in your area!

D E S I G N   B Y
Donald A. Gardner Architects, Inc.

PLAN HPT100094

A wonderful wraparound covered porch at the front and sides of this house and the open deck with a spa at the back provide plenty of outside living area. Inside, the spacious great room is appointed with a fireplace, cathedral ceiling and clerestory with arched window. The kitchen is centrally located for maximum flexibility in layout and features a food-preparation island for convenience. Besides the owners bedroom with access to the sun room, there are two second-level bedrooms that share a full bath.

Total: 2,218 sq. ft.
First Floor: 1,651 sq. ft.
Second Floor: 567 sq. ft.
Width: 55'-0" **Depth:** 53'-10"

97

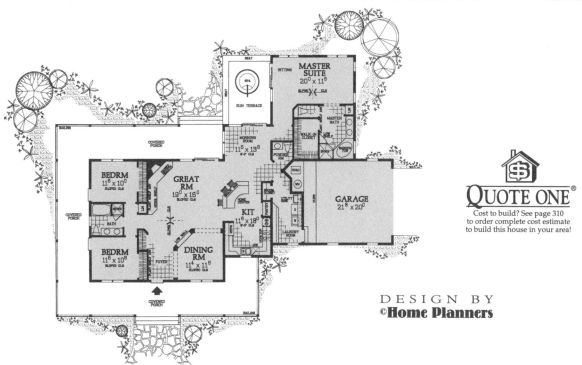

Quote One®

Cost to build? See page 310
to order complete cost estimate
to build this house in your area!

DESIGN BY
©Home Planners

PLAN HPT100095

Square Footage: 2,090
Width: 84'-6" **Depth:** 64'-0"

L·D

This classic farmhouse enjoys a wraparound porch that's perfect for enjoyment of the outdoors. To the rear of the plan, a sun terrace with a spa opens from the owners suite and the morning room. A grand great room offers a sloped ceiling and a corner fireplace with a raised hearth. The formal dining room is defined by a low wall and by graceful archways set off by decorative columns. The tiled kitchen has a centered island counter with a snack bar and adjoins a laundry area. Two family bedrooms reside to the side of the plan, and each enjoys private access to the covered porch. A secluded owners suite nestles in its own wing and features a sitting area with access to the rear terrace and spa.

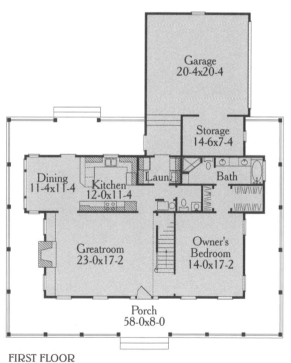

FIRST FLOOR

Garage
20-4x20-4

Storage
14-6x7-4

Dining
11-4x11-4

Kitchen
12-0x11-4

Laun.

Bath

Greatroom
23-0x17-2

Owner's
Bedroom
14-0x17-2

Porch
58-0x8-0

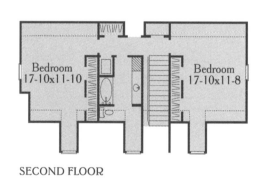

Bedroom
17-10x11-10

Bedroom
17-10x11-8

SECOND FLOOR

DESIGN BY
©Larry James & Associates, Inc.

A full wraparound porch lends itself to hours of contemplating nature in the great out-doors. Built-ins surround the fireplace in the great room, making it a perfect gathering place to stay warm on chilly days. Light pours into the dining area with access to the rear porch—a good location for the outdoor grill! The kitchen has a charming window over the sink and accesses the laundry area and a powder room for guests. A pampering owners suite completes the first floor with a luxurious bath featuring a triangle-shaped shower, dual-van-ity sinks and a roomy walk-in closet. Upstairs, two bedrooms share a full bath and have dormer windows. Please specify basement, crawlspace or slab foundation when ordering.

PLAN HPT100096

Total: 2,162 sq. ft.
First Floor: 1,339 sq. ft.
Second Floor: 823 sq. ft.
Width: 58'-0" **Depth:** 67'-2"

PLAN HPT100097

Country comforts abound inside and outside this three-bedroom home. Inside one can choose to curl up by a warming fire in the living area. The owners suite is buffered by the stair, walk-in closet and guest powder room, ensuring privacy. Luxuriate in the owners bath with its huge bathtub, separate shower and twin lavatory sinks. Sun fills the formal and informal eating areas through two bay windows. The U-shaped kitchen is conveniently located near the garage and laundry facilities. Bedrooms 2 and 3 share a full bath and access to the study on the second floor. Please specify basement, crawlspace or slab foundation when ordering.

Total: 2,091 sq. ft.
First Floor: 1,362 sq. ft.
Second Floor: 729 sq. ft.
Bonus Room: 384 sq. ft.
Width: 72'-0" **Depth:** 38'-0"

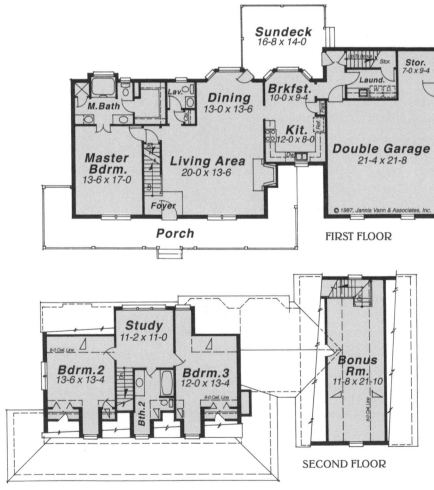

DESIGN BY
©**Jannis Vann & Associates, Inc.**

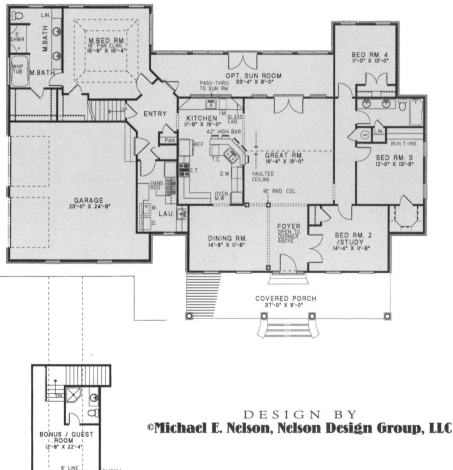

COVERED PORCH
37'-0" X 8'-0"

DESIGN BY
©Michael E. Nelson, Nelson Design Group, LLC

BONUS / GUEST
ROOM
12'-8" X 22'-4"

PLAN HPT100098

Palladian windows and sunburst windows set in dormers above a covered porch lend elegance to this lovely home. Columns add a graceful style to the foyer and formal dining room. To the right of the foyer is Bedroom 2—or a study—which shares a full bath with two family bedrooms. The efficient kitchen includes a large snack bar and a pass-through window to the optional sun room. A secluded owners suite features a private entry from the garage, a tray ceiling and a luxurious owners bath with a whirlpool tub, separate shower, dual-vanity sinks and a walk-in closet. Upstairs is an optional bonus/guest room. Please specify crawl-space or slab foundation when ordering.

Square Footage: 2,485
Bonus Room: 399 sq. ft.
Width: 76'-0" Depth: 56'-0"

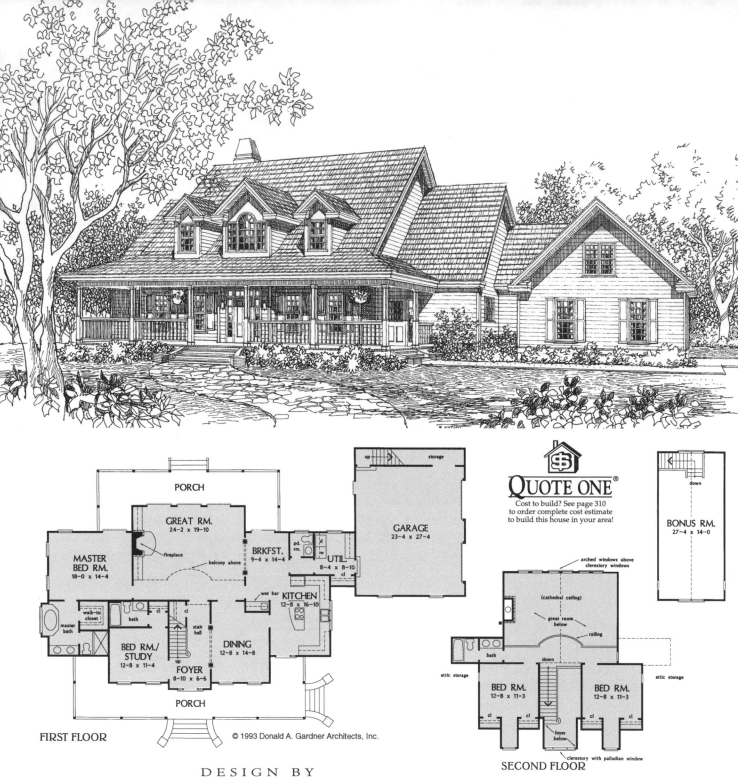

FIRST FLOOR

© 1993 Donald A. Gardner Architects, Inc.

PORCH

GREAT RM.
24-2 x 19-10

fireplace

balcony above

MASTER BED RM.
18-0 x 14-4

BRKFST.
9-4 x 14-4

pd. rm.

d

UTIL
8-4 x 8-10
cl

wet bar

KITCHEN
12-8 x 16-10

walk-in closet

bath

BED RM./STUDY
12-8 x 11-4

stair hall

DINING
12-8 x 14-8

master bath

FOYER
8-10 x 6-6

up

PORCH

up

storage

GARAGE
23-4 x 27-4

QUOTE ONE®
Cost to build? See page 310
to order complete cost estimate
to build this house in your area!

SECOND FLOOR

arched windows above clerestory windows

(cathedral ceiling)

great room below

railing

bath

attic storage

BED RM.
12-8 x 11-3

down

foyer below

BED RM.
12-8 x 11-3

attic storage

cl

clerestory with palladian window

down

BONUS RM.
27-4 x 14-0

DESIGN BY
Donald A. Gardner Architects, Inc.

PLAN HPT100099

Total: 2,658 sq. ft.
First Floor: 2,064 sq. ft.
Second Floor: 594 sq. ft.
Bonus Room: 483 sq. ft.
Width: 92'-0" **Depth:** 57'-8"

You'll find country living at its best when meandering through this four-bedroom farmhouse with its wraparound porch. A front Palladian dormer window and rear clerestory windows in the great room add exciting visual elements to the exterior while providing natural light to the interior. The large great room boasts a fireplace, bookshelves and a raised cathedral ceiling, allowing a curved balcony overlook above. The great room, owners bedroom and breakfast room are accessible to the rear porch for greater circulation and flexibility. Special features such as the large cooktop island in the kitchen, the wet bar, the generous bonus room over the garage and ample storage space set this plan apart.

© 1995 Donald A. Gardner Architects, Inc.

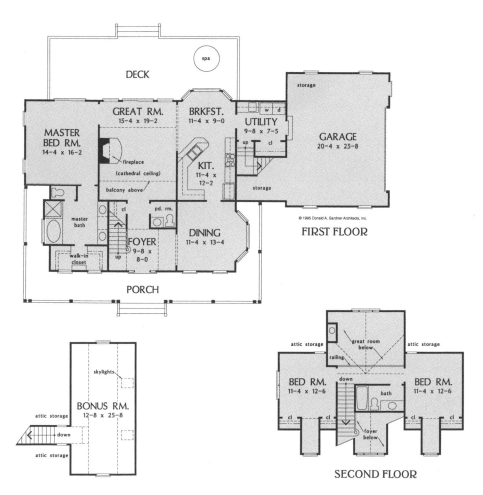

DECK

spa

GREAT RM.
15-4 x 19-2

BRKFST.
11-4 x 9-0

UTILITY
9-8 x 7-5

storage

w   d

GARAGE
20-4 x 25-8

MASTER
BED RM.
14-4 x 16-2

fireplace
(cathedral ceiling)

balcony above

KIT.
11-4 x 12-2

storage

master
bath

cl

pd. rm.

walk-in
closet

FOYER
9-8 x 8-0

DINING
11-4 x 13-4

up

PORCH

© 1995 Donald A. Gardner Architects, Inc.

FIRST FLOOR

skylights

BONUS RM.
12-8 x 25-8

attic storage

down

attic storage

attic storage

great room
below

attic storage

railing

BED RM.
11-4 x 12-6

down

BED RM.
11-4 x 12-6

bath

cl

cl

cl

cl

foyer
below

SECOND FLOOR

DESIGN BY
Donald A. Gardner Architects, Inc.

PLAN HPT100100

This farmhouse has plenty to offer, from its covered front porch to its rear deck with a spa. Special touches, such as multi-pane windows and mock shutters, add further charm to this three-bedroom home. Inside, the amenities continue, including a formal dining room to the right of the two-story foyer, a great room with a fireplace, and a breakfast nook located off the efficient kitchen. Both the formal and informal dining areas benefit from a bay window. The first-floor owners suite boasts a luxurious bath with a whirlpool tub, separate shower and walk-in closet. Upstairs, away from the owners bedroom for privacy, two family bedrooms share a full hall bath and a balcony overlook.

Total: 1,991 sq. ft.
First Floor: 1,480 sq. ft.
Second Floor: 511 sq. ft.
Bonus Room: 363 sq. ft.
Width: 73'-0" **Depth:** 51'-10"

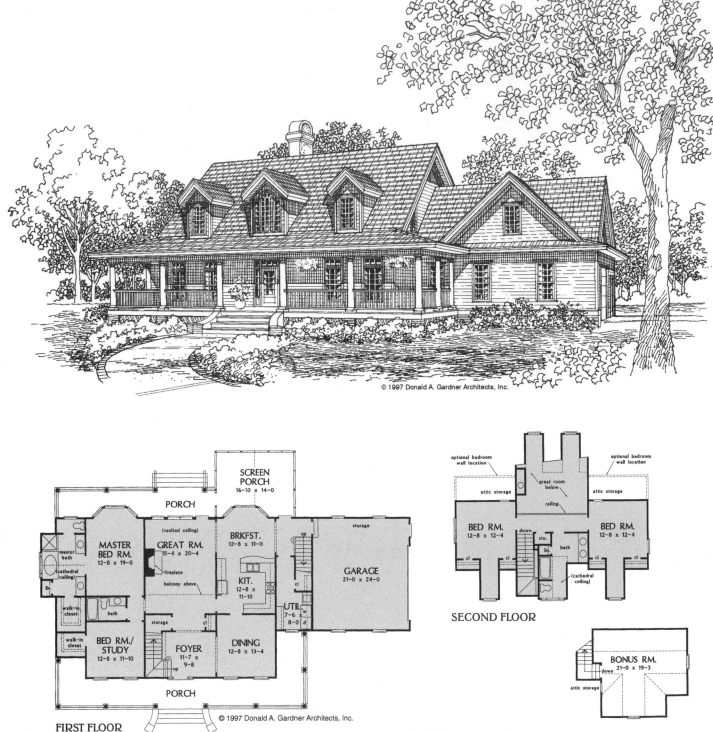

© 1997 Donald A. Gardner Architects, Inc.

SCREEN PORCH
16-10 x 14-0

PORCH

MASTER BED RM.
12-8 x 19-0

master bath

cathedral ceiling

lin.

walk-in closet

walk-in closet

bath

BED RM./STUDY
12-8 x 11-10

GREAT RM.
15-4 x 20-4

(vaulted ceiling)

fireplace

balcony above

storage

FOYER
11-7 x 9-8

up

BRKFST.
12-8 x 11-0

KIT.
12-8 x 11-10

DINING
12-8 x 13-4

UTIL.
7-6 x 8-0

up

cl

storage

GARAGE
21-0 x 24-0

FIRST FLOOR

PORCH

© 1997 Donald A. Gardner Architects, Inc.

optional bedroom wall location

optional bedroom wall location

great room below

attic storage

railing

attic storage

BED RM.
12-8 x 12-4

BED RM.
12-8 x 12-4

down

sto.

lin.

bath

(cathedral ceiling)

cl

cl

cl

cl

SECOND FLOOR

BONUS RM.
21-0 x 19-3

down

attic storage

DESIGN BY
Donald A. Gardner Architects, Inc.

PLAN HPT100101

Total: 2,596 sq. ft.
First Floor: 1,939 sq. ft.
Second Floor: 657 sq. ft.
Bonus Room: 386 sq. ft.
Width: 80'-10" **Depth:** 55'-8"

This country farmhouse offers an inviting wraparound porch for comfort and three gabled dormers for style. The foyer leads to a generous great room with an extended-hearth fireplace, cathedral ceiling and access to the back covered porch. The first-floor owners suite enjoys a sunny bay window and features a private bath with a cathedral ceiling, large oval tub set near a window, separate shower and dual-vanity sinks. Upstairs, two family bedrooms share an elegant bath that has a cathedral ceiling. An optional bonus room over the garage allows plenty of room to grow.

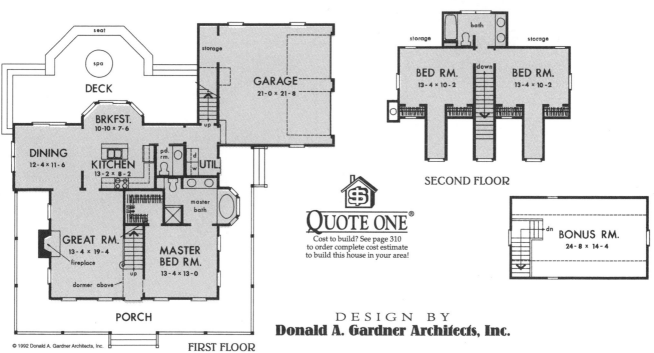

seat

spa

DECK

storage

GARAGE
21-0 × 21-8

BRKFST.
10-10 × 7-6

DINING
12-4 × 11-6

KITCHEN
13-2 × 8-2

pd. rm.

d w

UTIL.

up

master bath

GREAT RM.
13-4 × 19-4

fireplace

MASTER BED RM.
13-4 × 13-0

up

dormer above

PORCH

© 1992 Donald A. Gardner Architects, Inc.

FIRST FLOOR

bath

storage

storage

BED RM.
13-4 × 10-2

down

BED RM.
13-4 × 10-2

SECOND FLOOR

QUOTE ONE®

Cost to build? See page 310 to order complete cost estimate to build this house in your area!

dn

BONUS RM.
24-8 × 14-4

D E S I G N   B Y
Donald A. Gardner Architects, Inc.

L ook this plan over and you'll be amazed at how much livability can be found in less than 2,000 square feet. A wraparound porch welcomes visitors to the home. Inside lies an enormous great room with a fireplace. To the rear of the home, the breakfast and dining rooms have sliding glass doors to a large deck with room for a spa. The owners bedroom contains a walk-in closet and an airy bath with a whirlpool tub. Two bedrooms occupy the second floor, as well as a bonus room over the garage.

PLAN HPT100102

Total: 1,663 sq. ft.
First Floor: 1,145 sq. ft.
Second Floor: 518 sq. ft.
Bonus Room: 380 sq. ft.
Width: 59'-4" **Depth:** 56'-6"

PLAN HPT100103

Dutch gable rooflines and a gabled wraparound porch with star-burst trim provide an extra measure of farmhouse style. The clerestory window sheds light on the stairway leading from the foyer to the upstairs bedrooms and loft. On the main level, the foyer leads on the left to the study or guest bedroom that connects to the owners suite, on the right to the formal dining room, and to the massive great room in the center of the home where a warming fireplace creates a cozy centerpiece. The kitchen conveniently combines with the great room, the breakfast nook and the dining room. The owners suite includes access to the covered patio, a spacious walk-in closet and an owners bath with a whirlpool tub.

Total: 3,434 sq. ft.
First Floor: 2,347 sq. ft.
Second Floor: 1,087 sq. ft.
Width: 93'-6" **Depth:** 61'-0"

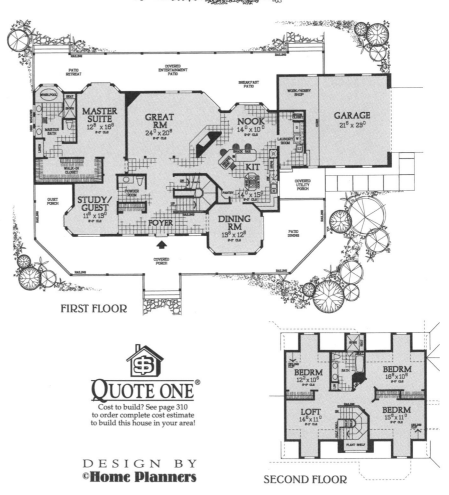

FIRST FLOOR

Quote One®
Cost to build? See page 310
to order complete cost estimate
to build this house in your area!

DESIGN BY
©**Home Planners**

SECOND FLOOR

©1993 Donald A. Gardner Architects, Inc.

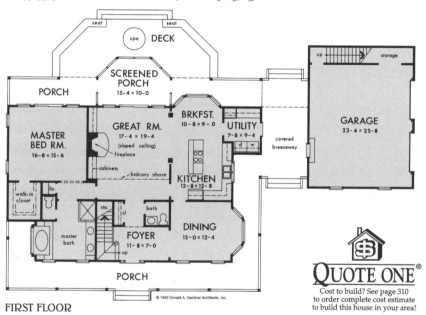

DECK
seat seat
spa

SCREENED PORCH
15-4 x 10-0

PORCH

MASTER BED RM.
16-8 x 15-6

GREAT RM.
17-4 x 19-4
(sloped ceiling)
fireplace
cabinets
balcony above

BRKFST.
10-8 x 9-0

UTILITY
7-8 x 9-4
d | w

GARAGE
22-4 x 25-8

up | storage

covered breezeway

walk-in closet
lin.
master bath

KITCHEN
12-8 x 12-8

sto.
cl
bath
up

FOYER
11-8 x 7-0

DINING
15-0 x 12-4

PORCH

© 1993 Donald A. Gardner Architects, Inc.

FIRST FLOOR

DESIGN BY
Donald A. Gardner Architects, Inc.

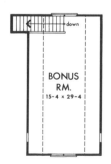

down

BONUS RM.
15-4 x 29-4

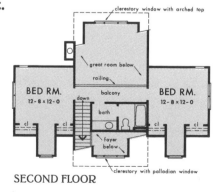

clerestory window with arched top

great room below

railing

BED RM.
12-8 x 12-0

balcony

down

BED RM.
12-8 x 12-0

bath

cl | cl

cl | cl

foyer below

clerestory with palladian window

SECOND FLOOR

PLAN HPT100104

The entrance foyer and great room enjoy Palladian clerestory windows that allow natural light to enter the well-planned interior of this country home. The spacious great room boasts a fireplace, built-in cabinets and an overlook from the second-floor balcony. The kitchen furnishes a cooktop island counter and is placed conveniently between the breakfast room and the formal dining room. A generous first-floor owners suite offers plenty of closet space and a lavish bath with a windowed whirlpool tub. Upstairs, two family bedrooms share a full bath. Bonus space over the garage awaits later development.

QUOTE ONE®
Cost to build? See page 310 to order complete cost estimate to build this house in your area!

Total: 2,188 sq. ft.
First Floor: 1,618 sq. ft.
Second Floor: 570 sq. ft.
Bonus Room: 495 sq. ft.
Width: 87'-0" **Depth:** 57'-0"

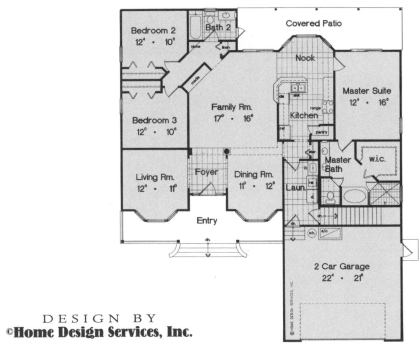

Bedroom 2
12⁴ • 10⁰

Bath 2

Covered Patio

Nook

Master Suite
12⁴ • 16⁸

Family Rm.
17⁰ • 16⁸

Kitchen

Bedroom 3
12⁰ • 10⁸

Master Bath

w.i.c.

Living Rm.
12⁴ • 11⁰

Foyer

Dining Rm.
11⁰ • 12⁸

Laun.

Entry

2 Car Garage
22⁴ • 21⁰

DESIGN BY
©Home Design Services, Inc.

PLAN HPT100105

Square Footage: 1,831
Width: 54'-0" **Depth:** 63'-8"

The front porch welcomes you to this house, clad in ship-lap siding at the front, with three traditional dormers. Inside, the dining and living rooms are both adorned with bay windows facing the front yard. A media alcove attracts interest as the focal point of the family room. Two family bedrooms share a full bath to the left of the family room. Read a book or newspaper in the sunlit breakfast nook with its bay window. The owners suite is privately located to the right of the kitchen, and the luxurious bath includes a large oval tub, generous shower, twin-vanity sinks and a roomy walk-in closet.

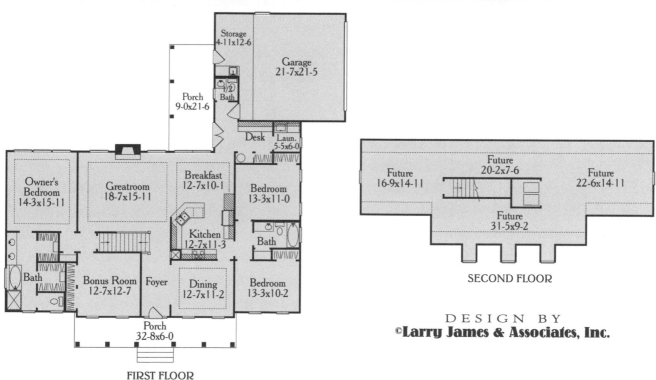

Storage 4-11x12-6

Garage 21-7x21-5

Porch 9-0x21-6

Bath

Desk

Laun. 5-5x6-0

Owner's Bedroom 14-3x15-11

Greatroom 18-7x15-11

Breakfast 12-7x10-1

Bedroom 13-3x11-0

Kitchen 12-7x11-3

Bath

Bath

Bonus Room 12-7x12-7

Foyer

Dining 12-7x11-2

Bedroom 13-3x10-2

Porch 32-8x6-0

FIRST FLOOR

Future 16-9x14-11

Future 20-2x7-6

Future 22-6x14-11

Future 31-5x9-2

SECOND FLOOR

DESIGN BY
©**Larry James & Associates, Inc.**

This lovely country home offers charming dormers and a covered porch. Inside, the formal dining room is to the right, and easily accesses the kitchen. A snack bar in the kitchen allows views of both the breakfast nook and the great room. Two windows frame the warming fireplace of the great room, adorned with a tray ceiling. The secluded owners suite on the left of the plan features a compartmented bath with His and Hers walk-in closets. Near the front of the house, a bonus room can be used as a fourth bedroom, hobby area or study. Please specify basement, crawlspace or slab foundation when ordering.

PLAN HPT100106

Square Footage: 2,127
Bonus Space: 1,095 sq. ft.
Width: 69'-0" **Depth:** 67'-7"

FIRST FLOOR

SECOND FLOOR

DESIGN BY
©**Drummond Designs, Inc.**

PLAN HPT100107

Total: 1,840 sq. ft.
First Floor: 980 sq. ft.
Second Floor: 860 sq. ft.
Width: 49'-8" **Depth:** 32'-0"

This traditional three-bedroom home features two full bathrooms and a powder room. A graceful front porch with a French-door entry welcomes guests. Living quarters downstairs include a well-designed eat-in kitchen with lots of counter space, a formal dining area, a spacious family room, a laundry room and a powder room. Three bedrooms reside upstairs. The owners bedroom features a large walk-in closet and a spacious private bath with two vanities, a shower stall and a separate bathtub. The additional bedrooms each have large closets and share a bathroom. This home is designed with a basement foundation.

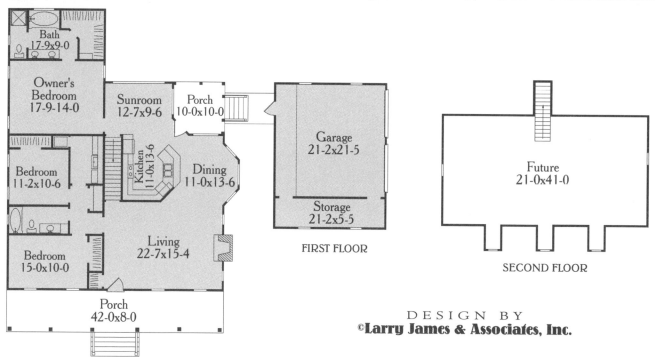

Bath
17-9x9-0

Owner's
Bedroom
17-9-14-0

Sunroom
12-7x9-6

Porch
10-0x10-0

Garage
21-2x21-5

Bedroom
11-2x10-6

Kitchen
11-0x13-6

Dining
11-0x13-6

Bedroom
15-0x10-0

Living
22-7x15-4

Storage
21-2x5-5

FIRST FLOOR

Porch
42-0x8-0

Future
21-0x41-0

SECOND FLOOR

DESIGN BY
©Larry James & Associates, Inc.

A sunburst over the entry door, a covered porch, three dormers and shutters give this home a comforting air. Inside, the living room contains a warming fireplace, framed by windows. Sunshine or moonlight fills the formal dining room through bay windows. The kitchen adjoins the dining room with a snack bar. Nearby, the owners bedroom has a private bath with a walk-in closet. Two bedrooms share a full bath accessed via the living room. Additional space is available upstairs with a bonus room. Please specify basement, crawlspace or slab foundation when ordering.

PLAN HPT100108

Square Footage: 1,879
Bonus Room: 965 sq. ft.
Width: 45'-0" **Depth:** 62'-0"

PLAN HPT100109

This twin-gabled farmhouse is sure to please, with its covered front porch, large screened back porch and many amenities. Inside, the foyer is flanked by a formal dining room and a cozy study. Double doors separate the foyer from the spacious great room, which is complete with a fireplace and twin French doors to the screened porch. The homeowner will definitely feel pampered in the owners suite. Here, two walk-in closets, a separate exercise room and a lavish bath wait to help with relaxation. Upstairs, an absolutely luxurious bath will make family or guests feel like royalty. Note the optional media room. Please specify basement, crawlspace or slab foundation when ordering.

Total: 3,706 sq. ft.
First Floor: 2,473 sq. ft.
Second Floor: 1,233 sq. ft.
Bonus Room: 155 sq. ft.
Width: 60'-0" **Depth:** 64'-2"

FIRST FLOOR

SECOND FLOOR

DESIGN BY
©**Michael E. Nelson, Nelson Design Group, LLC**

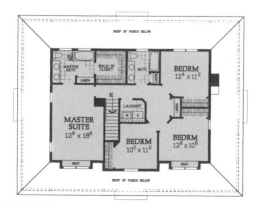

FIRST FLOOR

QUOTE ONE®

Cost to build? See page 310
to order complete cost estimate
to build this house in your area!

DESIGN BY
©**Home Planners**

SECOND FLOOR

PLAN HPT100110

Amenities fill this two-story country home, beginning with a full wrap-around porch that offers access to each room on the first floor. Formal living and dining rooms border the central foyer, each with French-door access to the covered porch. At the rear of the first floor, an open family area begins with a U-shaped kitchen and a bayed breakfast or morning area and continues to a large family room with a fireplace and access to the rear porch. Upstairs, three family bedrooms share a centrally located utility room and a full hall bath that has dual sinks. The owners suite features a box-bay window seat and a private bath with separate sinks and a walk-in closet. A half-bath on the first floor completes this exquisite design.

Total: 2,295 sq. ft.
First Floor: 1,160 sq. ft.
Second Floor: 1,135 sq. ft.
Width: 54'-0" **Depth:** 42'-0"

Double Garage
23-0 x 24-0

FIRST FLOOR

Brkfst.
17-0 x 10-0

Sundeck
14-0 x 12-0

Lav.

Kitchen
11-0 x 11-0

Family Rm.
21-0 x 14-0

Dining
12-0 x 13-0

Living
16-0 x 11-0

Bonus Rm.
23-0 x 24-0

SECOND FLOOR

Bdrm.3
12-0 x 13-0

Bath 2

M.Bath

Laund.

Bdrm.2
12-0 x 15-0

Bdrm.4
11-0 x 13-0

Master
Bdrm.
13-0 x 17-0

DESIGN BY
©Jannis Vann & Associates, Inc.

PLAN HPT100111

Total: 2,479 sq. ft.
First Floor: 1,250 sq. ft.
Second Floor: 1,229 sq. ft.
Bonus Room: 420 sq. ft.
Width: 52'-0" **Depth:** 64'-0"

A Palladian window over a wraparound porch lends classy style to this roomy four-bedroom home. Inside, the foyer leads to the formal dining room on the left and the living room to the right. A U-shaped kitchen is conveniently nearby the dining area and the breakfast room. A ribbon of windows and warming fireplace adorn the family room, which accesses both the rear deck and the wraparound covered porch. Upstairs, three family bedrooms share a hall bath near the beautiful owners bedroom, which features a spacious walk-in closet and a sumptuous private bath complete with a shower, large soaking tub and dual-vanity sink. Please specify basement or crawlspace foundation when ordering.

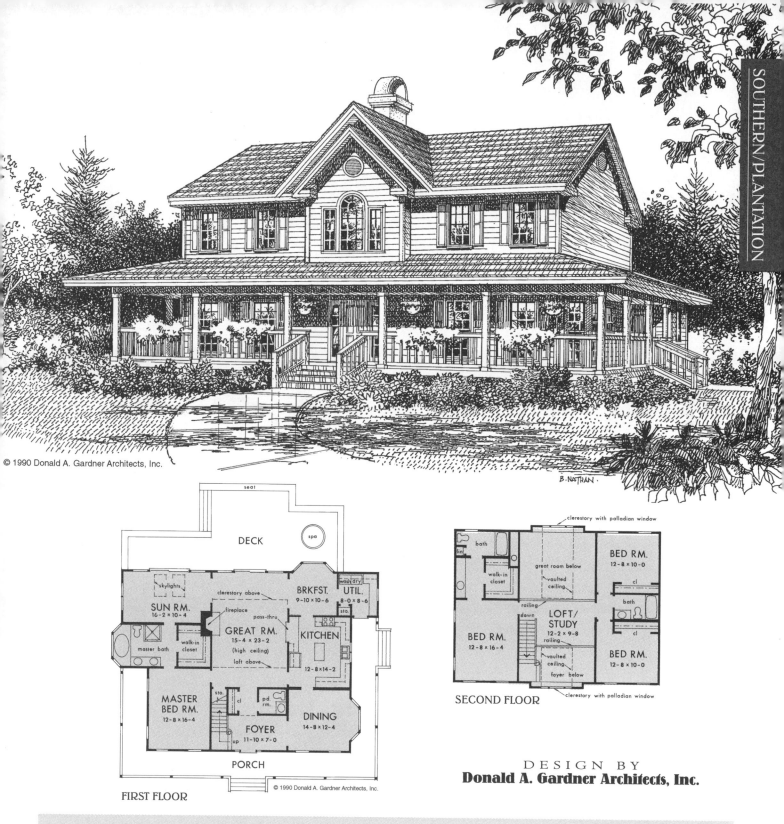

B. NATHAN.

FIRST FLOOR

- seat
- DECK
- spa
- skylights
- SUN RM. 16-2 × 10-4
- clerestory above
- fireplace
- BRKFST. 9-10 × 10-6
- UTIL. 8-0 × 8-6
- wash/dry
- sto.
- pass-thru
- GREAT RM. 15-4 × 23-2 (high ceiling)
- loft above
- KITCHEN 12-8 × 14-2
- walk-in closet
- master bath
- MASTER BED RM. 12-8 × 16-4
- sto.
- cl
- pd. rm.
- DINING 14-8 × 12-4
- FOYER 11-10 × 7-0 up
- PORCH

© 1990 Donald A. Gardner Architects, Inc.

SECOND FLOOR

- clerestory with palladian window
- bath
- lin
- great room below
- walk-in closet
- vaulted ceiling
- railing
- BED RM. 12-8 × 10-0
- cl
- bath
- cl
- BED RM. 12-8 × 16-4
- down
- LOFT/ STUDY 12-2 × 9-8
- railing
- vaulted ceiling
- foyer below
- BED RM. 12-8 × 10-0
- clerestory with palladian window

DESIGN BY
Donald A. Gardner Architects, Inc.

A wraparound covered porch at the front and sides of this home and the open deck with a spa and seating provide plenty of outside living area. A central great room features a vaulted ceiling, a fireplace and clerestory windows above. The loft/study on the second floor overlooks this gathering area. Besides a formal dining room, kitchen, breakfast room and sun room on the first floor, there is also a generous owners suite with a garden tub. Three second-floor bedrooms complete the sleeping accommodations. A walk-in closet and a private bath highlight one of these bedrooms, while the other two share a bath.

PLAN HPT100112

Total: 2,692 sq. ft.
First Floor: 1,734 sq. ft.
Second Floor: 958 sq. ft.
Width: 55'-0" **Depth:** 59'-10"

© 1992 Donald A. Gardner Architects, Inc.

PLAN HPT100113

This grand four-bedroom farmhouse with a wraparound porch has eye-catching features: a double-gabled roof, a Palladian window at the upper level, arched windows on the lower level, and an intricately detailed brick chimney. The large family room allows for more casual living. Look for a fireplace, wet bar and direct access to a porch and deck here. The lavish kitchen boasts a cooking island and serves the dining room, breakfast room and deck. The owners suite on the second level has a large walk-in closet and an owners bath with a whirlpool tub, separate shower and double-bowl vanity. Three additional bedrooms share a full bath.

Total: 2,561 sq. ft.
First Floor: 1,357 sq. ft.
Second Floor: 1,204 sq. ft.
Width: 80'-0" **Depth:** 57'-0"

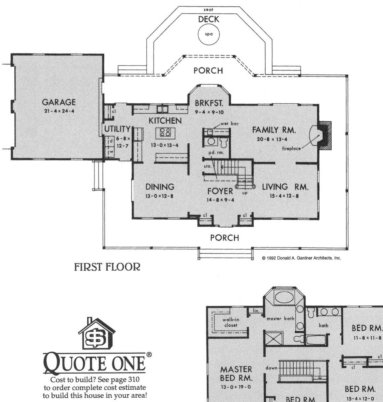

FIRST FLOOR

© 1992 Donald A. Gardner Architects, Inc.

QUOTE ONE®
Cost to build? See page 310
to order complete cost estimate
to build this house in your area!

SECOND FLOOR

DESIGN BY
Donald A. Gardner Architects, Inc.

FIRST FLOOR

DESIGN BY
©**Home Planners**

SECOND FLOOR

Quote One®
Cost to build? See page 310
to order complete cost estimate
to build this house in your area!

PLAN HPT100114

The combination of shutters, multi-pane windows and a luxurious wrap-around porch makes this farmhouse a real winner. Columns accent the formal living room, which offers access to the covered porch. At the rear of the plan, the formal dining room shares a through-fireplace with a large family room; both rooms have convenient access to the efficient kitchen. The private first-floor owners suite has plenty to offer—a walk-in closet, ultra tub, separate shower and access to the covered porch. Upstairs, three family bedrooms share a full hall bath that includes a compartmented toilet. A large utility room is conveniently located just off a multimedia loft.

Total: 2,290 sq. ft.
First Floor: 1,378 sq. ft.
Second Floor: 912 sq. ft.
Width: 74'-0" **Depth:** 46'-0"

L

PLAN HPT100115

Classic capstones and arched windows complement rectangular shutters and pillars on this traditional facade. The family room offsets a formal dining room and shares a see-through fireplace with the keeping room. A gourmet kitchen boasts a food-preparation island with a serving bar, a generous pantry and French-door access to the rear property. Upstairs, a sensational owners suite with a tray ceiling and a vaulted bath with a plant shelf, whirlpool spa and walk-in closet opens from a gallery hall with a balcony overlook. Bonus space offers the possibility of an adjoining sitting room. Three additional bedrooms share a full bath. Please specify basement or crawl-space foundation when ordering.

Total: 2,386 sq. ft.
First Floor: 1,223 sq. ft.
Second Floor: 1,163 sq. ft.
Bonus Room: 204 sq. ft.
Width: 50'-0" **Depth:** 46'-0"

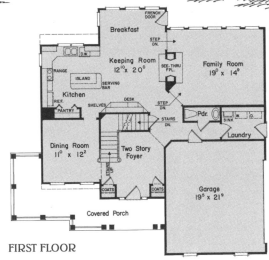

FIRST FLOOR

DESIGN BY
©**Frank Betz Associates, Inc.**

SECOND FLOOR

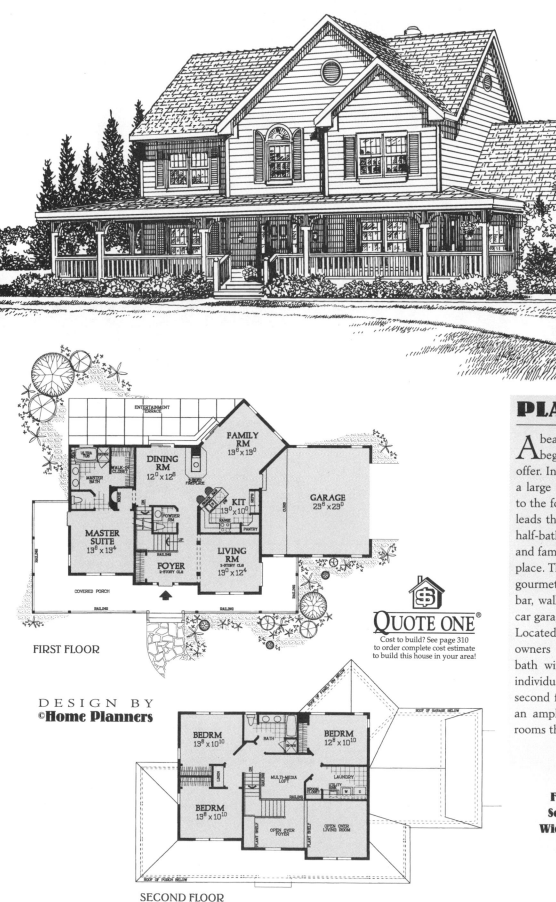

FIRST FLOOR

DESIGN BY
©**Home Planners**

QUOTE ONE®

Cost to build? See page 310
to order complete cost estimate
to build this house in your area!

SECOND FLOOR

PLAN HPT100116

A beautiful country facade is just the beginning of what this design has to offer. Inside, the two-story foyer includes a large coat closet and decorative entry to the formal living room. The foyer also leads through a hall—with a convenient half-bath—to the formal dining room and family room with its three-sided fireplace. The angled family room opens to a gourmet kitchen, which features a snack bar, walk-in pantry and access to a two-car garage with a workshop/storage area. Located on the first floor for privacy, the owners bedroom features a pampering bath with a separate tub and shower, individual sinks and a walk-in closet. The second floor contains a multimedia loft, an ample laundry area and three bedrooms that share a full bath.

Total: 2,290 sq. ft.
First Floor: 1,378 sq. ft.
Second Floor: 912 sq. ft.
Width: 74'-0" **Depth:** 46'-0"

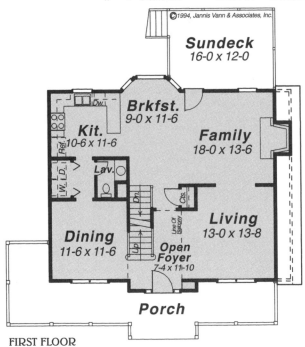

©1994, Jannis Vann & Associates, Inc.

Sundeck
16-0 x 12-0

Brkfst.
9-0 x 11-6

Kit.
10-6 x 11-6

Family
18-0 x 13-6

Dining
11-6 x 11-6

Lav.

Living
13-0 x 13-8

Line Of Balcony

Open Foyer
7-4 x 11-10

Porch

FIRST FLOOR

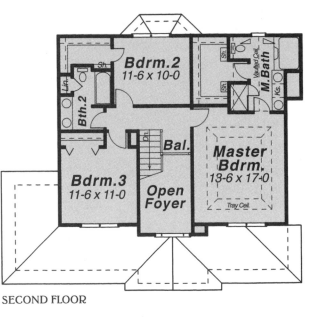

Bdrm.2
11-6 x 10-0

Sh.

Bth.2

Lin.

M. Bath
Vaulted Ceil.
Sh.
Ks.

Bal.

Bdrm.3
11-6 x 11-0

Open Foyer

Master Bdrm.
13-6 x 17-0

Tray Ceil.

SECOND FLOOR

DESIGN BY
©**Jannis Vann & Associates, Inc.**

PLAN HPT100117

Total: 1,880 sq. ft.
First Floor: 981 sq. ft.
Second Floor: 899 sq. ft.
Width: 44'-0" **Depth:** 38'-0"

A lovely keystone lintel over a Palladian window sets the stylish tone of this roomy three-bedroom home. Inside, light pours into the two story foyer, illuminating the stairway to the second floor. Upstairs, two family bedrooms share a hall bath near the beautiful owners bedroom with a tray ceiling. The owners bath is complete with a spacious shower, large walk-in closet, two-person soaking tub and dual-vanity sinks. On the first floor, the foyer leads to the formal dining room on the left and the living room to the right. A U-shaped kitchen sits conveniently near the dining area and the breakfast room. The breakfast room—lit by a bay window—opens to the large family room and its warming fireplace.

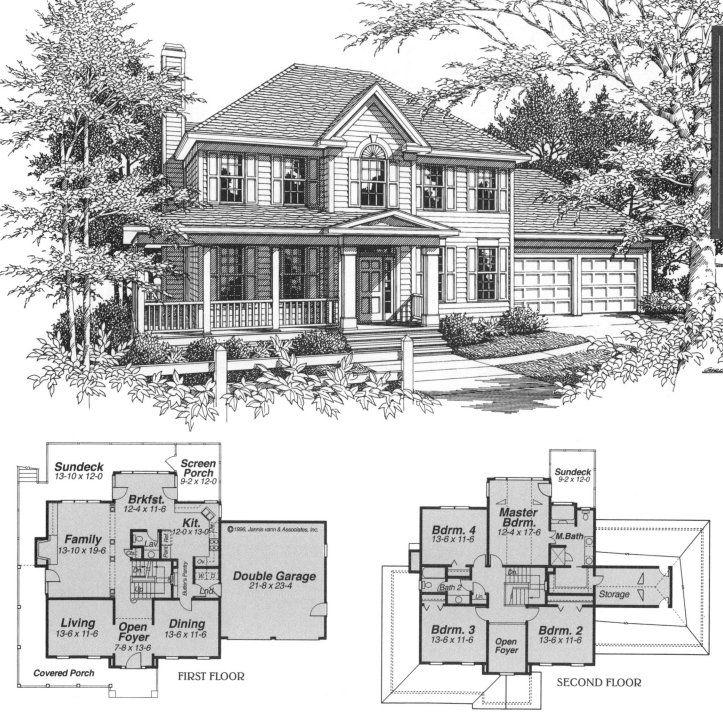

Sundeck 13-10 x 12-0

Screen Porch 9-2 x 12-0

Brkfst. 12-4 x 11-6

Kit. 12-0 x 13-0

©1996, Jannis vann & Associates, Inc.

Family 13-10 x 19-6

Lav.

Pantry Ref.

Ov.

Butler's Pantry

W D

Lnd.

Double Garage 21-8 x 23-4

Living 13-6 x 11-6

Open Foyer 7-8 x 13-6

Dining 13-6 x 11-6

Covered Porch

FIRST FLOOR

Sundeck 9-2 x 12-0

Bdrm. 4 13-6 x 11-6

Master Bdrm. 12-4 x 17-6

M.Bath

Bath 2

Lin.

Dn.

Storage

Bdrm. 3 13-6 x 11-6

Open Foyer

Bdrm. 2 13-6 x 11-6

SECOND FLOOR

DESIGN BY
©**Jannis Vann & Associates, Inc.**

A lovely keystone lintel over a Palladian window and thick pillars framing the doorway give this four-bedroom design a blissful country appeal. Inside, light pours into the two-story foyer, illuminating the stairway to the second floor. Upstairs, three family bedrooms share a hall bath near the breathtaking owners suite with a sloped ceiling and access to a private sun deck. On the first floor, the foyer leads to the formal dining room on the right and the living room to the left. An eye-catching butler's pantry connects the formal dining area to the kitchen. The sunny breakfast nook accesses both the screened porch and the sun deck at the rear of the house. Pillars mark the entry to the large family room.

PLAN HPT100118

Total: 2,416 sq. ft.
First Floor: 1,250 sq. ft.
Second Floor: 1,166 sq. ft.
Bonus Space: 144 sq. ft.
Width: 64'-0" **Depth:** 52'-0"

PLAN HPT100119

Three classic dormers set over a New Orleans-style double-decker porch begin this delightful five-bedroom home. Inside, be entertained in the formal dining and living rooms. The family room enjoys a fireplace and a ribbon of windows facing the rear yard. Light pours into the breakfast room from a full wall of windows. On the second floor, four family bedrooms—three share a full bath and one has a private bath—and an owners suite are tucked away from the everyday activities. The balcony is accessible by three of the four family bedrooms. The owners suite is complete with two walk-in closets, a sitting area and a luxurious bath with an oval tub set in a corner with steps. Please specify basement or slab foundation when ordering.

Total: 2,961 sq. ft.
First Floor: 1,286 sq. ft.
Second Floor: 1,675 sq. ft.
Width: 35'-0" **Depth:** 64'-0"

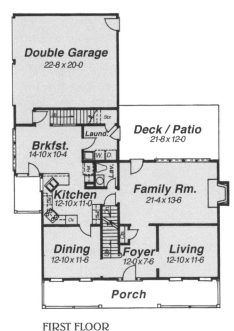

FIRST FLOOR

DESIGN BY
©Jannis Vann & Associates, Inc.

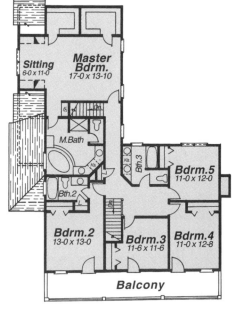

SECOND FLOOR

122

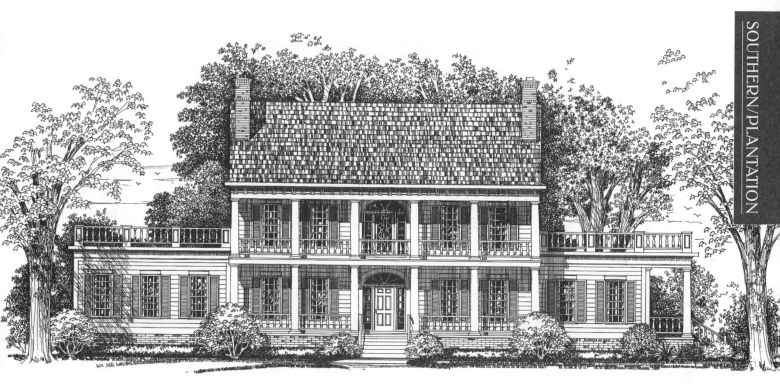

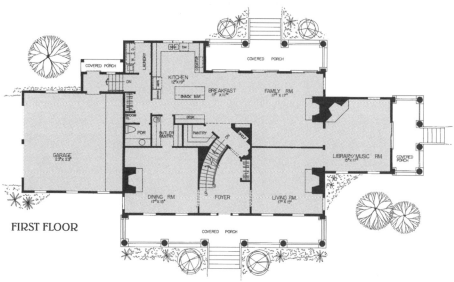

FIRST FLOOR

QUOTE ONE®

Cost to build? See page 310
to order complete cost estimate
to build this house in your area!

DESIGN BY
©Home Planners

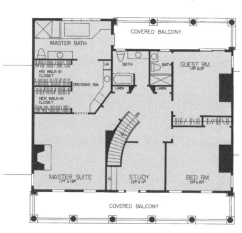

SECOND FLOOR

PLAN HPT100120

Make history with this modern version of Louisiana's "Rosedown House." Like its predecessor—built in the 1800s—this adaptation exhibits splendid Southern styling, but with today's most sought-after amenities. The formal zone of the house is introduced by a foyer with a graceful, curving staircase. The dining and living rooms flank the foyer—a fireplace highlights each. A library or music room offers a corner fireplace and access to a covered porch. A breakfast area is open to the family room and kitchen. Sleeping quarters upstairs include an owners suite with two walk-in closets and a private bath, a guest room with a private bath, and a family bedroom and study with a nearby hall bath.

Total: 3,833 sq. ft.
First Floor: 2,098 sq. ft.
Second Floor: 1,735 sq. ft.
Width: 95'-4" **Depth:** 48'-8"

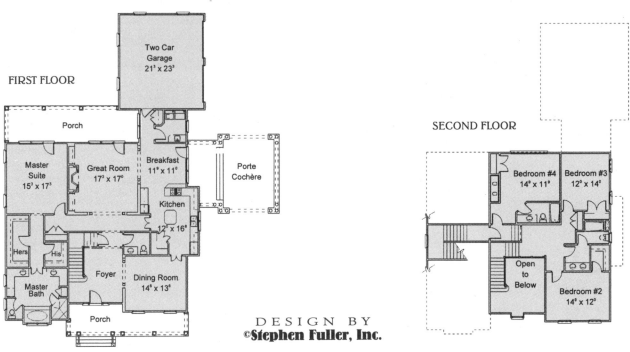

FIRST FLOOR

Two Car Garage
21³ x 23³

Porch

Master Suite
15³ x 17³

Great Room
17³ x 17⁰

Breakfast
11⁹ x 11⁰

Porte Cochère

Kitchen
12⁰ x 16⁸

Hers   His

Master Bath

Foyer

Dining Room
14⁹ x 13⁰

Porch

SECOND FLOOR

Bedroom #4
14⁹ x 11⁹

Bedroom #3
12⁰ x 14⁰

Open to Below

Bedroom #2
14⁹ x 12⁰

DESIGN BY
©**Stephen Fuller, Inc.**

PLAN HPT100121

Total: 3,250 sq. ft.
First Floor: 2,090 sq. ft.
Second Floor: 1,160 sq. ft.
Width: 70'-6" **Depth:** 79'-9"

The sweetly relaxed, slightly rambling composition of this Southern Vernacular-style home sets off farmhouse details such as lap siding, stone piers and wood-trimmed walls. Tapered columns on the front porch and an optional porte cochere lend an aura of hospitality. Inside, the two-story foyer leads to the spacious great room, where a vaulted ceiling creates a feeling of luxury and a focal-point fireplace adds warmth. The gourmet kitchen serves the dining room and the breakfast room with ease and features an island work counter and a walk-in pantry. The owners suite offers two large walk-in closets and a splendid bath with separate vanities. This home is designed with a basement foundation.

Victorian-Influenced Farmhouses

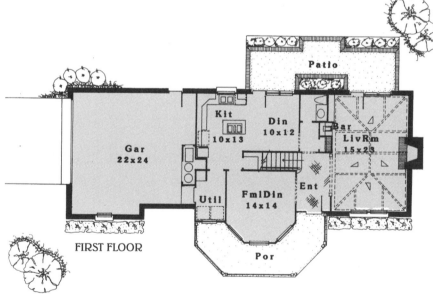

FIRST FLOOR

D E S I G N   B Y
©Fillmore Design Group

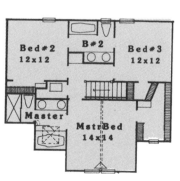

SECOND FLOOR

PLAN HPT100122

Farmhouse fresh with a touch of Victorian style best describes this charming home. A covered front porch wraps around the dining room's bay window and leads the way to the entrance. To the right of the entry is a living room that features a wet bar and a warming fireplace. At the rear of the plan, an L-shaped kitchen is equipped with an island cooktop, making meal preparation a breeze. Casual meals can be enjoyed in a dining area, which merges with the kitchen and accesses the rear patio. A powder room and utility room complete the first floor. Sleeping quarters contained on the second floor include a relaxing owners suite with a large walk-in closet, two family bedrooms and a connecting bath.

Total: 1,920 sq. ft.
First Floor: 1,082 sq. ft.
Second Floor: 838 sq. ft.
Width: 66'-10" **Depth:** 29'-5"

PLAN HPT100123

Fish-scale siding, pinnacles on top of the three gables, and wood detailing on the porch are just some of the charming Victorian elements of this four-bedroom home. Inside, built-in amenities abound—two coat closets frame the entry door and support a plant shelf above, an alcove in the dining room awaits your hutch, and a roomy pantry will easily store all your dried goods. Double doors open from the living room to the family room, lit with firelight from the fireplace. The L-shaped kitchen has an adjoining breakfast nook with bay windows. Upstairs, three family bedrooms, all with walk-in closets, share a full bath. The owners suite is complete with two walk-in closets and a luxurious bath.

Total: 2,531 sq. ft.
First Floor: 1,120 sq. ft.
Second Floor: 1,411 sq. ft.
Width: 57'-4" **Depth:** 33'-0"

FIRST FLOOR

SECOND FLOOR

DESIGN BY
©**Design Basics, Inc.**

126

FIRST FLOOR

SECOND FLOOR

DESIGN BY
©**Home Planners**

Quote One®

Cost to build? See page 310
to order complete cost estimate
to build this house in your area!

PLAN HPT100124

Covered porches at the front and rear are the first signal that this is a fine example of Folk Victorian styling. The interior grand plan for family living complements the exterior. A formal living room and attached dining room provide space for entertaining guests. The large family room with a fireplace is a gathering room for everyday activities. Both areas have access to outdoor spaces. Four bedrooms occupy the second floor. The owners suite features two lavatories, a window seat and three closets. One of the family bedrooms has its own private balcony and could be used as a study. Note the open staircase and convenient linen storage.

Total: 1,996 sq. ft.
First Floor: 1,096 sq. ft.
Second Floor: 900 sq. ft.
Width: 56'-0" **Depth:** 44'-0"

L·D

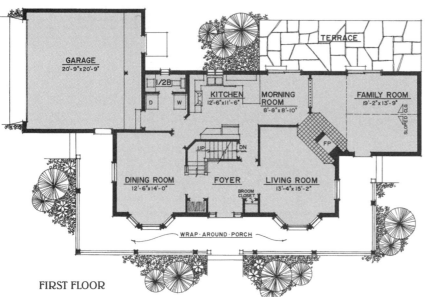

FIRST FLOOR

SECOND FLOOR

DESIGN BY
©R.L. Pfotenhauer

PLAN HPT102002

Total: 2,300 sq. ft.
First Floor: 1,308 sq. ft.
Second Floor: 992 sq. ft.
Width: 70'-8" **Depth:** 42'-10"

A covered wraparound porch welcomes you into this updated farmhouse. A traditional floor plan puts work and gathering areas downstairs and bedrooms upstairs. The living room and dining room stand at the front of the house, while the casual living areas at the back include the open kitchen with a breakfast nook and the family room with a double-facing fireplace shared with the living room. Close by is the half-bath and the laundry area. Sliding doors open from the family room and the breakfast nook to a terrace. Upstairs, the master bedroom has a walk-in closet and a bath with a separate tub and shower. Two more bedrooms share a second full bath.

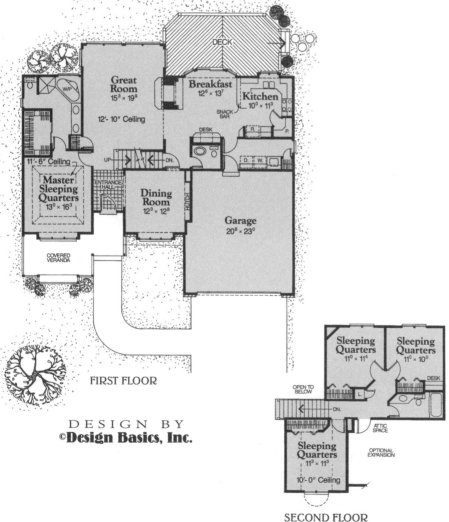

FIRST FLOOR

DESIGN BY
©**Design Basics, Inc.**

SECOND FLOOR

PLAN HPT100126

Victorian details and a covered veranda lend a peaceful flavor to the elevation of this popular home. A volume entry hall views the formal dining room and luxurious great room. Imagine the comfort of relaxing in the great room with a vaulted ceiling and abundant windows. The kitchen and breakfast area include a through-fireplace, snack bar, walk-in pantry and wrapping counters. The secluded owners suite features a tray ceiling, luxurious dressing/bath area and corner whirlpool tub. Upstairs, the family sleeping quarters possess special amenities unique to each.

Total: 1,999 sq. ft.
First Floor: 1,421 sq. ft.
Second Floor: 578 sq. ft.
Width: 52'-0" **Depth:** 47'-4"

PLAN HPT100127

Total: 2,353 sq. ft.
First Floor: 1,653 sq. ft.
Second Floor: 700 sq. ft.
Width: 54'-0" **Depth:** 50'-0"

Beautiful arches and elaborate detail give the elevation of this four-bedroom, 1½-story home an unmistakable elegance. Inside, the floor plan is equally appealing. Note the formal dining room with a bay window, visible from the entrance hall. The large great room presents a fireplace and a wall of windows with views of the rear property. A hearth room with a built-in bookcase adjoins the kitchen, which boasts a corner walk-in pantry and a spacious breakfast nook with a bay window. The first-floor owners suite features His and Hers wardrobes, a large whirlpool tub and double lavatories. Upstairs, the sleeping quarters share a full bath that includes compartmented sinks.

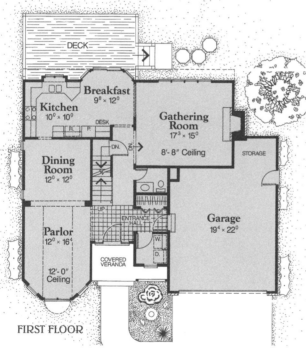

DECK

Breakfast 9⁸ × 12⁰

Kitchen 10⁰ × 10⁰

DESK

Gathering Room 17³ × 15⁰

8'-8" Ceiling

STORAGE

Dining Room 12⁰ × 12⁰

DN.

UP

Parlor 12⁰ × 16⁴

12'-0" Ceiling

ENTRANCE HALL

Garage 19⁴ × 22⁰

W. D.

COVERED VERANDA

FIRST FLOOR

SKYLIGHT   SKYLIGHT

W/P

9'-0" Ceiling

Master Sleeping Quarters 12⁰ × 17⁰

DN.

L

Sleeping Quarters 11⁰ × 10⁰

Sleeping Quarters 10⁰ × 11⁰

Sleeping Quarters 11⁰ × 12⁸

11'-6" Ceiling

SECOND FLOOR

DESIGN BY
©**Design Basics, Inc.**

E legant detail, a charming veranda and a tall brick chimney make a pleasing facade on this four-bedroom, two-story Victorian home. Yesterday's simpler lifestyle is reflected throughout this plan. From the large bayed parlor with a sloped ceiling to the sunken gathering room with a fireplace, there's plenty to appreciate about the floor plan. The L-shaped kitchen with its attached breakfast room furnishes plenty of storage space and easily serves the dining room through a discreet doorway. Upstairs, sleeping quarters include an owners suite with a private dressing area and a whirlpool bath, and three family bedrooms arranged to share a hall bath.

PLAN HPT100128

Total: 2,078 sq. ft.
First Floor: 1,113 sq. ft.
Second Floor: 965 sq. ft.
Width: 46'-0"   **Depth:** 41'-5"

PLAN HPT100129

A large covered porch with a wood railing complements this home's distinctive design personality. The living room is distinguished by the warmth of a bay window and French doors leading to the family room. In the well-appointed kitchen, an island cooktop will save you steps. The owners suite on the second floor delights with special ceiling treatment, a spacious bath and an enormous Palladian-style window. Please specify basement or block foundation when ordering.

Total: 1,998 sq. ft.
First Floor: 1,093 sq. ft.
Second Floor: 905 sq. ft.
Width: 55'-4" **Depth:** 37'-8"

FIRST FLOOR

DESIGN BY
©Design Basics, Inc.

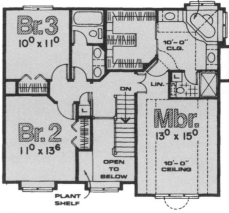

SECOND FLOOR

Storage
19'-8" X 7'-4"

Carport
20'-3" X 22'

Breakfast
12'-10" X 11'

Covered Porch

Util.

Ba.

Ma. Bath

Kitchen
12'-10" X 12'

Living
15'-3" X 25'

Master Bedroom
17'-8" X 13'

Dining
12'-10" X 14'

Foyer

Porch

FIRST FLOOR

Bedroom #2
12'-10" X 12'

Balcony

Bath

Bedroom #4
11'-6" X 14'

Unfinished Gameroom
17'-8" X 14'-8"

Bedroom #3
12'-10" X 13'

Bath

SECOND FLOOR

DESIGN BY
©**Chatham Home Planning, Inc.**

PLAN HPT100130

This nostalgic country design will bring a breath of fresh air to any neighborhood—in grand style. Past the wraparound porch, the open foyer expands to the stunning living area, with a central fireplace and views from all three sides. Double French doors lead to the wraparound porch. Steps away from a cheery breakfast nook, an angled breakfast bar also provides additional counter space for the kitchen, filled with convenient amenities. The owners suite offers a sizable walk-in closet, twin lavatories with a vanity, and a windowed whirlpool tub. Upstairs, a balcony hallway joins three family bedrooms and two full baths, and leads to a large, unfinished game room.

Total: 2,852 sq. ft.
First Floor: 1,729 sq. ft.
Second Floor: 1,123 sq. ft.
Bonus Room: 261 sq. ft.
Width: 60'-0" **Depth:** 67'-6"

133

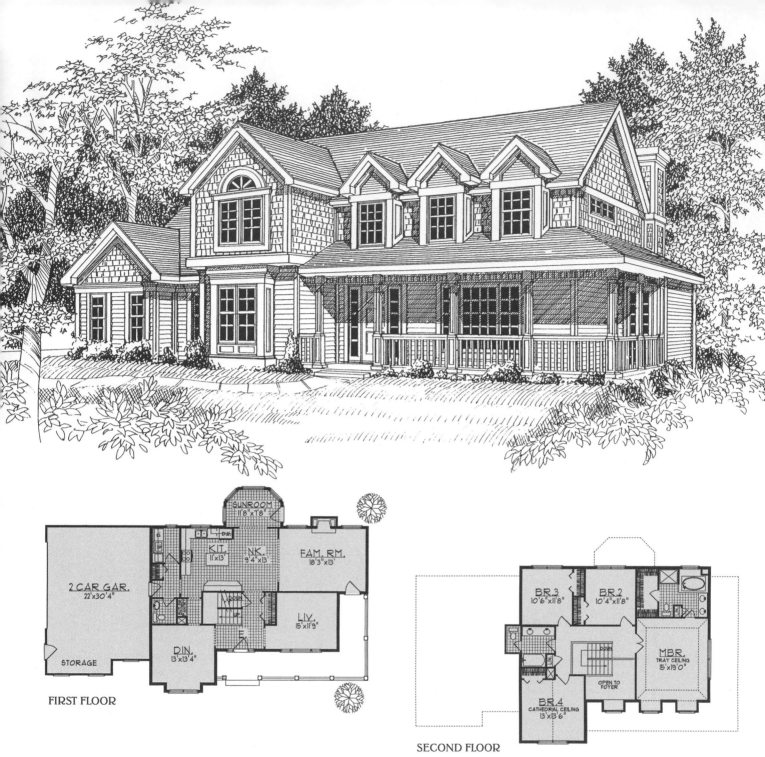

FIRST FLOOR

SECOND FLOOR

DESIGN BY
©**Ahmann Design, Inc.**

PLAN HPT100131

Total: 2,491 sq. ft.
First Floor: 1,333 sq. ft.
Second Floor: 1,158 sq. ft.
Width: 68'-0" **Depth:** 42'-6"

This two-story house is just the right home for a large family. The wraparound porch only adds to its charm. This home features a well-laid-out floor plan with amenities that include a formal living room, formal dining room, an inviting sun room and a huge cozy family room. The oversized kitchen with a center island is great for meal planning. The nook is conveniently open to the kitchen, which flows directly into the family room–great for family conversations. The second floor includes four bedrooms and an opening to the foyer. The owners bedroom is very large and features a private bath, which includes a whirlpool tub, walk-in shower and a roomy walk-in closet.

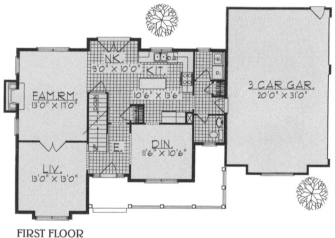

FIRST FLOOR

FAM.RM. 13'0" x 17'0"

NK. 9'0" x 10'0"

KIT. 10'6" x 13'6"

3 CAR GAR. 20'0" x 31'0"

LIV. 13'0" x 13'0"

DIN. 11'6" x 10'6"

DESIGN BY
©Ahmann Design, Inc.

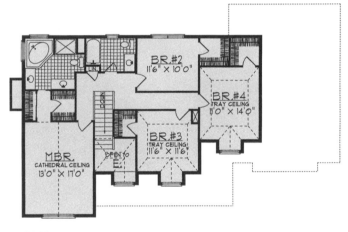

SECOND FLOOR

BR.#2 11'6" x 10'0"

BR.#4 TRAY CEILING 10'0" x 14'0"

BR.#3 TRAY CEILING 11'6" x 11'6"

MBR. CATHEDRAL CEILING 13'0" x 17'0"

This welcoming two-story home offers the spaciousness you have been looking for in a new home. The covered front porch leads to the foyer, which invites guests into the living room. The formal living room is perfect for entertaining—or move through the French doors into the family room for intimate gatherings around the fireplace. The formal dining room is available for special meals. The large open kitchen has a center island and a sunny nook for breakfast and lunch. The owners bedroom is your private retreat. Inside, you'll find a large walk-in closet and a private bath with two vanities, a corner spa tub and a shower. Three additional bedrooms share a full bath.

PLAN HPT100132

Total: 2,236 sq. ft.
First Floor: 1,065 sq. ft.
Second Floor: 1,171 sq. ft.
Width: 60'-0" **Depth:** 40'-0"

PLAN HPT100133

Reminiscent of the Gothic Victorian style of the mid-19th Century, this delightfully detailed, three-story house presents a wraparound veranda for summertime relaxing. A grand reception hall welcomes visitors and displays an elegant staircase. The parlor and family room, each with a fireplace, provide excellent formal and informal living facilities. The well-planned kitchen is only a couple of steps from the dining and breakfast rooms. The family room and the breakfast room both provide access to the rear terrace. The second floor holds four bedrooms and two baths plus a sewing room or a study. The third floor houses an additional bedroom or a studio with a half-bath, as well as a playroom.

Total: 3,606 sq. ft.
First Floor: 1,600 sq. ft.
Second Floor: 1,095 sq. ft.
Third Floor: 911 sq. ft.
Width: 88'-0" **Depth:** 42'-0"

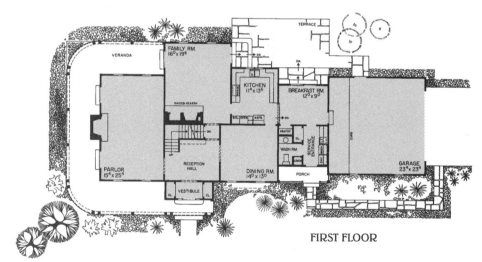

FIRST FLOOR

SECOND FLOOR

DESIGN BY
©**Home Planners**

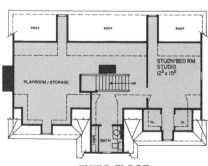

THIRD FLOOR

136

FIRST FLOOR

DESIGN BY
©**The Sater Design Collection**

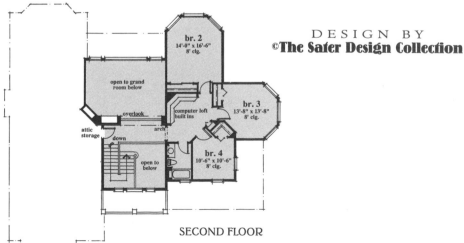

SECOND FLOOR

PLAN HPT100134

This romantic farmhouse, with its covered porches and decorative widow's walk, is designed with family living in mind. From the wraparound porch, the foyer first meets the front parlor through an arched doorway. The impressive formal dining room just beyond will be a delight for casual meals as well as formal affairs. The grand room offers rear-porch access, a corner fireplace, a built-in media center and a pass-through to the kitchen. The kitchen features a worktop island and a breakfast nook. The owners suite is lavishly appointed. Upstairs, a computer loft with built-ins serves as a common area to the three family bedrooms that share a full hall bath. Please specify basement or slab foundation when ordering.

Total: 3,183 sq. ft.
First Floor: 2,240 sq. ft.
Second Floor: 943 sq. ft.
Width: 69'-8" **Depth:** 61'-10"

137

PLAN HPT100135

Victorian detailing and a wraparound covered porch grace this three-bedroom farmhouse. An archway introduces the octagonal living room and its adjoining dining room. Sliding glass doors in the dining room lead to the porch; the living room enjoys a fireplace. A pocket door separates the kitchen and bayed breakfast nook from the dining room. Workspace in the kitchen is L-shaped for convenience. The family room opens to this area and features sliding glass doors to the rear yard and a fireplace. Reach the two-car garage through a service entrance near the laundry. Bedrooms are upstairs. The owners suite has a bay window, walk-in closet and a private bath with a corner whirlpool tub and double vanity. Two family bedrooms include one nestled in a windowed bay.

Total: 2,043 sq. ft.
First Floor: 1,056 sq. ft.
Second Floor: 987 sq. ft.
Width: 46'-6" **Depth:** 54'-6"

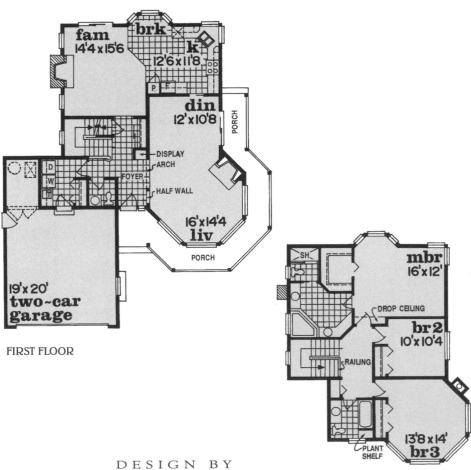

FIRST FLOOR

SECOND FLOOR

D E S I G N   B Y
©Select Home Designs

FIRST FLOOR

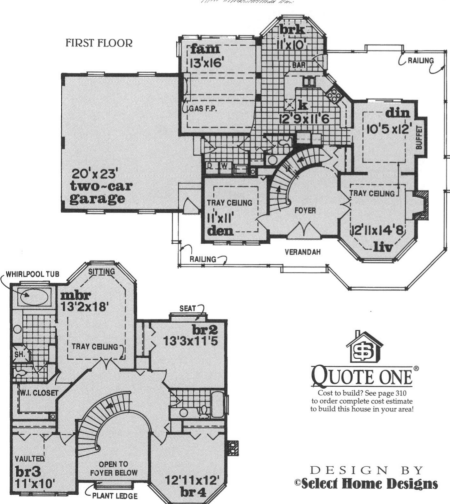

fam
13'x16'

GAS F.P.

brk
11'x10'

BAR

k
12'9"x11'6"

RAILING

din
10'5 x12'

BUFFET

20'x 23'
**two~car
garage**

TRAY CEILING
11'x11'
den

FOYER

TRAY CEILING

12'11"x14'8"
liv

RAILING

VERANDAH

WHIRLPOOL TUB   SITTING

mbr
13'2"x18'

TRAY CEILING

SEAT

br2
13'3"x11'5

SH.

W.I. CLOSET

VAULTED

br3
11'x10'

OPEN TO
FOYER BELOW

PLANT LEDGE

12'11"x12'
br4

SECOND FLOOR

PLAN HPT100136

A turret, wood detailing and a wrap-around veranda signal Victorian style for this home. The double-door entry opens to a foyer with a lovely curved staircase. The living room provides a fireplace, and the formal dining room has a buffet alcove and access to the veranda. The family room also furnishes a fireplace and sliding glass doors to the rear yard. On the second floor, a tray ceiling highlights the owners suite, and a sumptuous bath completes it with a whirlpool tub, separate shower and compartmented toilet. Three family bedrooms join the owners suite on this level, sharing a full bath—one bedroom has a built-in window seat, while another enjoys a bay window.

QUOTE ONE®
Cost to build? See page 310
to order complete cost estimate
to build this house in your area!

Total: 2,516 sq. ft.
First Floor: 1,324 sq. ft.
Second Floor: 1,192 sq. ft.
Width: 67'-6" **Depth:** 47'-6"

DESIGN BY
©**Select Home Designs**

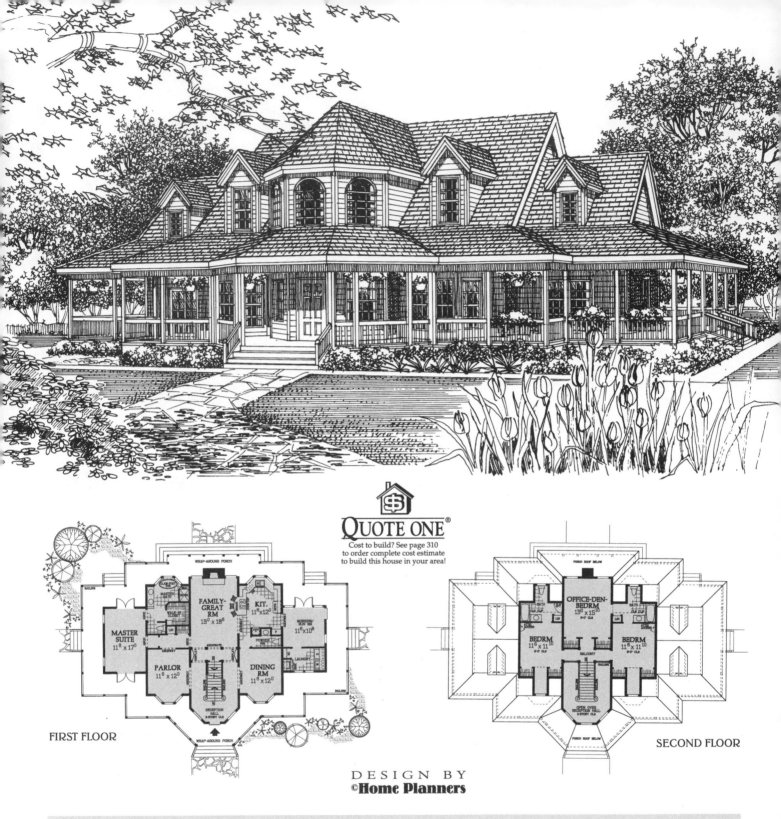

FIRST FLOOR

SECOND FLOOR

QUOTE ONE®

Cost to build? See page 310
to order complete cost estimate
to build this house in your area!

DESIGN BY
©**Home Planners**

PLAN HPT100137

Total: 2,658 sq. ft.
First Floor: 1,752 sq. ft.
Second Floor: 906 sq. ft.
Width: 74'-0" **Depth:** 51'-7"

L·D

Delightfully proportioned and superbly symmetrical, this Victorian farmhouse has lots of curb appeal. The wraparound porch offers rustic columns and railings, and broad steps present easy access to the front, rear and side yards. Archways, display niches and columns help define the great room, which offers a fireplace framed by views to the rear property. A formal parlor and a dining room flank the reception hall, and each offers a bay window. The owners suite boasts two sets of French doors to the wraparound porch, and a private bath with a clawfoot tub, twin lavatories, a walk-in closet and a stall shower. Upstairs, a spacious office/den adjoins two family bedrooms, each with a private bath.

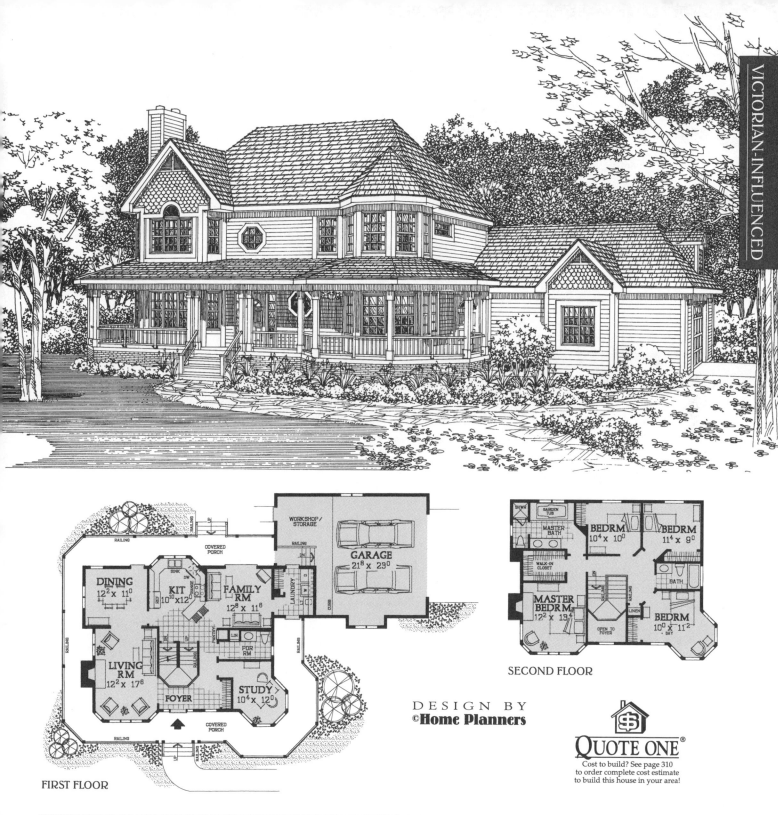

FIRST FLOOR

SECOND FLOOR

DESIGN BY
©**Home Planners**

QUOTE ONE®

Cost to build? See page 310
to order complete cost estimate
to build this house in your area!

Palladian window, fish-scale shingles and turret-style bays set off this country-style Victorian exterior. An impressive tiled entry opens to the formal rooms, which nestle to the left side of the plan. The turret houses a secluded study on the first floor and provides a sunny bay window for one of three family bedrooms upstairs. The second-floor owners suite boasts its own fireplace, a dressing area with a walk-in closet, and a lavish bath with a garden tub and twin vanities.

PLAN HPT100138

Total: 2,174 sq. ft.
First Floor: 1,186 sq. ft.
Second Floor: 988 sq. ft.
Width: 72'-0" **Depth:** 50'-10"

L·D

PLAN HPT100139

Victorian elements abound on this three-bedroom home, including a turret, fish-scale siding and a wrap-around porch. A view of the curved staircase is the focal point of the entry. To the right, a combined living room and dining area accesses the L-shaped kitchen. The kitchen has added counter space with the island/snack bar and is conveniently located near the garage. The triangular-shaped family room presents a fireplace framed by two windows. Nearby, the den—accessed through French doors—is set within the turret. Upstairs, two family bedrooms, one of which is the second floor of the turret, share a full bath. The owners bedroom includes a spacious bath with a walk-in closet, oversized soaking tub, twin-vanity sinks and a compartmented toilet.

Total: 2,362 sq. ft.
First Floor: 1,337 sq. ft.
Second Floor: 1,025 sq. ft.
Width: 47'-0" **Depth:** 72'-6"

FIRST FLOOR

SECOND FLOOR

DESIGN BY
©Alan Mascord Design Associates, Inc.

142

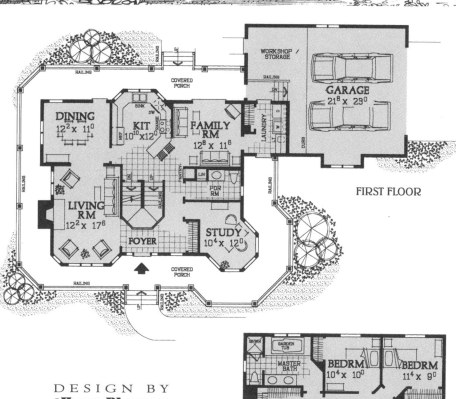

FIRST FLOOR

DINING
12² x 11⁰

KIT
10⁰ x12²

FAMILY RM
12⁸ x 11⁶

WORKSHOP / STORAGE

GARAGE
21⁸ x 29⁰

LIVING RM
12² x 17⁶

FOYER

STUDY
10⁴ x 12⁰

COVERED PORCH

PDR RM

LAUNDRY

RAILING

DESIGN BY
©**Home Planners**

MASTER BATH

GARDEN TUB

BEDRM
10⁴ x 10⁰

BEDRM
11⁴ x 9⁰

WALK-IN CLOSET

MASTER BEDRM
12² x 13⁴

BATH

LINEN

OPEN TO FOYER

BEDRM
10⁰ x 11²

SECOND FLOOR

PLAN HPT100140

This Victorian-style exterior offers you a wonderful floor plan. The detailing includes a wraparound porch, muntin windows and turret-style bays. Inside, an impressive tiled entry opens to the formal rooms, which nestle to the left side of the plan and enjoy natural light from an abundance of windows. More than just a pretty face, the turret houses a secluded study on the first floor and provides a sunny bay window for a family bedroom upstairs. The second-floor owners suite boasts its own fireplace, a dressing area with a walk-in closet, and a lavish bath with a garden tub and twin vanities. The two-car garage offers space for a workshop or extra storage.

Total: 2,174 sq. ft.
First Floor: 1,186 sq. ft.
Second Floor: 988 sq. ft.
Width: 72'-4" **Depth:** 51'-2"

L•D

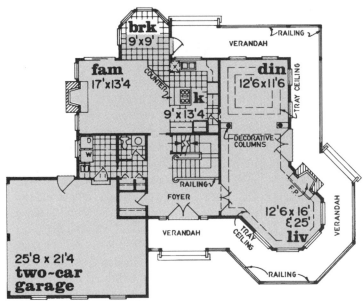

FIRST FLOOR

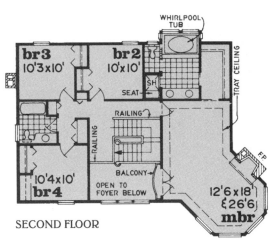

SECOND FLOOR

DESIGN BY
©Select Home Designs

PLAN HPT100141

Total: 2,560 sq. ft.
First Floor: 1,290 sq. ft.
Second Floor: 1,270 sq. ft.
Width: 65'-0" **Depth:** 53'-4"

With both farmhouse flavor and Victorian details, this plan features a wraparound veranda and a large bayed area on the first and second floors. The living room is nestled in one of these bays and hosts a tray ceiling, a masonry fireplace and French-door access to the veranda. A pair of columns separates the living and dining rooms. Note the tray ceiling in the dining room. The kitchen has a handy center work island and is open to both the breakfast bay and family room. A fireplace is enjoyed from all angles. The owners suite is tucked into the bay on the second floor. Its amenities include a fireplace, a walk-in closet and a private bath with a whirlpool tub. Three family bedrooms share a full bath.

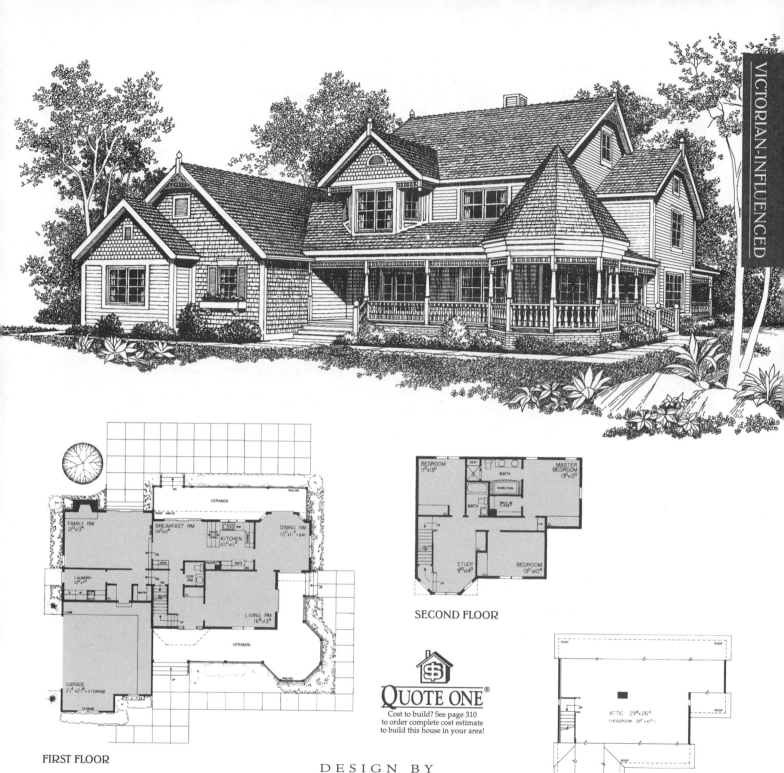

FIRST FLOOR

SECOND FLOOR

ATTIC

QUOTE ONE®
Cost to build? See page 310
to order complete cost estimate
to build this house in your area!

DESIGN BY
©**Home Planners**

Covered porches, front and back, are a fine preview to the livable nature of this Victorian design. Living areas are defined in a family room with a fireplace, the formal living and dining rooms, and the kitchen with a breakfast room. An ample laundry room, a garage with a storage area, and a powder room round out the first floor. Three second-floor bedrooms are joined by a study and two full baths. The owners suite on this floor offers two closets, including an ample walk-in, as well as a relaxing bath with a tile-rimmed whirlpool tub and a separate shower with a seat.

PLAN HPT100142

Total: 2,391 sq. ft.
First Floor: 1,375 sq. ft.
Second Floor: 1,016 sq. ft.
Attic: 303 sq. ft.
Width: 62'-7" **Depth:** 54'-0"

PLAN HPT100143

A wraparound porch with lattice work, bay windows and a turret lend this roomy three-bedroom farmhouse Victorian style. The gazebo section of the front porch would be a perfect location for a table and chairs. Inside, a ribbon of windows pours light into the living room. The dining area has a bay window and sits conveniently near the kitchen and breakfast areas. The family room has an eye-catching corner fireplace. Upstairs, two family bedrooms share a full hall bath, while the owners suite contains a private bath, large walk-in closet and a sitting alcove, placed within the turret.

Total: 1,764 sq. ft.
First Floor: 887 sq. ft.
Second Floor: 877 sq. ft.
Width: 61'-0" **Depth:** 46'-0"

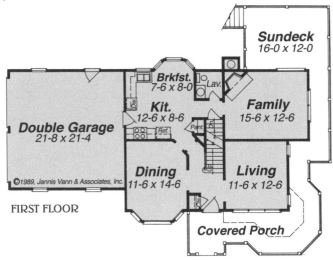

Sundeck 16-0 x 12-0
Brkfst. 7-6 x 8-0
Lav.
Kit. 12-6 x 8-6
Family 15-6 x 12-6
Double Garage 21-8 x 21-4
Ref.
Pant.
Dining 11-6 x 14-6
Living 11-6 x 12-6
©1989, Jannis Vann & Associates, Inc.

FIRST FLOOR

Covered Porch

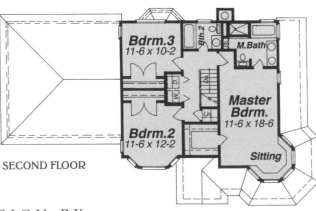

Bdrm.3 11-6 x 10-2
Bth.2
M.Bath
W.D.
Lin.
Master Bdrm. 11-6 x 18-6
Bdrm.2 11-6 x 12-2
Sitting

SECOND FLOOR

DESIGN BY
©**Jannis Vann & Associates, Inc.**

FIRST FLOOR

Sundeck
18-7 x 12-0

Brkfst.
10-0 x 15-6

Lav.

Kit.
9-6 x 13-6

Family Rm.
19-6 x 13-6

©1995, Jannis Vann & Associates, Inc.

Dining
13-6 x 14-6

Foyer
10-8 x 7-6

Living
13-6 x 11-6

Porch

SECOND FLOOR

Bdrm.2
11-6 x 11-2

Bth.2

M.Bath

Bdrm.3
11-6 x 11-6

Bdrm.4
11-4 x 11-4

Master
Bdrm.
13-6 x 17-6

Balc.
6-0 x 10-0

Turit
7-6 x 7-6

DESIGN BY
©**Jannis Vann & Associates, Inc.**

PLAN HPT100144

With both farmhouse flavor and Victorian details, this plan features a wraparound veranda and a bayed area on the first and second floors as well as a turret on the second floor. Inside, the living room's many windows pour light in. The dining area begins with a bay window and is conveniently near the kitchen and breakfast area—also with a bay window. The U-shaped kitchen features an island workstation, ensuring plenty of space for cooking projects. A nearby lavatory is available for guests. The family room has an eye-catching corner-set fireplace. Upstairs, three family bedrooms share a full hall bath, while the owners suite has a private bath and balcony, a large walk-in closet and a sitting alcove, placed within the turret.

Total: 2,364 sq. ft.
First Floor: 1,155 sq. ft.
Second Floor: 1,209 sq. ft.
Width: 46'-0" **Depth:** 36'-8"

PLAN HPT100145

Rich with Victorian details—scalloped shingles, a wraparound veranda and turrets—this beautiful facade conceals a modern floor plan. Archways announce a distinctive living room with a lovely tray ceiling and help define the dining room. An octagonal den across the foyer provides a private spot for reading or studying. The U-shaped island kitchen holds an octagonal breakfast bay and a pass-through breakfast bar to the family room. Upstairs, three family bedrooms share a hall bath—one bedroom is within a turret. The owners suite is complete with a sitting room with a bay window, along with a fancy bath set in another of the turrets.

Total: 2,632 sq. ft.
First Floor: 1,362 sq. ft.
Second Floor: 1,270 sq. ft.
Width: 79'-0" **Depth:** 44'-0"

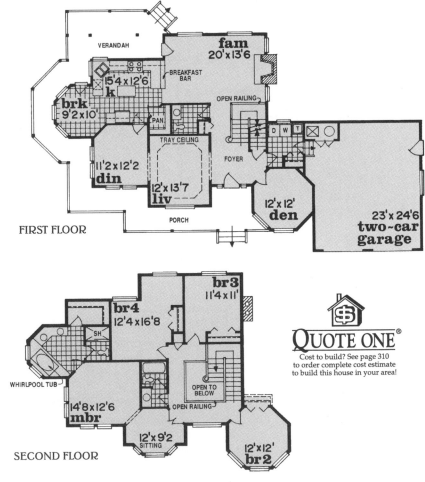

QUOTE ONE®
Cost to build? See page 310
to order complete cost estimate
to build this house in your area!

DESIGN BY
©Select Home Designs

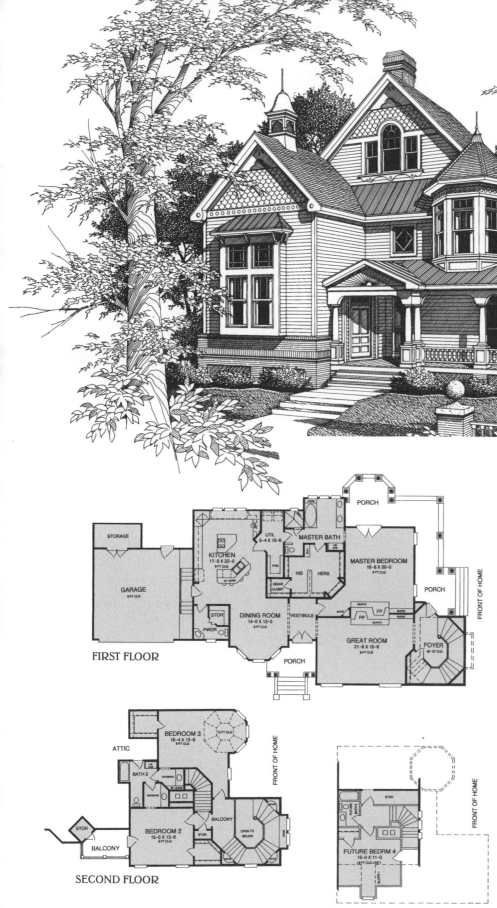

FIRST FLOOR

STORAGE

GARAGE
9 FT CLG

KITCHEN
17-0 X 22-0
9 FT CLG

UTIL
5-4 X 15-6

MASTER BATH

MASTER BEDROOM
16-6 X 20-0
9 FT CLG

PORCH

STOR

PWDR

DINING ROOM
14-0 X 13-0
9 FT CLG

VESTIBULE

GREAT ROOM
21-6 X 15-6
9 FT CLG

FOYER

PORCH

PORCH

FRONT OF HOME

SECOND FLOOR

ATTIC

BEDROOM 3
16-4 X 13-6
9 FT CLG

BATH 2

STOR

BALCONY

BEDROOM 2
15-0 X 13-6
9 FT CLG

BALCONY

STOR

OPEN TO BELOW

FRONT OF HOME

THIRD FLOOR

STOR

FUTURE BEDRM 4
15-0 X 11-0

FRONT OF HOME

DESIGN BY
©**Larry E. Belk Designs**

PLAN HPT100146

With equally appealing front and side entrances, a charming Victorian facade invites entry to this stunning home. The foyer showcases the characteristic winding staircase and opens to the large great room with a masonry fireplace. An enormous kitchen features a cooktop island and a breakfast bar large enough to seat four. The amenity-filled owners suite, also with a masonry fireplace, is located on the first floor. The second floor contains two bedrooms—one with access to the outdoor balcony on the side of the home. The third floor is completely expandable. Please specify crawlspace or slab foundation when ordering.

Total: 3,064 sq. ft.
First Floor: 2,194 sq. ft.
Second Floor: 870 sq. ft.
Bonus Room: 251 sq. ft.
Width: 50'-11" **Depth:** 91'-2"

PLAN HPT100147

Designed for a narrow lot, this charming home with a wraparound porch and rear garage is reminiscent of an earlier time. The entry foyer offers access to the formal parlor, dining room, kitchen and great room. For family convenience, the stairs are located to the rear of the home, offering quick access to the garage, laundry room and breakfast room. A large great room with a fireplace and built-in entertainment cabinet is convenient to the wraparound porch. Four bedrooms on the second floor, including a large owners bedroom suite, completes this exciting Victorian-style home.

Total: 2,561 sq. ft.
First Floor: 1,331 sq. ft.
Second Floor: 1,230 sq. ft.
Width: 36'-0" **Depth:** 67'-6"

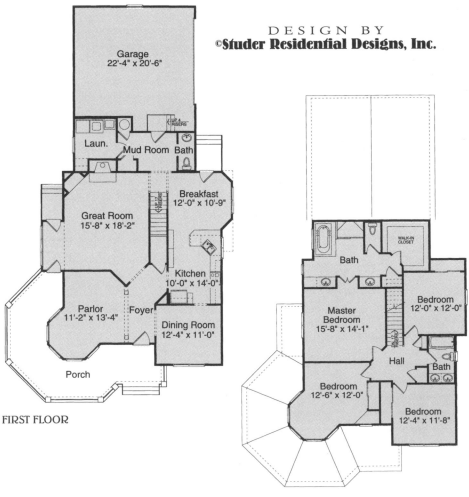

DESIGN BY
©Studer Residential Designs, Inc.

Garage 22'-4" x 20'-6"

Laun. Mud Room Bath

Great Room 15'-8" x 18'-2"

Breakfast 12'-0" x 10'-9"

Kitchen 10'-0" x 14'-0"

Parlor 11'-2" x 13'-4" Foyer

Dining Room 12'-4" x 11'-0"

Porch

FIRST FLOOR

WALK-IN CLOSET

Bath

Master Bedroom 15'-8" x 14'-1"

Bedroom 12'-0" x 12'-0"

Hall Bath

Bedroom 12'-6" x 12'-0"

Bedroom 12'-4" x 11'-8"

SECOND FLOOR

150

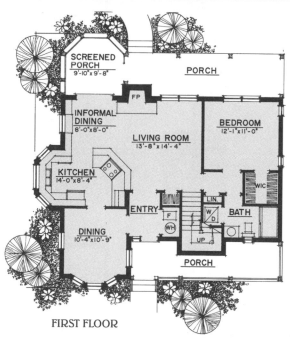

FIRST FLOOR

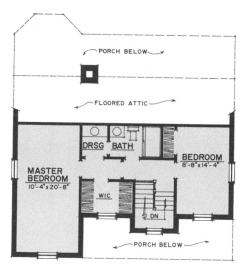

SECOND FLOOR

DESIGN BY
©**R.L. Pfotenhauer**

Front and rear porches and bay windows lend this three-bedroom home Victorian flavor. Inside, the entry leads to the formal dining room with a bay window, and the living room. The kitchen adjoins both the formal and informal dining area and is open to the living room via a snack bar. The informal eating area opens to the screened porch, expanding the living space to the outdoors. On the right of the first floor is a bedroom with a walk-in closet and full bath—perfect for a guest room or possibly an optional owners suite. Upstairs, a family bedroom and an owners bedroom share a full bath.

PLAN HPT100148

Total: 1,582 sq. ft.
First Floor: 949 sq. ft.
Second Floor: 633 sq. ft.
Width: 40'-3" **Depth:** 40'-6"

PLAN HPT100149

This sweet lakeside cottage is sure to please with its quaint charm and convenient floor plan. A covered porch greets family and friends and offers a place to sit and enjoy the summer breezes. Inside, the living room—with its warming fireplace—flows nicely into the kitchen/dining area. A snack bar, pantry and plenty of cabinet and counter space are just some of the features found here. The first-floor owners suite boasts a bay window, walk-in closet and private bath. Upstairs, two bedrooms share a bath and a linen closet.

Total: 1,317 sq. ft.
First Floor: 836 sq. ft.
Second Floor: 481 sq. ft.
Width: 38'-2" **Depth:** 34'-0"

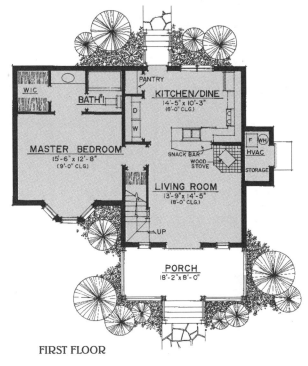

FIRST FLOOR

DESIGN BY
©R.L. Pfotenhauer

SECOND FLOOR

152

PLAN HPT100150

The exterior of this three-bedroom home presents a unique mixture of farmhouse and Victorian elements, including fish-scale siding, dormer windows, trusses in the gables and a detailed wood porch. Inside, the great room possesses a warming fireplace. The owners bedroom is nearby, with private access to the rear deck and owners bathroom. The split-bedroom design allows for a private owners bedroom by placing Bedrooms 2 and 3 upstairs with a shared bath. Bonus space on the second level of this plan makes it an intriguing option for a growing family. Bay-window accents, a rear deck and screened porch provide a fresh, indoor/outdoor livability.

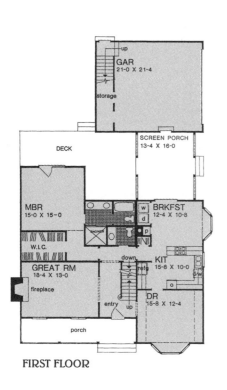

FIRST FLOOR

DESIGN BY
©**Home Planners**

ALTERNATE PLAN FOR
CRAWLSPACE

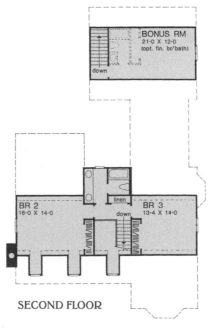

SECOND FLOOR

Total: 2,299 sq. ft.
First Floor: 1,563 sq. ft.
Second Floor: 736 sq. ft.
Bonus Room: 280 sq. ft.
Width: 44'-0" **Depth:** 72'-0"

153

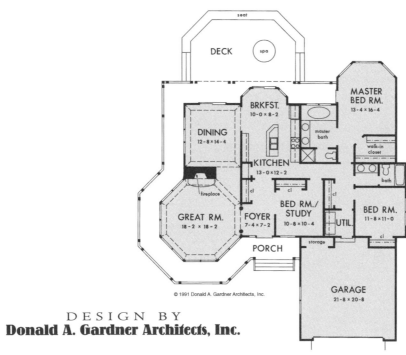

DESIGN BY
Donald A. Gardner Architects, Inc.

PLAN HPT100151

Square Footage: 1,865
Width: 61'-6" **Depth:** 74'-8"

This distinctive Victorian exterior conceals an open, contemporary floor plan. The entrance foyer with round columns offers visual excitement. The octagonal great room has a high tray ceiling and a fireplace. A generous kitchen with an angular island counter is centrally located, providing efficient service to the dining room, breakfast room and deck. The luxurious owners bedroom suite enjoys a large walk-in closet and a compartmented bath. Two additional bedrooms—one that would make a lovely study by including an entrance off the foyer—and a full hall bath round out this favorite plan.

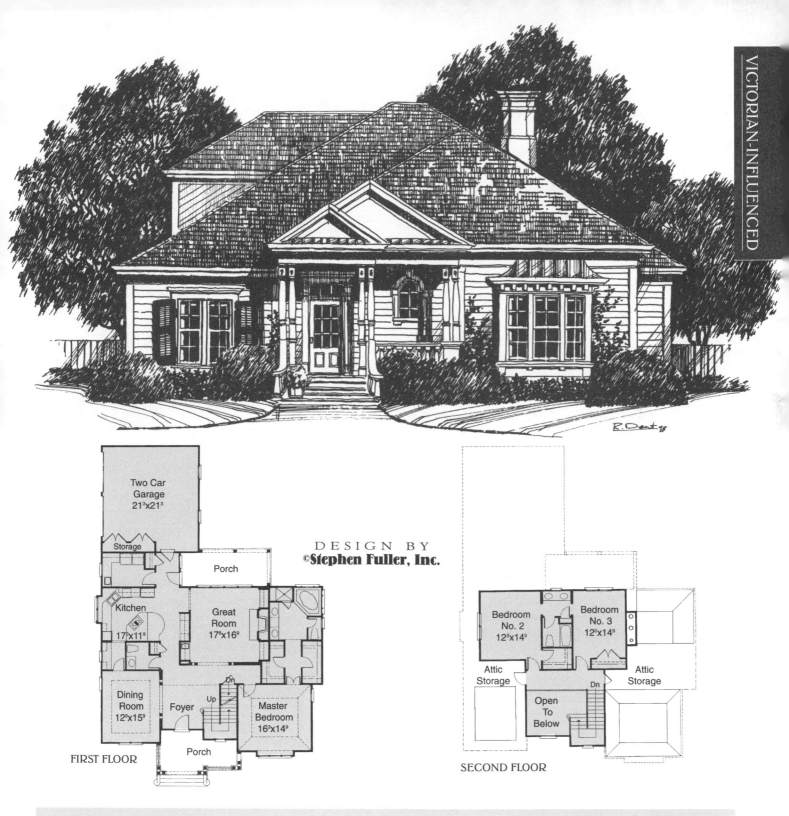

DESIGN BY
©**Stephen Fuller, Inc.**

FIRST FLOOR

Two Car Garage 21³x21³

Storage

Porch

Kitchen 17⁶x11⁹

Great Room 17⁶x16⁹

Dining Room 12⁹x15⁹

Foyer

Up

Dn

Master Bedroom 16³x14⁹

Porch

SECOND FLOOR

Bedroom No. 2 12³x14⁹

Bedroom No. 3 12⁰x14⁹

Attic Storage

Open To Below

Dn

Attic Storage

On the first floor of this cozy home, the foyer opens through columns to a dining room on the left and, straight ahead, to a great room with a fireplace. In the kitchen, an angled cooktop facilitates meal preparations. A laundry room sits near the exit to a two-car garage where storage closets are an added bonus. The owners bedroom pampers with dual walk-in closets and a private bath with a double-bowl vanity, separate shower and compartmented toilet. This home is designed with a walkout basement foundation.

PLAN HPT100152

Total: 2,504 sq. ft.
First Floor: 1,859 sq. ft.
Second Floor: 645 sq. ft.
Width: 49'-9" **Depth:** 74'-3"

PLAN HPT100153

Classic country character complements this delightful home, complete with rustic stone corners, a covered front porch and interesting gables. The entry opens to formal living areas that include a large dining room to the right, and straight ahead to a spacious living room warmed by a fireplace. A gallery leads the way into the efficient kitchen enhanced with a snack bar and large pantry. Casual meals can be enjoyed overlooking the covered veranda and rear grounds from the connecting breakfast room. The other side of the gallery accesses the luxurious owners suite and three second bedrooms—all with walk-in closets. The second floor contains a loft and an optional bonus room to be developed as needed.

Total: 2,709 sq. ft.
First Floor: 2,539 sq. ft.
Second Floor: 170 sq. ft.
Bonus Room: 469 sq. ft.
Width: 98'-0" **Depth:** 53'-11"

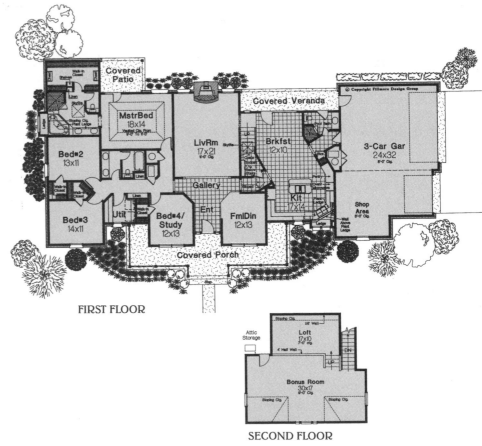

FIRST FLOOR

SECOND FLOOR

DESIGN BY
©Fillmore Design Group

European-Inspired Farmhouses

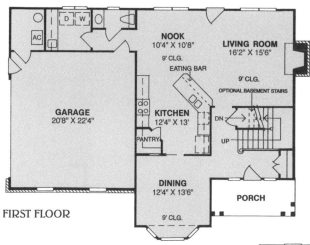

FIRST FLOOR

GARAGE
20'8" X 22'4"

NOOK
10'4" X 10'8"
9' CLG.

LIVING ROOM
16'2" X 15'6"

EATING BAR

9' CLG.

OPTIONAL BASEMENT STAIRS

KITCHEN
12'4" X 13'

DN

UP

PANTRY

DINING
12'4" X 13'6"
9' CLG.

PORCH

AC

D W

DESIGN BY
©**Design Basics, Inc.**

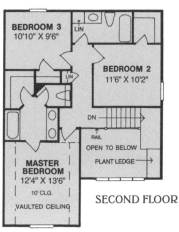

SECOND FLOOR

BEDROOM 3
10'10" X 9'6"

LIN

BEDROOM 2
11'6" X 10'2"

LIN

DN

RAIL

OPEN TO BELOW

PLANT LEDGE

MASTER BEDROOM
12'4" X 13'6"
10' CLG.

VAULTED CEILING

PLAN HPT100154

Alovely bay window, shutters and an arched lintel give this three-bedroom home great curb appeal. To the left of the entry, a light-filled dining room with bay windows accesses the kitchen. The kitchen joins the living room and breakfast nook via a breakfast bar, creating a spacious and open atmosphere. A fireplace warms the living room. Upstairs, two family bedrooms share a bath near the owners bedroom. The owners bedroom has a lavish bath with a walk-in closet, compartmented toilet and twin-vanity sinks. Please specify basement, crawlspace or slab foundation when ordering.

Total: 1,689 sq. ft.
First Floor: 979 sq. ft.
Second Floor: 710 sq. ft.
Width: 48'-0" **Depth:** 38'-0"

PLAN HPT100155

This classic Americana design employs wood siding, a variety of window styles and a detailed front porch. Inside, the large two-story foyer flows into the formal dining room with arched window accents and the living room highlighted by a bay window. A short passage with a wet bar accesses the family room with its wall of windows, French doors and fireplace. The large breakfast area and open island kitchen are spacious and airy as well as efficient. Upstairs, the owners suite's sleeping and sitting rooms feature architectural details including columns, tray ceilings and a fireplace. The elegant owners bath contains a raised oval tub, dual vanities and a separate shower. A generous walk-in closet is located beyond the bath. This home is designed with a walkout basement foundation.

Total: 3,200 sq. ft.
First Floor: 1,570 sq. ft.
Second Floor: 1,630 sq. ft.
Width: 59'-10" **Depth:** 43'-4"

DESIGN BY
©**Stephen Fuller, Inc.**

FIRST FLOOR

SECOND FLOOR

FIRST FLOOR

DECK

BREAKFAST
11'-0" x 6'-0"

FAMILY ROOM
15'-6" x 17'-0"

KITCHEN
12'-6" x 13'-8"

LNDR.
6'-0" X 7'-6"

PWDR

PAN.

COAT

FOYER
11'-6" X 15'-0"

DN

UP

TWO-CAR GARAGE
20'-0" x 25'-8"

LIVING ROOM
10'-2" x 13'-0"

DINING ROOM
10'-2" x 12'-0"

STOOP

SECOND FLOOR

MASTER SUITE
15'-6" x 15'-0"

BEDROOM No.2
11'-6" x 12'-6"

BEDROOM No.4
12'-6" x 10'-0"

M. BATH

OPEN TO BELOW

DN

BATH

BEDROOM No.3
15'-4" x 13'-0"

MASTER CLOSET

DESIGN BY
©Stephen Fuller, Inc.

PLAN HPT100156

This traditional home combines an attractive, classic exterior with an open and sophisticated interior design. To the right of the foyer reside both the living and dining rooms with their individual window treatments. Enter the kitchen from the dining room through a corner butler's pantry for added convenience while entertaining. The open design flows from the breakfast area to the family room with two large bay windows. The open foyer staircase leads to the upper level, beginning with the owners suite. The owners bath contains a luxurious tub, separate shower and dual vanities, as well as a large linen closet. All three secondary bedrooms share a hall bath that includes a separate vanity and bathing area. This home is designed with a walkout basement foundation.

Total: 2,395 sq. ft.
First Floor: 1,156 sq. ft.
Second Floor: 1,239 sq. ft.
Width: 57'-3" **Depth:** 39'-0"

FIRST FLOOR

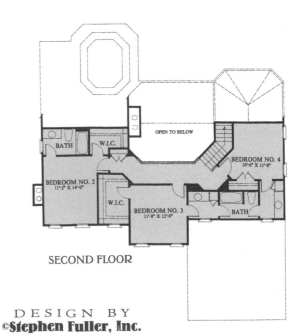

SECOND FLOOR

DESIGN BY
©Stephen Fuller, Inc.

PLAN HPT100157

Total: 2,790 sq. ft.
First Floor: 1,840 sq. ft.
Second Floor: 950 sq. ft.
Width: 58'-6" **Depth:** 62'-0"

The appearance of this early American home brings the past to mind with its wraparound porch, wood siding and flower-box detailing. Inside, columns frame the great room and dining room. Left of the foyer lies the living room with a warming fireplace. The angular kitchen joins a sunny breakfast nook. The owners suite has a spacious private bath and walk-in closet. Three family bedrooms, with large walk-in closets and private bath access, complete this level. This home is designed with a walkout basement foundation.

160

FIRST FLOOR

Deck
16-0 x 12-0

Vaulted
Living
Area
15-4 x 21-6

Brkfst.
11-8 x 11-6

Dining
13-4 x 11-6

Master
Bdrm.
15-4 x 19-6

Deck
12-0 x 24-0

Kit.
11-8 x 11-10

Library/
Bdrm. 5
13-8 x 10-6

Open
Foyer
11-2 x 10-6

M. Bath

Double Garage
21-4 x 23-8

Porch

SECOND FLOOR

Bdrm.2
13-8 x 11-6

Open To
Vaulted
Living

Balcony

Linen

Bdrm.3
13-8 x 11-6

Open
Foyer

Bdrm.4
13-6 x 13-6

Plant Shelf

DESIGN BY
©Jannis Vann & Associates, Inc.

This European-influenced farmhouse is as charming on the inside as it is outside. Keystones decorate several of the lintels over windows, including the central Palladian window. Inside, a library or fifth bedroom opens to the left through double doors. A vaulted living area features a warming fireplace and a ribbon of windows viewing the rear yard. Tucked behind the living room is the owners suite adorned with a tray ceiling and bay window, and featuring a fireplace, private access to the front porch, and a private bath. The dining room is to the left of the living room, past elegant columns, and located near the kitchen and breakfast room.

PLAN HPT100158

Total: 3,058 sq. ft.
First Floor: 2,047 sq. ft.
Second Floor: 1,011 sq. ft.
Width: 69'-8" **Depth:** 56'-5"

PLAN HPT100159

There's a feeling of old Charleston in this stately home—particularly on the quiet side porch that wraps around the kitchen and breakfast room. The interior of this home revolves around a spacious great room with a welcoming fireplace. The left wing is dedicated to the owners suite, which boasts wide views of the rear property. A corner kitchen easily serves planned events in the formal dining room as well as family meals in the breakfast area. Three family bedrooms, one with a private bath and the others sharing a bath, are tucked upstairs. This home is designed with a basement foundation.

Total: 2,845 sq. ft.
First Floor: 1,804 sq. ft.
Second Floor: 1,041 sq. ft.
Width: 59'-10" **Depth:** 71'-0"

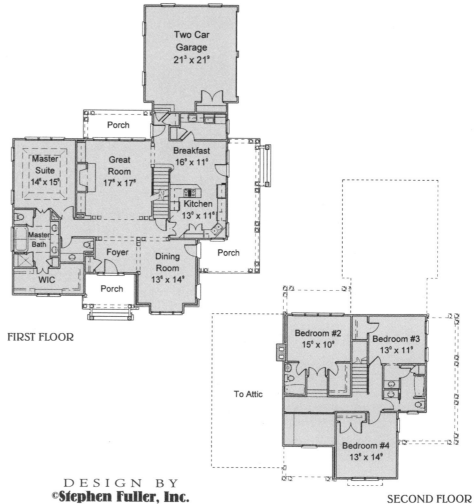

FIRST FLOOR

SECOND FLOOR

DESIGN BY
©**Stephen Fuller, Inc.**

162

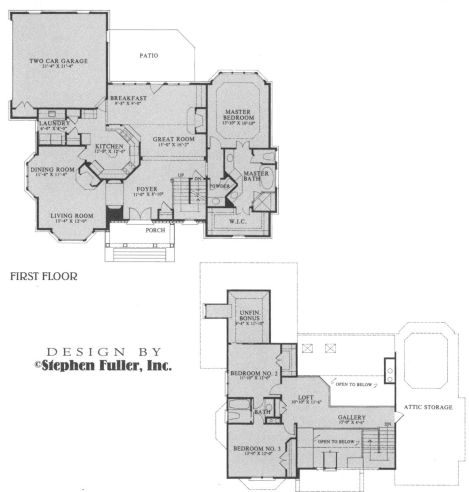

FIRST FLOOR

DESIGN BY
©Stephen Fuller, Inc.

SECOND FLOOR

PLAN HPT100160

This attractive home features a columned front porch and wood framing. Straight ahead from the foyer, the great room opens to the vaulted breakfast area. The octagonal kitchen is designed to promote the flow of family traffic. The dining room and living room share a hearth. The owners bedroom at the right rear of the home beckons with a large bay window and a lavish bath. The upper level is comprised of a gallery and a loft open to the great room and foyer below. Beyond the loft, two bedrooms share a bath and an unfinished bonus room. This home is designed with a walk-out basement foundation.

Total: 2,375 sq. ft.
First Floor: 1,725 sq. ft.
Second Floor: 650 sq. ft.
Bonus Room: 140 sq. ft.
Width: 60'-6" **Depth:** 50'-6"

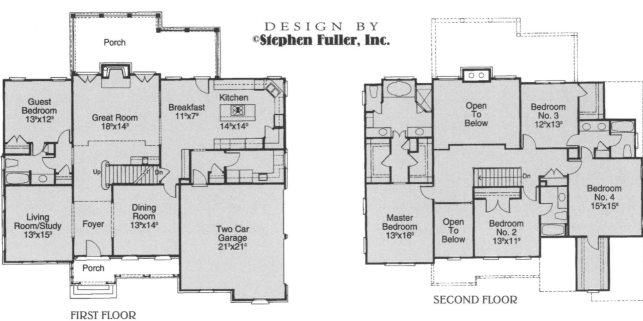

Porch

Guest Bedroom
13⁹x12³

Great Room
18⁰x14³

Breakfast
11⁰x7⁹

Kitchen
14³x14⁰

Up   Dn

Living Room/Study
13⁹x15⁰

Foyer

Dining Room
13⁹x14⁰

Two Car Garage
21³x21⁰

Porch

FIRST FLOOR

DESIGN BY
©**Stephen Fuller, Inc.**

Open To Below

Bedroom No. 3
12⁰x13⁰

Dn

Master Bedroom
13⁹x16⁰

Open To Below

Bedroom No. 2
13⁹x11⁰

Bedroom No. 4
15³x15⁰

SECOND FLOOR

PLAN HPT100161

Total: 3,499 sq. ft.
First Floor: 1,809 sq. ft.
Second Floor: 1,690 sq. ft.
Width: 58'-3" **Depth:** 58'-3"

Though charming, the front porch of this country cottage provides more than just a pretty facade. Rain or shine, the protective cover will inspire you to enjoy the outdoors. Inside, space for formal entertaining is provided by the living room/study and dining room that flank the foyer. A guest bedroom and an adjacent bath are conveniently located to the rear of the living room/study. An island cooktop enhances the efficient, U-shaped kitchen, which easily serves the breakfast room, the dining room, and the great room with its centered fireplace. The second floor contains three family bedrooms, two full baths, and a relaxing owners suite. This home is designed with a walkout basement foundation.

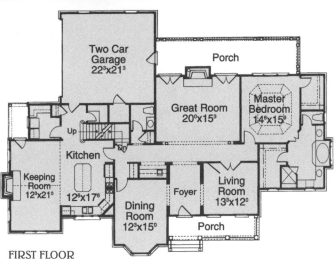

FIRST FLOOR

DESIGN BY
©**Stephen Fuller, Inc.**

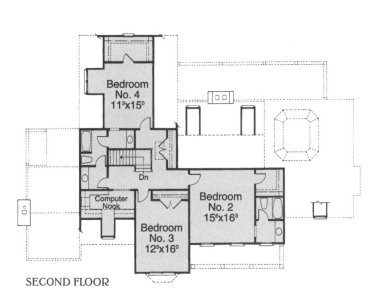

SECOND FLOOR

A charming country cottage exterior conceals a roomy interior. Formal living and dining rooms frame the foyer, which opens to the great room. There, French doors to the rear covered porch flank a centered fireplace. The kitchen's central food-preparation island overlooks a spacious keeping room with its own hearth. A few steps away—and just off the foyer—the formal dining room offers a bay window with views to the front yard. The first-floor owners suite provides a private outdoor area. On the second floor, three family bedrooms share a gallery hall, which leads to a computer nook. This home is designed with a basement foundation.

PLAN HPT100162

Total: 3,626 sq. ft.
First Floor: 2,286 sq. ft.
Second Floor: 1,340 sq. ft.
Width: 80'-0" **Depth:** 56'-9"

PLAN HPT100163

Arched sunburst windows within twin dormers set off one side of the front exterior, while a bay window and curved keystone lintel lend this home grace and charm. Inside, the foyer is open to the living room and dining area. The dining room features a bay window and access to the kitchen, powder room and breakfast nook. The tiled kitchen shares the light from the bay window of the breakfast nook, and French doors set in this bay window access the rear yard. Nearby, the family room has a cozy fireplace and a view of the rear yard through yet another set of bay windows. Upstairs, three family bedrooms share a bath while the owners suite has a luxurious private bath. Please specify basement or slab foundation when ordering.

Total: 1,879 sq. ft.
First Floor: 946 sq. ft.
Second Floor: 933 sq. ft.
Width: 55'-4" **Depth:** 35'-0"

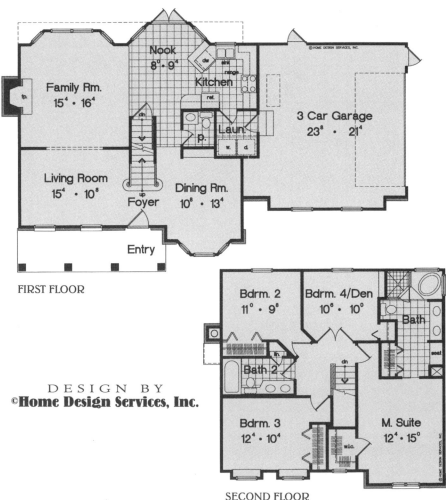

FIRST FLOOR

DESIGN BY
©Home Design Services, Inc.

SECOND FLOOR

166

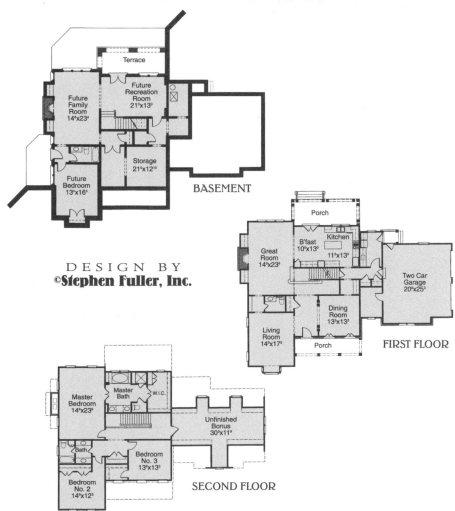

Terrace

Future Family Room 14⁵x23⁹

Future Recreation Room 21⁵x13⁰

Storage 21⁵x12¹⁰

Future Bedroom 13⁰x16⁶

BASEMENT

DESIGN BY
©**Stephen Fuller, Inc.**

Porch

Great Room 14⁵x23⁹

B'fast 10⁵x13⁰

Kitchen 11⁵x13⁰

Two Car Garage 20⁰x25³

Living Room 14⁵x17³

Dining Room 13³x13³

Porch

FIRST FLOOR

Master Bedroom 14⁵x23⁹

Master Bath

W.I.C.

Unfinished Bonus 30³x11⁹

Bath

Bedroom No. 3 13³x13³

Bedroom No. 2 14⁵x12³

SECOND FLOOR

PLAN HPT100164

The fieldstone exterior and cupola evoke rural Southern appeal. Inside, formal and informal spaces are separated by a graceful central stair hall that opens off the front foyer. French doors lead from the front porch to a formal dining room. The living room leads to a cheerful great room that features a fireplace and built-in bookcases. An adjoining breakfast area opens to a columned rear porch. Upstairs, a spacious owners suite overlooks the rear yard. Two additional bedrooms share a convenient hall bath. This home is designed with a walkout basement foundation.

Total: 3,153 sq. ft.
First Floor: 1,704 sq. ft.
Second Floor: 1,449 sq. ft.
Bonus Room: 455 sq. ft.
Width: 70'-9" **Depth:** 56'-0"

167

PLAN HPT100165

It's hard to get beyond the covered front porch of this home, but doing so reveals a bright two-story entry open to the central hall. Just to the left, a living room features French doors connecting to the family room. The efficient kitchen with a snack bar and pantry is open to the bay-windowed breakfast area with a planning desk. The salad sink and counter space double as a service for the formal dining room. The owners bedroom features a raised ceiling and an arched window. Its adjoining bath contains a walk-through closet and a corner whirlpool tub. Three family bedrooms and a hall bath complete this level.

Total: 2,387 sq. ft.
First Floor: 1,303 sq. ft.
Second Floor: 1,084 sq. ft.
Width: 54'-0" **Depth:** 42'-0"

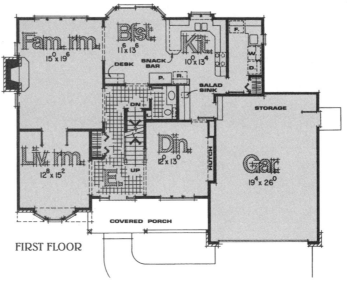

FIRST FLOOR

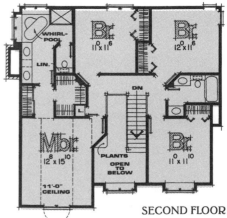

SECOND FLOOR

DESIGN BY
©Design Basics, Inc.

FIRST FLOOR

DESIGN BY
©**Design Basics, Inc.**

SECOND FLOOR

PLAN HPT100166

The classic look of this two-story home with its large covered entry gives this house excellent curb appeal. Inside, the elegant, transom-lit foyer is flanked by the living and dining rooms, each with large, boxed windows. Double doors lead from the living room to the family room, which shares a through-fireplace with the kitchen. This hearth area makes the kitchen a gathering spot. Upstairs, three secondary bedrooms boast unusual window treatments. The luxurious owners suite with a vaulted ceiling and skylit bath with a whirlpool tub rounds out the plan.

Total: 2,496 sq. ft.
First Floor: 1,299 sq. ft.
Second Floor: 1,197 sq. ft.
Width: 55'-8" **Depth:** 38'-0"

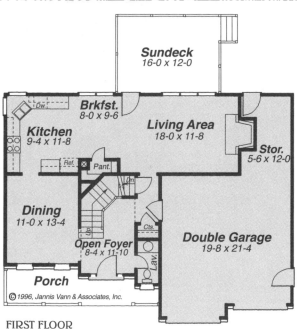

Sundeck 16-0 x 12-0

Brkfst. 8-0 x 9-6

Living Area 18-0 x 11-8

Kitchen 9-4 x 11-8

Stor. 5-6 x 12-0

Dw.

Ref.

Pant.

Dn.

Dining 11-0 x 13-4

Open Foyer 8-4 x 11-10

Cts.

Lav.

Double Garage 19-8 x 21-4

Porch

© 1996, Jannis Vann & Associates, Inc.

FIRST FLOOR

D E S I G N B Y
© **Jannis Vann & Associates, Inc.**

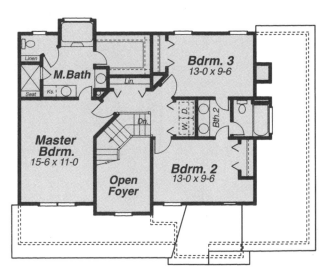

Linen

M.Bath

Seat Ks.

Lin.

Bdrm. 3 13-0 x 9-6

Dn.

W. D.

Bth.2

Master Bdrm. 15-6 x 11-0

Open Foyer

Bdrm. 2 13-0 x 9-6

SECOND FLOOR

PLAN HPT100167

Total: 1,683 sq. ft.
First Floor: 797 sq. ft.
Second Floor: 886 sq. ft.
Width: 44'-0" **Depth:** 34'-5"

Welcome yourself home to this charming farmhouse. Just inside the foyer is a powder room and a coat closet. To the left, a spacious formal dining room conveniently accesses the kitchen and breakfast area. The L-shaped kitchen consists of a roomy walk-in pantry and a corner sink with two windows. Three bedrooms are nestled upstairs, away from the busy activity areas on the first floor. The owners bedroom has an amazing bath, with an oversized soaking tub set in a box-bay window, twin-vanity sinks, a roomy shower, compartmented toilet and large walk-in closet. Bedrooms 2 and 3 share a full bath, which includes a tub set in a box-bay window. Please specify basement, crawlspace or slab foundation when ordering.

DESIGN BY
©**Stephen Fuller, Inc.**

Two Car Garage
21³x24³

Breakfast
12⁰x10⁰

Porch

Kitchen
14³x10⁶

Dining Room
14³x12⁰

Foyer

Porch

Great Room
16³x18⁰

Master Bedroom
15³x16⁰

FIRST FLOOR

Dn

Open To Below

Gallery

Attic Storage

Bedroom No. 2
12⁰x12⁰

Bedroom No. 3
13⁰x13³

SECOND FLOOR

On the first floor of this home, a great room opens up to provide maximum livability for the family. A fireplace and built-ins, as well as volume ceilings, make it a winner. The kitchen serves an octagonal breakfast room, which opens to a side porch. The kitchen also serves the dining room at the front of the house. In the owners bedroom, a detailed ceiling and views out two sides create a lofty feeling. Dual walk-in closets and a full bath with a corner garden tub are sure to satisfy. Two additional bedrooms and a full bath reside upstairs. This home is designed with a walkout basement foundation.

PLAN HPT100168

Total: 2,459 sq. ft.
First Floor: 1,824 sq. ft.
Second Floor: 635 sq. ft.
Width: 52'-9" **Depth:** 68'-9"

PLAN HPT100169

This American country-style home, with wood siding and shuttered windows, echoes images of the warmth of traditional Southern living. The two-story foyer opens to a dining room and formal parlor. Pass the open-rail stairs to the large family room with its fireplace and hearth, flanking bookcases, and squared column supports. The spacious kitchen's breakfast area opens to the outside. There is also an "option room" which may serve as the guest quarters with private bath, a private study or a children's den. Upstairs, the owners suite has its own sitting area and an unusual vaulted ceiling. Two other bedrooms share a bath; a fourth has a private bath and access to the second-floor porch. This home is designed with a walkout basement foundation.

Total: 3,610 sq. ft.
First Floor: 1,850 sq. ft.
Second Floor: 1,760 sq. ft.
Width: 56'-0" **Depth:** 55'-0"

DESIGN BY
©Stephen Fuller, Inc.

FIRST FLOOR

SECOND FLOOR

FIRST FLOOR

Two Car Garage
21³x21³

Porch

Breakfast
10⁰x12³

Kitchen
12³x13⁶

Family Room
14⁹x19⁶

Dn

Dining Room
14³x12⁰

Up

Foyer

Living Room
14³x11⁰

Porch

SECOND FLOOR

Bedroom No. 2
13⁰x12⁰

Bedroom No. 3
11⁹x12⁶

Dn

Master Bedroom
14⁶x16³

Alcove
11⁰x8⁶

Sitting
14⁶x6⁹

D E S I G N   B Y
©**Stephen Fuller, Inc.**

PLAN HPT100170

Double doors provide entry to this fine traditional home. The living room with a bay window creates a formal entertaining area. The kitchen satisfies with ample proportions and a nearby breakfast nook. In the family room, a warming hearth is sure to please. Three bedrooms reside upstairs with the owners suite gaining a lot of attention. It includes a sitting area and a roomy private bath with a corner shower and angled oversized tub beside it. This home is designed with a walkout basement foundation.

Total: 2,705 sq. ft.
First Floor: 1,407 sq. ft.
Second Floor: 1,298 sq. ft.
Width: 46'-3" **Depth:** 72'-3"

OPTIONAL GUEST SUITE

FIRST FLOOR

SECOND FLOOR

DESIGN BY
©Frank Betz Associates, Inc.

PLAN HPT100171

Total: 2,910 sq. ft.
First Floor: 1,471 sq. ft.
Second Floor: 1,439 sq. ft.
Bonus Room: 297 sq. ft.
Width: 60'-0" **Depth:** 45'-6"

Large keystones set within lintels over the windows and doorways lure eyes to this engaging four-bedroom home. A naturally illuminated two-story foyer is adorned with a plant shelf. An arched opening to the left leads to the living room for formal entertaining. Another arch to the right introduces the roomy dining room, with access to the kitchen via a butler's pantry. The focal point of the two-story family room is the large fireplace with built-in bookshelves to each side and plant shelves above. The second-floor owners suite showcases a tray ceiling, a light-filled sitting room, two walk-in closets and a luxurious bath. Please specify basement or crawlspace foundation when ordering.

Breakfast

Bedroom 4/ Study 11² x 12⁴

Bath

PANTRY

FRENCH DOOR

Family Room 18² x 13⁰

FPL.

W.i.c.

RANGE

Kitchen

DW.

REF.

OPEN RAIL

STAIRS UP

Garage 19⁵ x 22⁴

STAIRS DN.

COATS

Dining Room 11⁶ x 10⁸

Two Story Foyer

Living Room 11⁶ x 10⁸

Covered Porch

FIRST FLOOR

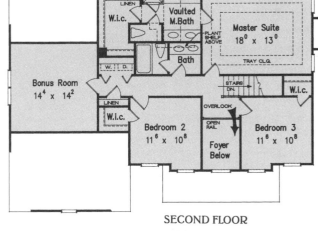

QUOTE ONE®

Cost to build? See page 310
to order complete cost estimate
to build this house in your area!

RADIUS WINDOW

SHWR.

LINEN

W.i.c.

Vaulted M.Bath

PLANT SHELF ABOVE

Master Suite 18⁰ x 13⁰

Bath

TRAY CLG.

W. D.

Bonus Room 14⁴ x 14²

STAIRS DN.

W.i.c.

LINEN

W.i.c.

Bedroom 2 11⁶ x 10⁸

OVERLOOK

OPEN RAIL

Foyer Below

Bedroom 3 11⁶ x 10⁸

SECOND FLOOR

DESIGN BY
©Frank Betz Associates, Inc.

This grand two-story home proves that tried and true traditional style is still the best! Thoughtful planning brings formal living areas to the forefront and places open, casual living areas to the rear of the plan. Bedroom 4 serves as a multi-purpose room, providing the flexibility desired by today's homeowner. The second floor is devoted to the relaxing owners suite, two secondary bedrooms, a full hall bath and a balcony overlook. Please specify basement, crawlspace or slab foundation when ordering.

PLAN HPT100172

Total: 2,052 sq. ft.
First Floor: 1,135 sq. ft.
Second Floor: 917 sq. ft.
Bonus Room: 216 sq. ft.
Width: 52'-4" **Depth:** 37'-6"

PLAN HPT100173

A wraparound porch, Palladian window set in a second-floor gable, and varying rooflines add picturesque charm to this spacious four-bedroom home. The parlor and dining room surround the foyer. A truly grand room features a fireplace framed by built-in cabinets and a circular wall of windows. The kitchen has an island workstation, walk-in pantry and serving bar to simplify food preparation. Nearby are a hearth room with its own fireplace, and a breakfast nook with a bay window. Upstairs, four bedrooms are positioned around a large exercise room featuring a circle of windows viewing the rear yard. The owners suite is absolutely spectacular with a huge sitting room adorned with a fireplace and tray ceiling, another tray ceiling over the owners bedroom, dressing room, His and Hers walk-in closets and lavish bath. Please specify basement or crawlspace foundation when ordering.

Total: 5,466 sq. ft.
First Floor: 2,732 sq. ft.
Second Floor: 2,734 sq. ft.
Width: 85'-0" **Depth:** 85'-6"

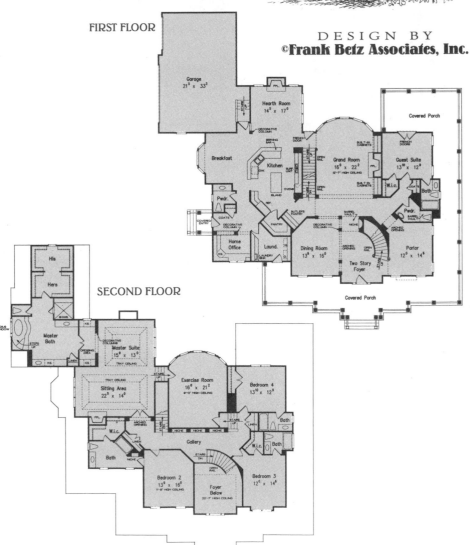

DESIGN BY
©**Frank Betz Associates, Inc.**

FIRST FLOOR

SECOND FLOOR

DESIGN BY
©Frank Betz Associates, Inc.

PLAN HPT100174

Here's a new country home with a fresh face and a dash of Victoriana. Inside, the foyer leads to an elegant dining room and a spacious living room with French doors to the covered rear porch. The heart of the home is a two-story family room with a focal-point fireplace and its own French door to the rear property. A breakfast room offers a walk-in pantry and shares a snack bar with the kitchen, which leads to the formal dining room through a butler's pantry. The second-floor owners suite features an impressive private bath with a vaulted ceiling and an optional sitting room. Please specify basement or crawlspace foundation when ordering.

Total: 2,608 sq. ft.
First Floor: 1,351 sq. ft.
Second Floor: 1,257 sq. ft.
Width: 60'-0" **Depth:** 46'-4"

177

PLAN HPT100175

This charming cottage-style home features sweeping rooflines and an undeniably exquisite exterior. Inside, a two-story foyer opens through a large arch to the living room with a ten-foot coffered ceiling. Another arch defines the dining room. A see-through fireplace sits between the living room and the breakfast area, which features a bay window and a coffered ceiling. A large kitchen, utility room and walk-in pantry complete the area. The owners bedroom, with a ten-foot ceiling, sitting area and luxury owners bath, is located on the opposite side of the home. Bedroom 2 and Bath 2 are located nearby. Bedrooms 3 and 4 occupy the second floor with an expandable game room.

Total: 2,462 sq. ft.
First Floor: 1,934 sq. ft.
Second Floor: 528 sq. ft.
Width: 64'-10" **Depth:** 59'-8"

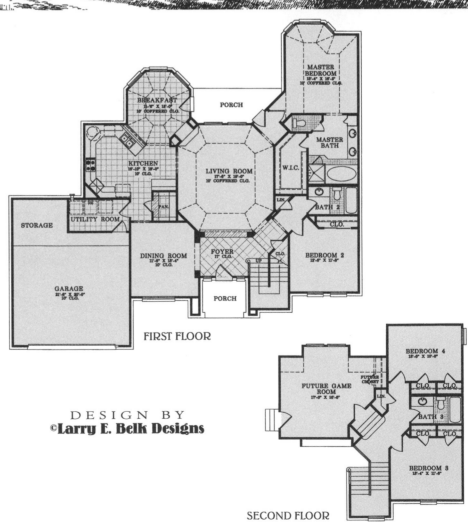

FIRST FLOOR

DESIGN BY
©**Larry E. Belk Designs**

SECOND FLOOR

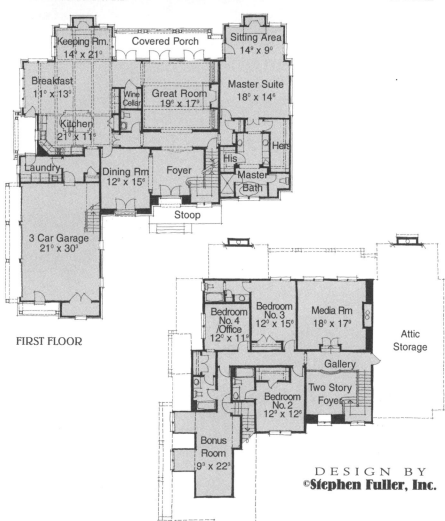

FIRST FLOOR

Keeping Rm. 14⁰ x 21⁰

Covered Porch

Sitting Area 14⁰ x 9⁰

Breakfast 11⁰ x 13⁰

Wine Cellar

Great Room 19⁶ x 17⁹

Master Suite 18⁰ x 14⁶

Kitchen 21⁰ x 11⁰

Hers

Laundry

Dining Rm 12⁹ x 15⁶

Foyer

His

Master Bath

Stoop

3 Car Garage 21⁰ x 30³

SECOND FLOOR

Bedroom No. 4 /Office 12⁰ x 11⁹

Bedroom No. 3 12⁰ x 15⁶

Media Rm 18⁰ x 17⁹

Attic Storage

Gallery

Bedroom No. 2 12⁹ x 12⁶

Two Story Foyer

Bonus Room 9³ x 22³

DESIGN BY
©**Stephen Fuller, Inc.**

PLAN HPT100176

This magnificent home captures the charm of French country design with its high hipped roof and brick detailing. Inside, the two-story foyer leads directly to the spacious great room with a fireplace and three sets of double doors to the rear porch. The formal dining room sits to the left of the foyer and near the L-shaped kitchen, which serves a bright breakfast room. The main-floor owners suite takes the entire right wing of the house. It includes a large sitting area with porch access and an opulent bath. Upstairs, a gallery hall leads to a media room, three more bedrooms (each with a private bath) and a bonus room over the garage. This home is designed with a basement foundation.

Total: 4,271 sq. ft.
First Floor: 2,963 sq. ft.
Second Floor: 1,308 sq. ft.
Bonus Room: 358 sq. ft.
Width: 72'-0"   **Depth:** 76'-6"

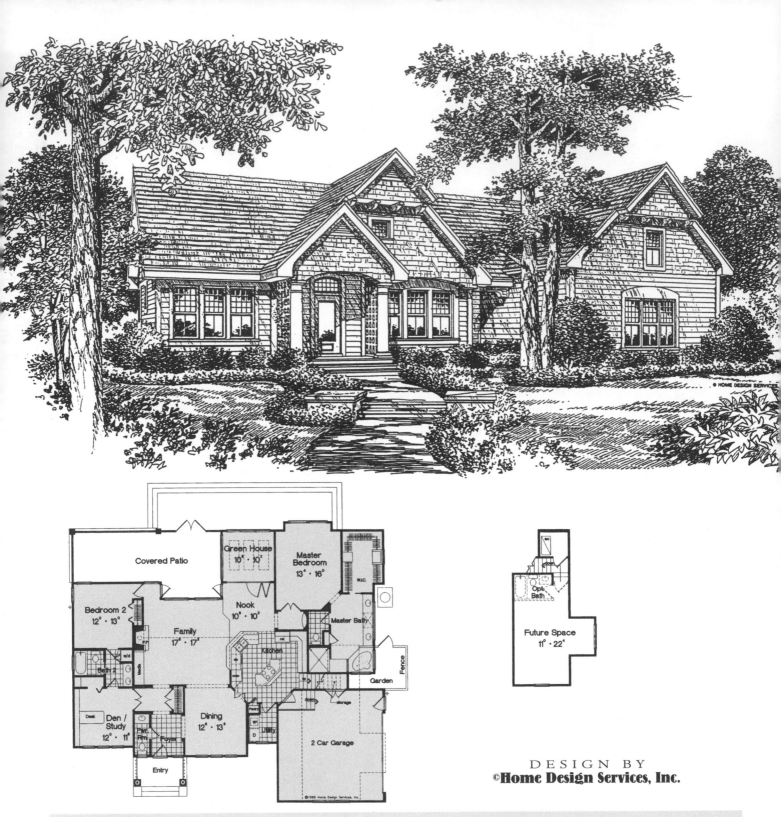

Covered Patio

Green House
10⁴ · 10²

Master
Bedroom
13⁴ · 16⁰

W.I.C.

Bedroom 2
12⁰ · 13⁰

Nook
10⁰ · 10²

Family
17⁰ · 17⁰

Master Bath

Kitchen

Bath 2

Fence

Garden

Den / Study
12⁰ · 11⁰

Dining
12⁰ · 13⁰

Foyer

Utility

storage

2 Car Garage

Entry

Opt.
Bath

Future Space
11⁰ · 22⁴

DESIGN BY
©Home Design Services, Inc.

PLAN HPT100177

Square Footage: 1,997
Bonus Room: 310 sq. ft.
Width: 64'-4" **Depth:** 63'-0"

The center of the hub of this charming plan is the spacious kitchen with an island and serving bar. The nearby breakfast nook accesses the greenhouse with its wall of windows and three large skylights. A built-in media center beside a warming fireplace is the focal point of the family room. Bedroom 2 shares a full bath with the den/study, which might also be a third bedroom. The owners suite features large His and Hers vanity sinks, a corner tub with an open walk-in shower, and a supersized walk-in closet. Future space over the garage can expand the living space as your family grows. Please specify basement, crawlspace or slab foundation when ordering.

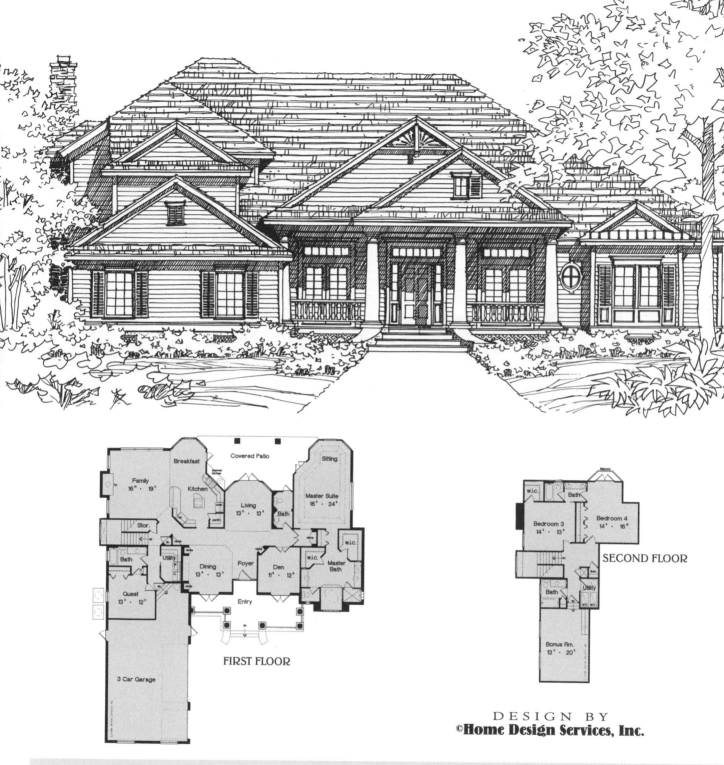

FIRST FLOOR

SECOND FLOOR

D E S I G N   B Y
©Home Design Services, Inc.

Country accents and a full veranda create the charm of Southern living in this four-bedroom home. The foyer leads to the living room, dining area and den, each with a set of French doors opening to a covered patio/entry. The dining room is fitted with furniture and art niches, great for displaying family heirlooms. Nearby, the kitchen, breakfast nook and family room create an open atmosphere. Double doors announce the entrance to the owners suite, which is crowned by a tray ceiling and features a sitting room placed within bay windows, and a lavish bath with a grand soaking tub, oversized shower, private toilet chamber and twin-vanity sinks.

PLAN HPT100178

Total: 3,557 sq. ft.
First Floor: 2,761 sq. ft.
Second Floor: 796 sq. ft.
Bonus Room: 284 sq. ft.
Width: 74'-0" **Depth:** 85'-0"

PLAN HPT100179

If you've ever traveled the European countryside, past rolling hills that range in hue from apple green to deep, rich emerald, you may have come upon a home much like this one. Stone accents combined with stucco, and shutters that frame multi-pane windows add a touch of charm that introduces the marvelous floor plan found inside. The foyer opens to a great room that offers a panoramic view of the veranda beyond. To the left is a formal dining room; to the right, a quiet den. Just steps away, a sitting room introduces the grand owners suite. A kitchen with a nook, the laundry room and a large shop area complete the first floor. The second floor contains two family bedrooms, two full baths and a bonus room.

Total: 3,517 sq. ft.
First Floor: 2,698 sq. ft.
Second Floor: 819 sq. ft.
Bonus Room: 370 sq. ft.
Width: 90'-6" **Depth:** 84'-0"

FIRST FLOOR

SECOND FLOOR

DESIGN BY
©Alan Mascord Design Associates, Inc.

PLAN HPT100180

Palladian windows, arched dormers and multi-level gables add interest to the exterior of this four-bedroom home. The foyer is framed with the dining room on the left—adorned with a tray ceiling—and the living room ahead with a unique waffle ceiling. To the right are the den/study and the owners suite. The luxurious owners bath contains a large double vanity with make-up area and a round soaking tub with a curved glass-block wall—the focal point of the room—and a spacious shower. The large island kitchen provides plenty of counter space and opens to the breakfast nook and family room with great views to the covered patio area. Bedroom 4 would be perfect as a guest suite with its private bath and entrance from the family room and rear yard. Bedrooms 2 and 3 share a full bath.

Square Footage: 3,458
Bonus Room: 466 sq. ft.
Width: 83'-4" **Depth:** 90'-8"

DESIGN BY
©Home Design Services, Inc.

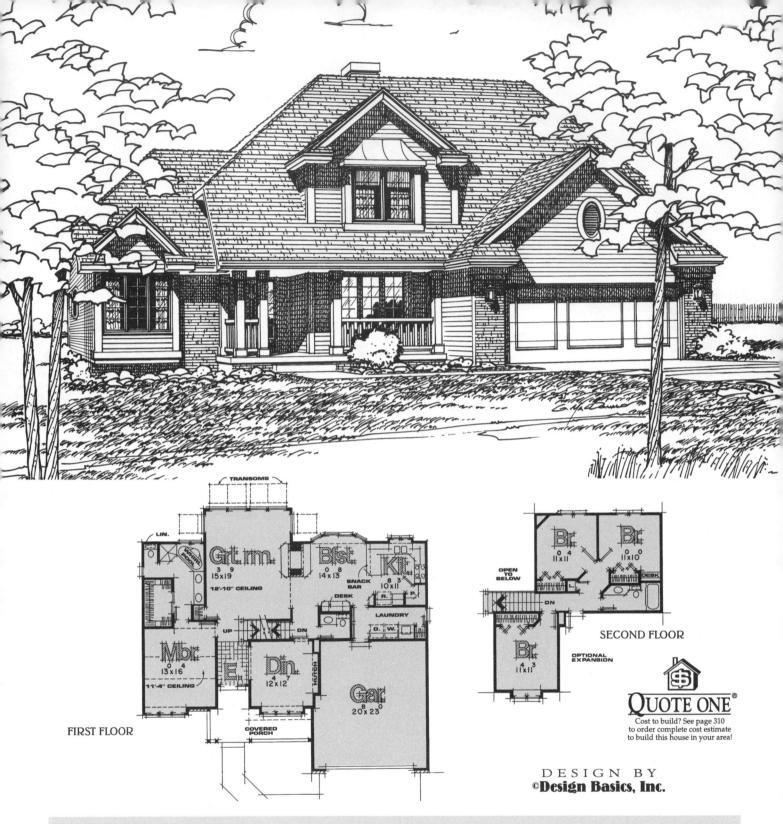

FIRST FLOOR

SECOND FLOOR

OPTIONAL EXPANSION

Quote One®
Cost to build? See page 310
to order complete cost estimate
to build this house in your area!

DESIGN BY
©**Design Basics, Inc.**

PLAN HPT100181

Total: 1,999 sq. ft.
First Floor: 1,421 sq. ft.
Second Floor: 578 sq. ft.
Width: 52'-0" **Depth:** 47'-4"

Growing families will love this unique plan. Start with the living areas—a spacious great room with high ceilings, windows overlooking the backyard, a through-fireplace to the kitchen and access to the rear deck. A dining room with hutch space accommodates formal occasions. The hearth kitchen features a well-planned work area and a bay-windowed breakfast area. The owners suite with a whirlpool tub and a walk-in closet is located on the first floor for privacy, while three family bedrooms upstairs share a full bath. Please specify basement or slab foundation when ordering.

FIRST FLOOR

- 12'ceiling
- Master 14x16
- vaulted clg.
- Family Room 20x15/6
- 18'ceiling
- Balcony above
- Breakfast Keeping Room 18/4x12/6
- Stoop
- Kitchen 13/4x11
- Pantry
- W D
- sink
- Dining 13/4x11
- Foyer
- Open Above
- dn. up
- Garage 21/4x22
- Porch
- Drive

SECOND FLOOR

- BR.#3 13/4x11
- Family Room Below
- Balcony
- Bookcase
- dn.
- Foyer Below
- BR.#2 13/4x11
- Gameroom Office BR.#4 13/4x22

DESIGN BY
©**Greg Marquis & Associates**

This large farmhouse with a wraparound porch begins with a cozy look outside and continues with an equally cozy feel inside. The breakfast/keeping room with a fireplace offers expansive views of the backyard. A walk-in pantry and laundry room with a utility sink are convenient pluses. The upstairs balcony overlooks the two-story family room, which provides a second fireplace. The first-floor vaulted owners suite is located for privacy and features twin walk-in closets and a deluxe bath. Upstairs, two bedrooms each have walk-in closets and share a full bath. A separate bonus room—great for teenagers—serves as a guest suite, home office or game room with its own private bath.

PLAN HPT100182

Total: 2,659 sq. ft.
First Floor: 1,627 sq. ft.
Second Floor: 1,032 sq. ft.
Width: 63'-0"   **Depth:** 50'-0"

PLAN HPT100183

From its large front porch to its rear porch and deck, this lavish farmhouse bids welcome. The foyer offers entrance to both the formal living and dining rooms and opens into the heart of the home—he spacious family room with its central fireplace and rear-yard access. A well-equipped kitchen features a desk, an island cooktop and a large breakfast area with views to the outside. The owners bedroom boasts a separate sitting room, a huge walk-in closet and a luxurious bath with separate sinks and a whirlpool tub. All three of the upstairs family bedrooms include walk-in closets and, while Bedrooms 3 and 4 share a full hall bath that has dual sinks, Bedroom 2 features its own bath.

Total: 4,219 sq. ft.
First Floor: 3,045 sq. ft.
Second Floor: 1,174 sq. ft.
Width: 77'-0" **Depth:** 53'-0"

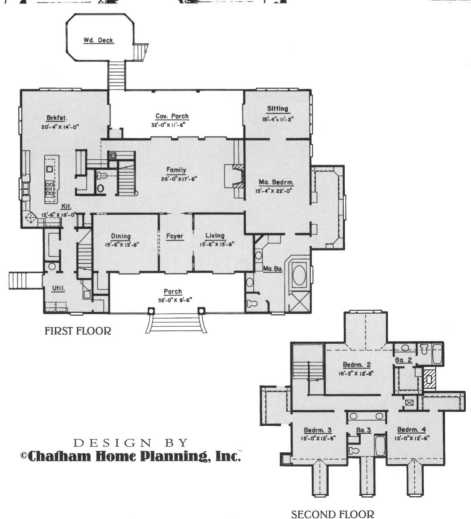

FIRST FLOOR

SECOND FLOOR

DESIGN BY
©Chatham Home Planning, Inc.

PLAN HPT100184

This Southern Louisiana design offers a distinctive exterior with tall, transomed windows, dormers and stately columns. The interior combines comfort and high elegance, with nine-foot ceilings adding an aura of hospitality throughout the main floor. Formal living and dining areas flank the foyer, while the spacious great room with a centered fireplace resides at the rear. A windowed whirlpool tub, twin lavatories and a generous walk-in closet highlight the plush owners suite. This home is finished in stucco and brick for low maintenance. Please specify crawlspace or slab foundation when ordering.

Total: 2,824 sq. ft.
First Floor: 2,120 sq. ft.
Second Floor: 704 sq. ft.
Width: 67'-0" **Depth:** 64'-2"

FIRST FLOOR

DESIGN BY
©**Chatham Home Planning, Inc.**

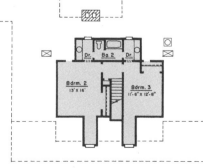

SECOND FLOOR

PLAN HPT100185

Symmetry and balance best describe this brick home accented by gabled roofs and dormers. Three sets of French doors under a covered porch provide entry to a foyer and great room, perfect for entertaining on a grand scale. A wall of windows and a set of French doors with access to the rear patio are the focal points of the great room. A cheery fire in the great room's large fireplace—with a built-in bookcase—will brighten any occasion. A rear covered porch opens to a large patio accessible from the breakfast nook. Nearby, the well-appointed kitchen includes a snack/serving bar. The owners suite is complete with picture windows, dual walk-in closets and a private bath with a whirlpool tub and separate shower. Please specify basement, crawlspace or slab foundation when ordering.

Square Footage: 2,184
Bonus Room: 572 sq. ft.
Width: 68'-0" **Depth:** 62'-0"

DESIGN BY
©**Larry James & Associates, Inc.**

GARAGE
22-0 x 20-4

seat

DECK

covered breezeway

master bath

walk-in closet

walk-in closet

GREAT RM.
15-4 x 25-4

fireplace

KIT./BRKFST.
18-8 x 15-8

BED RM.
11-8 x 10-2

walk-in closet

bath

MASTER BED RM.
14-8 x 14-2

(cathedral ceiling)

cl.

FOYER
5-0 x 9-8

DINING
13-4 x 12-0

d w

lin.

cl

SUN RM.
15-4 x 11-8

optional opening

BED RM.
11-8 x 12-8

skylights

(cathedral ceiling)

PORCH

DESIGN BY
Donald A. Gardner Architects, Inc.

PLAN HPT100186

Twin dormers set over a relaxing porch are complemented by sunburst windows within twin gables, creating a stylish country appeal. The foyer leads into the dining area, sun room and great room. Lounge in front of the fire in the great room or enjoy views of the backyard. The split floor plan allows for plenty of privacy in the owners suite, situated to the left of the great room. The owners bedroom is complete with two walk-in closets and a luxurious bath. Two family bedrooms, sharing a full bath, finish the floor plan.

Square Footage: 2,053
Width: 67'-4" **Depth:** 66'-4"

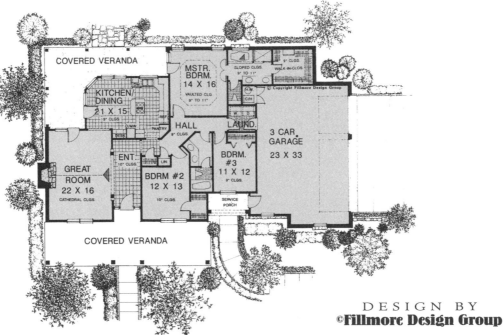

DESIGN BY
©Fillmore Design Group

PLAN HPT100187

Square Footage: 1,830
Width: 75'-0" **Depth:** 52'-3"

Characteristics that include a cupola, shutters, arched transoms and an exterior of combined stone and lap siding give this one-story home its country identity. To the left of the entry is the great room. Here, a cathedral ceiling and a fireplace extend an invitation for family and friends alike to relax and enjoy themselves. The kitchen and dining room are located nearby. Kitchen amenities include an island cooktop, built-in planning desk and pantry, while the multi-windowed dining room overlooks and provides access to the covered veranda. A hall leads to sleeping quarters that include two secondary bedrooms and a luxurious owners suite. Room for the family fleet is provided by the three-car garage.

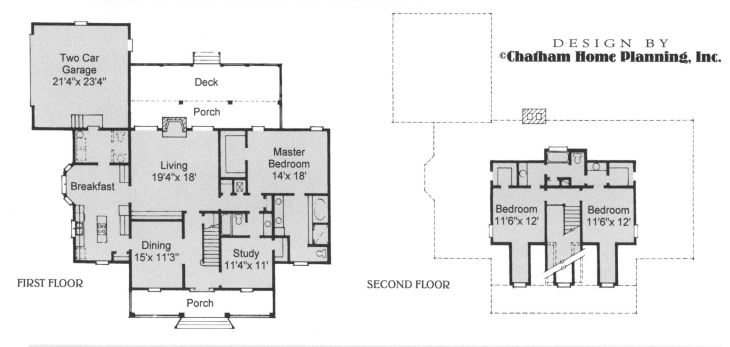

DESIGN BY
©**Chatham Home Planning, Inc.**

Two Car Garage 21'4"x 23'4"

Deck

Porch

Breakfast

Living 19'4"x 18'

Master Bedroom 14'x 18'

Dining 15'x 11'3"

Study 11'4"x 11'

FIRST FLOOR

Porch

SECOND FLOOR

Bedroom 11'6"x 12'

Bedroom 11'6"x 12'

This Southern cottage combines style and comfort and offers flexibility with an optional bedroom/study area. Nine-foot ceilings expand the plan throughout the first floor. The family chef will appreciate the large gourmet kitchen with an island cabinet and walk-in pantry. The breakfast nook will be a wonderful place to read a book with natural light from the bay window. There's room to relax with privacy in the spacious owners suite, complete with a sumptuous bath. Upstairs, two family bedrooms enjoy private dressing areas and walk-in closets, but share the main bathroom area. Please specify crawlspace or slab foundation when ordering.

PLAN HPT100188

Total: 2,533 sq. ft.
First Floor: 1,916 sq. ft.
Second Floor: 617 sq. ft.
Width: 66'-0" **Depth:** 66'-0"

PLAN HPT100189

Throughout the home, beautiful windows bring the outdoors in. French doors lead to the library with a bayed window, built-in desk and bookcases. Homeowners will relish the combination breakfast/hearth room and kitchen concept. Special finishing touches include the bayed sitting area and tray ceiling in the owners suite. The owners dressing/bath area is enhanced by His and Hers vanities, an oval whirlpool tub beneath the arched window, and a deluxe walk-in closet with windows. Three family bedrooms, each with a walk-in closet, and two full baths complete the second floor.

Total: 3,669 sq. ft.
First Floor: 1,679 sq. ft.
Second Floor: 1,990 sq. ft.
Width: 75'-2" **Depth:** 65'-0"

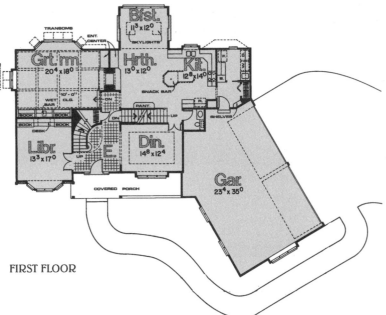

FIRST FLOOR

DESIGN BY
©**Design Basics, Inc.**

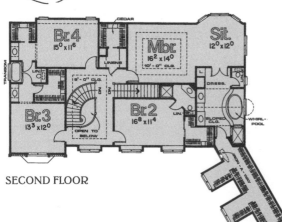

SECOND FLOOR

192

Country-Style Capes and Cottages

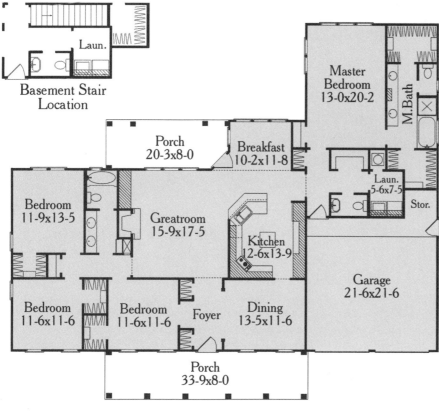

Basement Stair Location

Laun.

Porch
20-3x8-0

Breakfast
10-2x11-8

Master
Bedroom
13-0x20-2

M.Bath

Bedroom
11-9x13-5

Greatroom
15-9x17-5

Kitchen
12-6x13-9

Laun.
5-6x7-5

Stor.

Bedroom
11-6x11-6

Bedroom
11-6x11-6

Foyer

Dining
13-5x11-6

Garage
21-6x21-6

Porch
33-9x8-0

DESIGN BY
©**Larry James & Associates, Inc.**

PLAN HPT100190

Six columns and a steeply pitched roof lend elegance to this four-bedroom home. To the right of the foyer, the dining area sits conveniently near the efficient kitchen. The kitchen island and serving bar add plenty of workspace to the food-preparation zone. Natural light will flood the breakfast nook through a ribbon of windows facing the rear yard. Escape to the relaxing owners suite, with its luxurious bath set between His and Hers walk-in closets. The great room is at the center of this L-shaped plan, and is complete with a warming fireplace and built-ins. Three family bedrooms enjoy private walk-in closets and share a fully appointed bath. Please specify basement, crawlspace or slab foundation when ordering.

Square Footage: 2,267
Width: 71'-2" **Depth:** 62'-0"

Storage
21-6x11-0

Garage
21-6x25-6

Porch
19-2x12-0

Master Bedroom/ Sitting Room
12-9x23-8

M.Bath
10-0x13-6

Laun.
9-0x8-7

1/2 Bath

Kitchen
18-0x11-6

Greatroom
19-1x17-5

Bath

Bedroom
12-0x13-6

Breakfast
14-0x9-0

Dining
11-6x13-6

Foyer

Bedroom
11-6x13-6

Bedroom
12-0x11-7

Porch
31-5x8-0

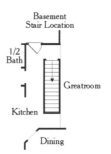

Basement Stair Location

1/2 Bath

Greatroom

Kitchen

Dining

DESIGN BY
©**Larry James & Associates, Inc.**

PLAN HPT100191

Square Footage: 2,555
Width: 66'-1" Depth: 77'-7"

A steeply pitched roof and transoms over multi-pane windows give this house great curb appeal. To the left of the foyer, the formal dining room provides through-access to the kitchen and breakfast area. A large island/snack bar adds plenty of counter space to the food-preparation area. Double French doors frame the fireplace in the great room, leading to the skylit covered porch at the rear of the home. The owners suite boasts a light-filled sitting room and luxurious bath with two walk-in closets, a garden tub and a shower. Three secondary bedrooms, at the front of the design, all have walk-in closets. Please specify basement, crawlspace or slab foundation when ordering.

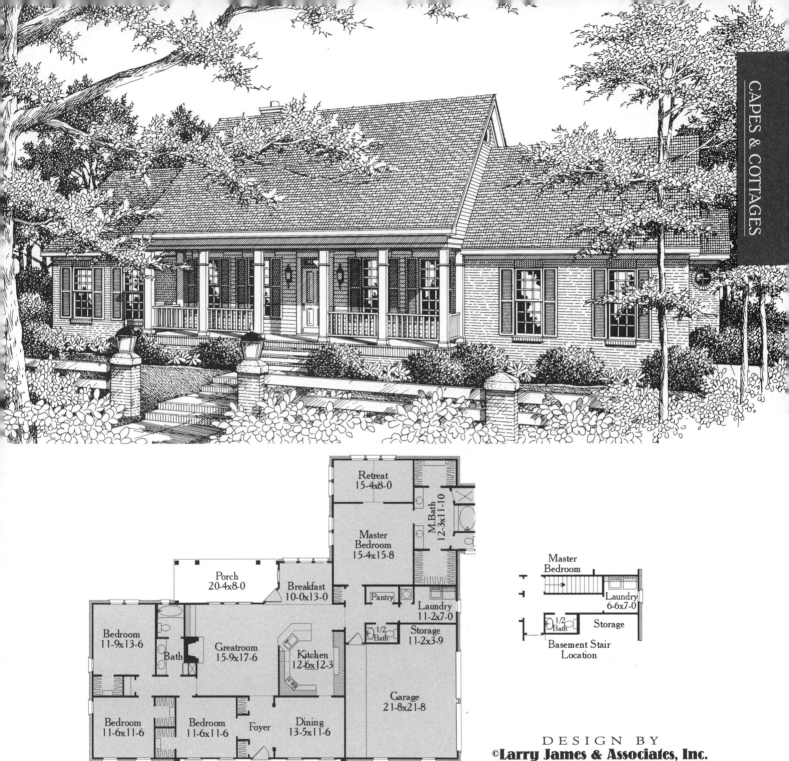

DESIGN BY
©Larry James & Associates, Inc.

A porch full of columns gives a relaxing emphasis to this country home. To the right of the foyer, the dining area resides conveniently near the efficient kitchen. The kitchen island, walk-in pantry and serving bar add plenty of workspace to the food-preparation zone. Natural light will flood the breakfast nook through a ribbon of windows facing the rear yard. Escape to the relaxing owners suite featuring a private sun room/retreat and a luxurious bath set between His and Hers walk-in closets. The great room at the center of this L-shaped plan is complete with a warming fireplace and built-ins. Please specify basement, crawlspace or slab foundation when ordering.

PLAN HPT100192

Square Footage: 2,506
Width: 72'-2" **Depth:** 66'-4"

PLAN HPT100193

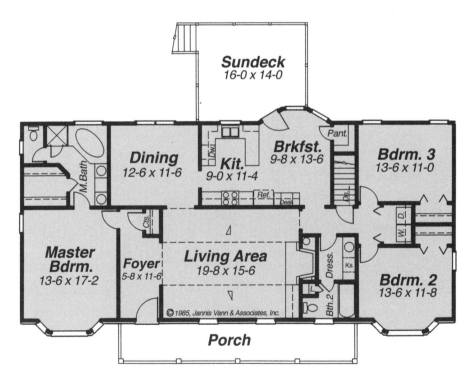

A raised porch greets visitors and welcomes them to sit a while and enjoy a quiet conversation. The foyer leads to a secluded owners bedroom to the left. The owners suite features a bay window and a luxurious bath, including a walk-in closet, twin-vanity sinks, large oval tub, separate shower and compartmented toilet. The living room's focal point is the fireplace, set below a sloping roof. The formal dining area is conveniently nearby the U-shaped kitchen and breakfast nook. Sunlight will flood both the kitchen—with a snack bar and walk-in pantry—and the breakfast area through a bay window. Bedrooms 2 and 3 share a fully appointed bath, completing this relaxing country design.

Square Footage: 1,778
Width: 62'-0"   Depth: 48'-0"

DESIGN BY
©**Jannis Vann & Associates, Inc.**

PLAN HPT100194

Compact yet comfortable, this country cottage possesses many appealing amenities. From the covered front porch that invites relaxed living, the entrance opens to the living room with access to the dining room and snack bar at the rear. Two bedrooms are secluded to the right of the plan with the kitchen and bathroom/laundry facilities located on the left side. A second porch off the kitchen provides room for more casual dining and quiet moments. This home is designed with a basement foundation.

Square Footage: 920
Width: 38'-0" **Depth:** 28'-0"

5,70 X 3,50
19'-0" X 11'-8"

3,65 X 3,50
12'-2" X 11'-8"

4,60 X 3,60
15'-4" X 12'-0"

2,70 X 3,00
9'-0" X 10'-0"

DESIGN BY
©Drummond Designs, Inc.

197

PLAN HPT100195

This home-sweet-home features a welcoming front porch across its entire length. Once you enter, you'll be greeted by ten-foot ceilings in the large family room and a cozily angled fireplace. The vaulted eat-in kitchen, with its popular L-shape and work island, includes an ample pantry and a laundry room. Note the large owners bedroom with a walk-in closet. Each of the other two bedrooms also have walk-in closets. Out back, a covered walkway runs next to the deck and connects the angled two-car garage with the living space in a most charming way.

Square Footage: 1,475
Width: 43'-0" **Depth:** 43'-0"

OPTIONAL MASTER BATH

DESIGN BY
©Greg Marquis & Associates

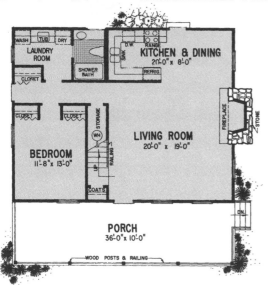

WASH | TUB | DRY

LAUNDRY ROOM

CLOSET

KITCHEN & DINING
20'-0" x 8'-0"

D.W.
RANGE
SINK
REFRIG.

SHOWER BATH

CLOSET   CLOSET

STORAGE

FIREPLACE
STONE

BEDROOM
11'-8" x 13'-0"

WH
UP
RAILING

LIVING ROOM
20'-0" x 19'-0"

COATS

DN

PORCH
36'-0" x 10'-0"

WOOD POSTS & RAILING

FIRST FLOOR

DESIGN BY
©**Home Planners**

QUOTE ONE®

Cost to build? See page 310
to order complete cost estimate
to build this house in your area!

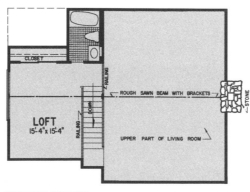

CLOSET

RAILING

LOFT
15'-4" x 15'-4"

DOWN

ROUGH SAWN BEAM WITH BRACKETS

STONE

UPPER PART OF LIVING ROOM

SECOND FLOOR

PLAN HPT100196

This charming farmhouse design will be economical to build and a pleasure to occupy. Like most vacation homes, this design features an open plan. The large living area includes a living room, a dining room and a massive stone fireplace. A partition separates the kitchen from the living room. The first floor also holds a bedroom, a full bath and a laundry room. Upstairs, a spacious sleeping loft overlooks the living room. Don't miss the large front porch—this will be a favorite spot for relaxing.

Total: 1,309 sq. ft.
First Floor: 1,036 sq. ft.
Second Floor: 273 sq. ft.
Width: 39'-0" **Depth:** 38'-0"

◄━■D■━►

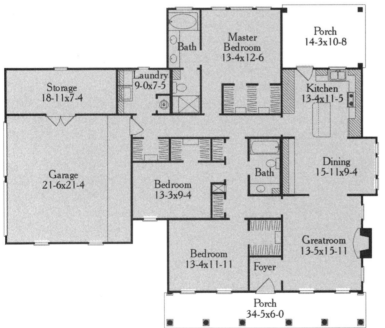

Storage
18-11x7-4

Laundry
9-0x7-5

Bath

Master
Bedroom
13-4x12-6

Porch
14-3x10-8

Kitchen
13-4x11-5

Garage
21-6x21-4

Bedroom
13-3x9-4

Bath

Dining
15-11x9-4

Greatroom
13-5x15-11

Bedroom
13-4x11-11

Foyer

Porch
34-5x6-0

Bedroom
13-3x9-4

Basement Stair
Location

DESIGN BY
©Larry James & Associates, Inc.

PLAN HPT100197

Square Footage: 1,675
Width: 63'-11" **Depth:** 54'-8"

A full porch of columns gives a relaxing emphasis to this country home. Inside, the great room provides a cozy fireplace framed by windows. An open floor plan connects the great room, dining room and kitchen. The island/snack bar adds to the available work space in the kitchen. Walk-in closets dominate this plan, with one in each of three bedrooms, and one by the laundry room. The two-car garage also holds a storage area for family treasures. The owners suite offers a wonderful view of the rear yard, and a compartmentalized bathroom with both a shower and a garden tub. Please specify basement, crawlspace or slab foundation when ordering.

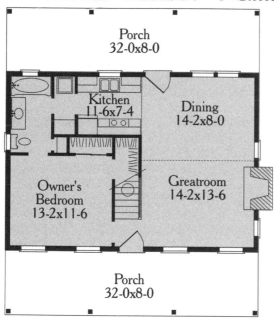

Porch
32-0x8-0

Kitchen
11-6x7-4

Dining
14-2x8-0

Owner's
Bedroom
13-2x11-6

Greatroom
14-2x13-6

Porch
32-0x8-0

FIRST FLOOR

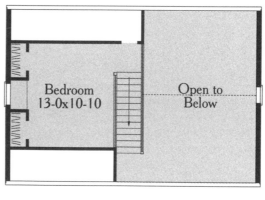

Bedroom
13-0x10-10

Open to
Below

SECOND FLOOR

DESIGN BY
©Larry James & Associates, Inc.

The steeply pitched roof, shuttered windows and two full covered porches lend this two-bedroom plan great country charm. The covered front and rear porches are perfect places for quiet time or entertaining guests in the great outdoors. A warming fireplace, with windows on each side, is the focal point of the great room and the dining area. The owners bedroom, located on the first floor, directly accesses the full bathroom. A galley kitchen leads directly into the dining room. One family bedroom is nested upstairs. Please specify basement, crawlspace or slab foundation when ordering.

PLAN HPT100198

Total: 923 sq. ft.
First Floor: 720 sq. ft.
Second Floor: 203 sq. ft.
Width: 32'-0" **Depth:** 38'-6"

PLAN HPT100199

With its twin gables, covered porch and shutters, this three-bedroom plan would look good on any lot. Rest a while in quiet contemplation on the porch, or go inside to relax by the fireplace in the great room. A rear covered porch lends additional living space to the design and would be a great location for a barbecue. The kitchen adjoins the light-filled dining area by a snack bar, and includes a pantry conveniently located near the carport entry. The owners suite is complete with His and Hers walk-in closets, a garden tub, shower and twin-vanity sinks. Two secondary bedrooms share a bath near the front of the home. There is room to grow with the optional bonus room upstairs. Please specify basement, crawlspace or slab foundation when ordering.

Square Footage: 1,806
Bonus Space: 1,362 sq. ft.
Width: 48'-0"   **Depth:** 80'-0"

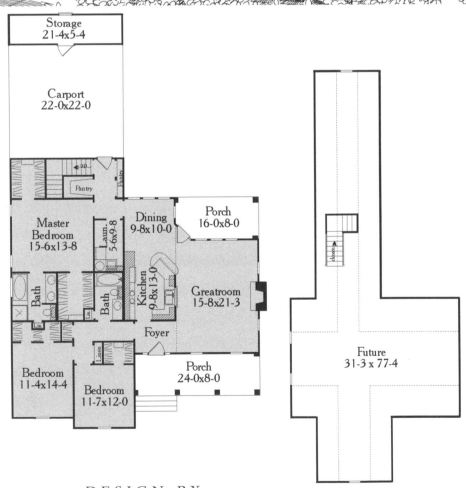

DESIGN BY
©Larry James & Associates, Inc.

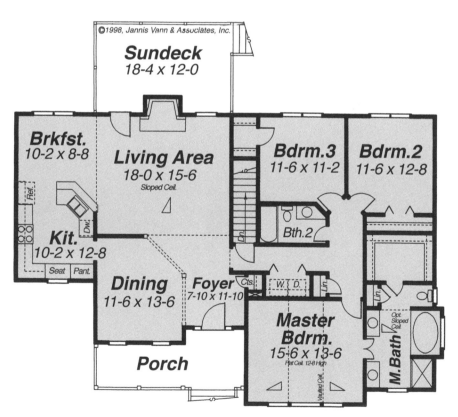

©1998, Jannis Vann & Associates, Inc.

Sundeck
18-4 x 12-0

Brkfst.
10-2 x 8-8

Living Area
18-0 x 15-6
Sloped Ceil.

Bdrm.3
11-6 x 11-2

Bdrm.2
11-6 x 12-8

Ref.

Dw.

Kit.
10-2 x 12-8

Seat Pant.

Dining
11-6 x 13-6

Foyer
7-10 x 11-10

Cts.

Bth.2

W.D.

Lin.

Dn.

Master Bdrm.
15-6 x 13-6
Flat Ceil. 12-8 High

Opt. Sloped Ceil.

M.Bath

Porch

Vaulted Ceil.

D E S I G N   B Y
©**Jannis Vann & Associates, Inc.**

PLAN HPT100200

Abeautiful Palladian window and the arched porch add an elegant style to this charming one-story home. Inside, the foyer opens directly to the formal dining room and living area. A fireplace, framed by a window and a door, is the focus of the living room. Nearby, the breakfast area joins the kitchen with a serving bar. The owners bedroom features the Palladian window of the front exterior, and a well-appointed bath includes a large walk-in closet, oversized soaking tub, separate shower and twin-vanity sinks. Two family bedrooms share a full bath and complete this simple design.

Square Footage: 1,772
Width: 57'-0" **Depth:** 38'-0"

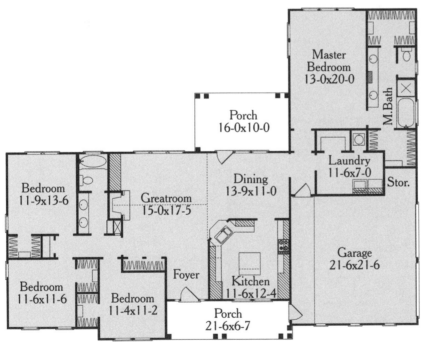

Master
Bedroom
13-0x20-0

M.Bath

Porch
16-0x10-0

Laundry
11-6x7-0

Dining
13-9x11-0

Stor.

Bedroom
11-9x13-6

Greatroom
15-0x17-5

Garage
21-6x21-6

Foyer

Bedroom
11-6x11-6

Bedroom
11-4x11-2

Kitchen
11-6x12-4

Porch
21-6x6-7

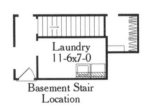

Laundry
11-6x7-0

Basement Stair
Location

DESIGN BY
©Larry James & Associates, Inc.

PLAN HPT100201

Square Footage: 2,093
Width: 71'-2" **Depth:** 56'-4"

Welcome your family home to this wonderful four-bedroom cottage. Step through the entry door with its transom and sidelights to a well-lit foyer. A ribbon of windows greets the eye in the great room, and a warming fireplace spreads comfort. A pass-through window to the kitchen is an added convenience. The owners suite enjoys a private wing, luxurious bath and His and Hers walk-in closets. On the opposite side of the plan, three secondary bedrooms—all with walk-in closets—share a full bath. Please specify basement, crawlspace or slab foundation when ordering.

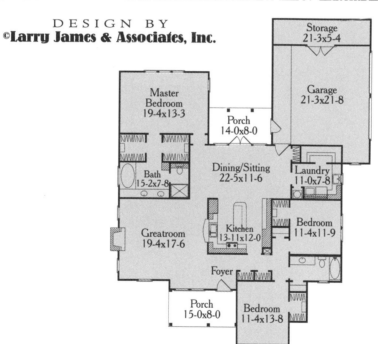

Storage
21-3x5-4

Garage
21-3x21-8

Master
Bedroom
19-4x13-3

Porch
14-0x8-0

Bath
15-2x7-8

Dining/Sitting
22-5x11-6

Laundry
11-0x7-8

Greatroom
19-4x17-6

Kitchen
13-11x12-0

Bedroom
11-4x11-9

Foyer

Porch
15-0x8-0

Bedroom
11-4x13-8

Shutters, multi-pane glass windows and cross-hatched railing on the front porch make this a beautiful country cottage. To the left of the foyer is a roomy great room and a warming fireplace, framed by windows. To the right of the foyer, two family bedrooms feature walk-in closets and share a fully appointed bath. The efficient kitchen centers around a long island workstation and opens to the large dining/sitting room. The rear porch adds living space to view the outdoors. French doors, a fireplace and columns complete this three-bedroom design. Please specify basement, crawlspace or slab foundation when ordering.

PLAN HPT100202

Square Footage: 2,053
Width: 57'-8" **Depth:** 71'-10"

PLAN HPT100203

This country cottage has charm packed into every square foot. A front porch ushers you into a large family room with a fireplace. The kitchen features a cooktop island with an adjoining eating bar, large pantry and built-in desk. The dining area looks out to the patio, providing an outdoor dining area. Three bedrooms with ample closets and two baths create plenty of room for quiet retreats.

Square Footage: 1,393
Width: 42'-0" **Depth:** 42'-0"

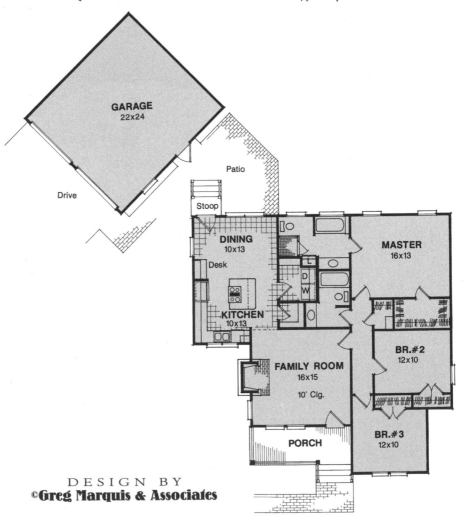

GARAGE
22x24

Drive

Patio

Stoop

DINING
10x13

Desk

KITCHEN
10x13

MASTER
16x13

FAMILY ROOM
16x15

10' Clg.

BR.#2
12x10

PORCH

BR.#3
12x10

DESIGN BY
©Greg Marquis & Associates

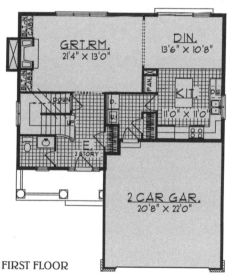

FIRST FLOOR

GRT. RM.
21'4" X 13'0"

DIN.
13'6" X 10'8"

KIT.
11'0" X 11'0"

DOWN

UP

E.
2 STORY

2 CAR GAR.
20'8" X 22'0"

DESIGN BY
©**Ahmann Design, Inc.**

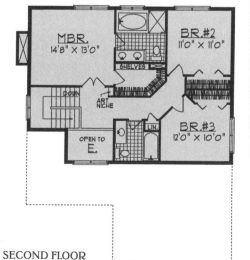

MBR.
14'8" X 13'0"

BR. #2
11'0" X 11'0"

SHELVES

DOWN

ART
NICHE

OPEN TO
E.

LIN.

BR. #3
12'0" X 10'0"

SECOND FLOOR

PLAN HPT100204

This charming two-story home offers the spaciousness you've been looking for in a three-bedroom home. The great room is extra large for your family gatherings and has a fireplace with a built-in entertainment center. The dining room just off the kitchen has nine-foot patio doors. The large open kitchen offers an island, pantry and easy access to the main-floor laundry center. Upstairs, the owners bedroom is your private retreat. Inside you'll find a large walk-in closet and a private bath with a double vanity, spa tub and separate shower. Two additional bedrooms share a full bath. There is plenty of space for future expansion in the lower level.

Total: 1,709 sq. ft.
First Floor: 886 sq. ft.
Second Floor: 823 sq. ft.
Width: 38'-0"   **Depth:** 44'-0"

PLAN HPT100205

This modest home takes a creative look at space to design an efficient floor plan that's comfortable yet compact. The vaulted family room contains a lovely corner fireplace and sliding glass doors to the rear yard. A galley kitchen is designed for efficiency and includes a hidden laundry center and a window over the sink. The breakfast room offers an optional bay window. The owners suite enjoys a tray ceiling and a large walk-in closet. Two family bedrooms and a hall bath round out the plan. Please specify basement, crawlspace or slab foundation when ordering.

Square Footage: 1,070
Width: 48'-0" **Depth:** 36'-0"

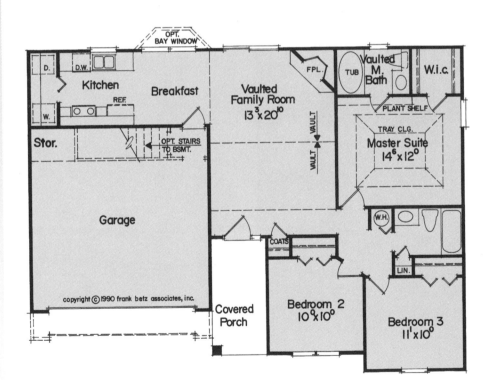

DESIGN BY
©**Frank Betz Associates, Inc.**

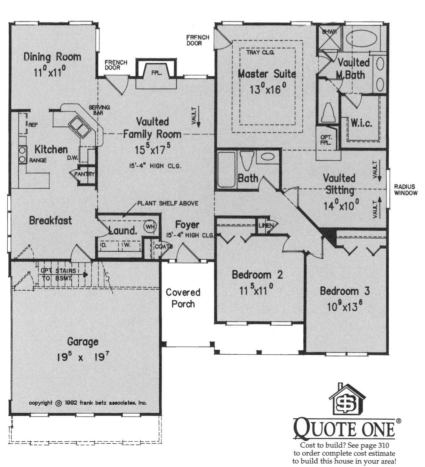

Dining Room
11⁰x11⁰

FRENCH DOOR

FPL.

SERVING BAR

REF

Kitchen

RANGE D.W.

PANTRY

Breakfast

PLANT SHELF ABOVE

Laund.

WH

OPT STAIRS TO BSMT

I.D. I.W.

COATS

Garage
19⁵ x 19⁷

copyright © 1992 frank betz associates, inc.

Covered Porch

Vaulted Family Room
15⁵x17⁵

15'-4" HIGH CLG.

Foyer
15'-4" HIGH CLG.

VAULT

FRENCH DOOR

TRAY CLG.

Master Suite
13⁰x16⁰

SHWR

Vaulted M.Bath

W.i.c.

OPT. FPL.

Bath

Vaulted Sitting
14⁰x10⁰

VAULT

VAULT

VAULT

RADIUS WINDOW

LINEN

Bedroom 2
11⁵x11⁰

Bedroom 3
10⁹x13⁶

PLAN HPT100206

Asymmetrical gables, a columned porch and an abundance of windows brighten the exterior of this compact home. An efficient kitchen boasts a pantry and a serving bar that it shares with the formal dining room and the vaulted family room. A sunny breakfast room and nearby laundry room complete the living zone. Be sure to notice extras such as the focal-point fireplace in the family room and a plant shelf in the laundry room. The sumptuous owners suite offers a door to the backyard, a vaulted sitting area and a pampering bath. Two family bedrooms share a hall bath. Please specify basement, crawlspace or slab foundation when ordering.

Square Footage: 1,671
Width: 50'-0" **Depth:** 51'-0"

Quote One®
Cost to build? See page 310 to order complete cost estimate to build this house in your area!

DESIGN BY
©**Frank Betz Associates, Inc.**

DESIGN BY
©**Stephen Fuller, Inc.**

PLAN HPT100207

Square Footage: 2,919
Width: 70'-10" **Depth:** 66'-6"

This plan was made for entertaining. Its entry and center hall are lined with columns that help define, but not limit, the great room, dining room and bedroom wing. A beam ceiling, a fireplace and covered rear-porch access highlight the great room. This room also opens to a sun room and the bay-windowed breakfast room. A large, gourmet-style kitchen makes a great work center. Bedrooms include two family suites with a shared bath and private vanity areas and the owners suite with a tray ceiling in the bedroom. The owners bath offers His and Hers walk-in closets, a garden whirlpool tub, separate shower, compartmented toilet and make-up vanity. This home is designed with a walkout basement foundation.

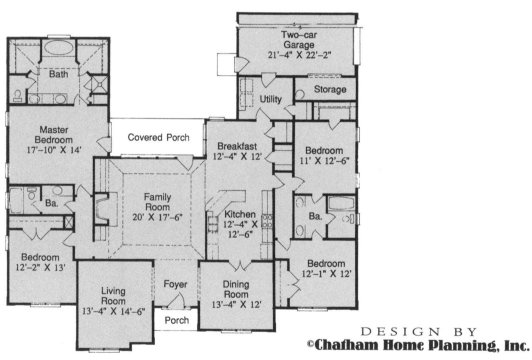

DESIGN BY
©**Chatham Home Planning, Inc.**

Heavy corner quoins make a rustic impression that is dressed up by a subtly asymmetrical design and arches on the windows. The centerpiece of the home is a magnificent family room with a tray ceiling, fireplace, built-in shelves and access to the rear covered porch. Adjacent, the breakfast room connects to the kitchen, which serves the formal dining room through elegant double doors. Two secondary bedrooms secluded on the far right of the plan each provide private access to a full bath with twin vanities. To the far left are a third bedroom and the spacious owners suite, which features His and Hers walk-in closets, an oval tub, separate shower, compartmented toilet and twin vanities.

PLAN HPT100208

Square Footage: 2,558
Width: 63'-6" **Depth:** 71'-6"

PLAN HPT100209

An exceptional use of cedar shingles, horizontal cedar siding and brick highlights the exterior of this one-story home. The floor plan provides many amenities found normally on much larger homes. Note, for example, the vaulted great room with a fireplace and the plant shelf above the entry. The owners bedroom is also vaulted. The covered patio off the formal dining room lends itself to great outdoor living even in inclement weather. Opening off the entry with a pair of French doors is a den, which could be used as a third bedroom.

Square Footage: 1,316
Width: 46'-0" **Depth:** 50'-0"

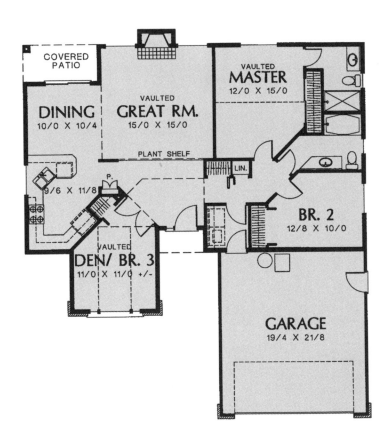

DESIGN BY
©Alan Mascord Design Associates, Inc.

Storage

Garage

Opt. Breakfast

REF

Kitchen

RANGE

D.W.

Vaulted Dining Room 10⁰x10³

PASS THRU

FLAT CLG.

TRAY CLG.

Master Suite 11¹x14⁰

VAULT

Vaulted Family Room 18⁸x13²

PLANT SHELF ABOVE

COATS

D. W.

TUB

M. Bath

VAULT VAULT

PLANT SHELF

W.i.c.

LIN.

Bath

LIN.

LIN.

Bedroom 2 10¹x10³

Bedroom 3 10³x10⁰

DESIGN BY
©**Frank Betz Associates, Inc.**

PLAN HPT100210

You could not ask for better detailing in a smaller, one-story European traditional home. A tall, ornamented chimney is prominent at the front; the mixture of wood siding and brick, plus shuttered windows, adds a note of authenticity. The well-designed floor plan makes optimal use of space. Vaulted ceilings in both the dining room and family room create spaciousness in an already open plan. The kitchen may be complemented by an optional breakfast area if you choose. High ceilings in the owners bedroom and bath lend elegance to this lovely retreat.

Square Footage: 1,135
Width: 60'-0" **Depth:** 33'-6"

DESIGN BY
©**Ahmann Design, Inc.**

PLAN HPT100211

Square Footage: 1,540
Width: 60'-4" **Depth:** 46'-0"

This simple-to-build three-bedroom ranch home is ideal for a first-time builder. When entering this home through the covered porch area, you'll view the cozy living room, which features a vaulted ceiling, a corner gas fireplace and large windows to the backyard. The kitchen in this home is well designed and usable. The dining area has two slider doors to exit to either the backyard or the screened porch. Three bedrooms include the owners suite with its own private bath and roomy walk-in closet. The other two bedrooms feature ample closet space and share a full bath. This home also offers storage space in the garage for sporting equipment or a workshop, and the main-floor laundry is a standard in homes today.

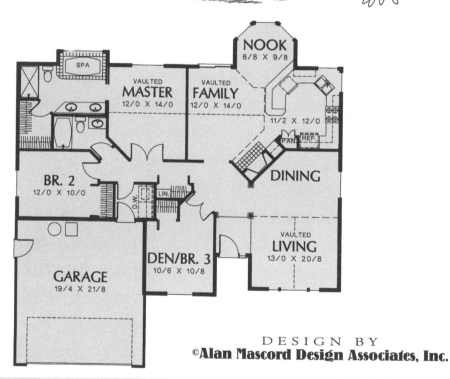

DESIGN BY
©**Alan Mascord Design Associates, Inc.**

This charming traditional home offers front-facing gables and a comfortable blend of shingles and vertical siding. Inside, a columned foyer opens to a vaulted living room, which offers a Palladian window and adjoins the formal dining room. An angled fireplace with an extended-tile hearth highlights the vaulted family room, which leads to a bayed breakfast nook. The nearby kitchen enjoys a windowed corner double sink and ample counter and pantry space. The owners suite boasts a tile-rimmed spa tub as well as a separate shower and sizable walk-in closet. A family bedroom easily accesses a hall bath. A quiet den, third bedroom or guest room opens from the central hall through French doors.

PLAN HPT100212

Square Footage: 1,565
Width: 50'-0" **Depth:** 52'-10"

— L —

PLAN HPT100213

The front covered porch of this home possesses a sweet disposition, set off by a charming single dormer. Inside, a spacious great room with an optional gas fireplace can handle a crowd and still be cozy enough for just the family. Casual dining will take place in the breakfast room or at the snack bar, served by the U-shaped kitchen. The family bedrooms to one side of the home share a full hall bath. Above the garage is much-needed storage space. This comfortable, narrow floor plan is a perfect starter home. Please specify crawlspace or slab foundation when ordering.

Square Footage: 985
Width: 27'-0" **Depth:** 65'-2"

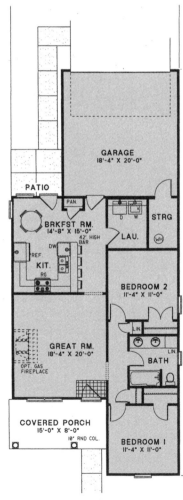

DESIGN BY
©Michael E. Nelson, Nelson Design Group, LLC

216

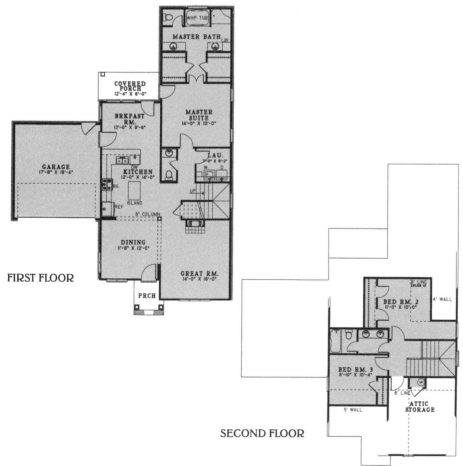

FIRST FLOOR

WHP TUB

MASTER BATH

COVERED PORCH
12'-4" X 6'-0"

BRKFAST RM.
12'-0" X 9'-6"

MASTER SUITE
14'-0" X 13'-0"

GARAGE
17'-8" X 18'-4"

KITCHEN
12'-0" X 14'-0"

LAU.
7'-0" X 8'-2"

ISLAND

8" COLUMN

DINING
11'-8" X 12'-0"

UP

GREAT RM.
14'-0" X 16'-0"

PRCH

SECOND FLOOR

BED RM. 2
11'-0" X 10'-0"

BED RM. 3
9'-10" X 10'-4"

ATTIC STORAGE

5' WALL

8' LINE

PLAN HPT100214

The many charms of this design include the owners suite at the rear of the plan, an L-shaped kitchen with a work island, a breakfast room that opens to both the rear porch and the garage, and the double-bowl vanity in the compartmented bath shared by the upstairs bedrooms. The owners suite is somewhat separated from the rest of the floor plan by a powder room and laundry room. It offers a lavish bath, entered through double French doors, and two walk-in closets. Separate vanities and a whirlpool tub add to the attractions. Please specify basement, crawlspace or slab foundation when ordering.

Total: 1,771 sq. ft.
First Floor: 1,334 sq. ft.
Second Floor: 437 sq. ft.
Bonus Room: 224 sq. ft.
Width: 45'-0" **Depth:** 62'-2"

DESIGN BY
©**Michael E. Nelson, Nelson Design Group, LLC**

PLAN HPT100215

An oversized dormer with a sunburst window enhances the charm of the raised and covered porch of this three-bedroom home. Inside, the living room contains a fireplace that can also be viewed from the formal dining area. The U-shaped kitchen and sunny breakfast nook open to the rear sun deck, perfect for an outdoor barbecue grill. Privacy is ensured for the owners suite with the split floor plan and a powder room for guests. A luxurious owners bath ensures relaxation with a large soaking tub, separate shower, twin-vanity sinks and a roomy walk-in closet. Two family bedrooms on the second floor share a full bath and a sitting area.

Total: 1,735 sq. ft.
First Floor: 1,045 sq. ft.
Second Floor: 690 sq. ft.
Width: 40'-4" **Depth:** 32'-0"

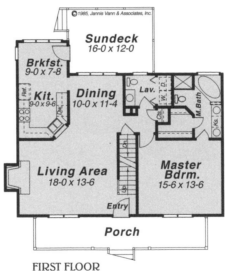

© 1985, Jannis Vann & Associates, Inc.

Sundeck
16-0 x 12-0

Brkfst.
9-0 x 7-8

Kit.
9-0 x 9-6

Dining
10-0 x 11-4

Lav.   W.D.

M. Bath

Clo.

Cls.

Living Area
18-0 x 13-6

Master Bdrm.
15-6 x 13-6

Entry

Porch

FIRST FLOOR

D E S I G N   B Y
© **Jannis Vann & Associates, Inc.**

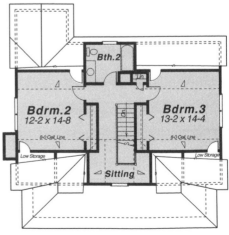

Bth.2

Lin.

Bdrm.2
12-2 x 14-8

Bdrm.3
13-2 x 14-4

8-0 Ceil. Line

8-0 Ceil. Line

Low Storage

Low Storage

Sitting

SECOND FLOOR

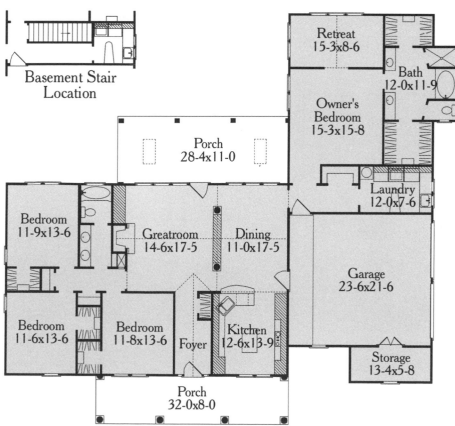

Basement Stair
Location

Porch
28-4x11-0

Bedroom
11-9x13-6

Greatroom
14-6x17-5

Dining
11-0x17-5

Retreat
15-3x8-6

Bath
12-0x11-9

Owner's
Bedroom
15-3x15-8

Laundry
12-0x7-6

Garage
23-6x21-6

Bedroom
11-6x13-6

Bedroom
11-8x13-6

Foyer

Kitchen
12-6x13-9

Storage
13-4x5-8

Porch
32-0x8-0

DESIGN BY
©Larry James & Associates, Inc.

PLAN HPT100216

Columns, transom windows and an eyebrow dormer lend this house a stylish country charm. Inside, a built-in media center, fireplace, skylights and columns add to the wonderful livability of this home. Escape to the relaxing owners suite featuring a private sitting room and a luxurious bath set between His and Hers walk-in closets. Three bedrooms share a bath on the other side of the plan, ensuring privacy. Please specify basement, crawlspace or slab foundation when ordering.

Square Footage: 2,360
Width: 75'-2" **Depth:** 68'-0"

DESIGN BY
©Stephen Fuller, Inc.

PLAN HPT100217

Square Footage: 2,935
Width: 71'-0" **Depth:** 66'-0"

This spacious one-story home easily accommodates a large family, providing all the luxuries and necessities for gracious living. For formal occasions, a grand dining room sits just off the entry foyer and features a vaulted ceiling. The great room offers a beautiful ceiling treatment and access to the rear deck. For more casual times, the kitchen, breakfast nook and adjoining keeping room with a fireplace fill the bill. The owners suite is spacious and filled with amenities that include a sitting room, walk-in closet and access to the rear deck. Two family bedrooms share a full bath. Each of these bedrooms provides its own lavatory. This home is designed with a walkout basement foundation.

DECK

seat

BED RM.
13-0 x 11-0

SUN RM.
15-8 x 11-0

skylights

BRKFST.
12-0 x 12-0

MASTER BED RM.
14-0 x 16-0

(cathedral ceiling)

master bath

skylight

walk-in closet

storage

bath

BED RM.
11-4 x 10-0

GREAT RM.
18-0 x 18-0

fireplace

(cathedral ceiling)

KITCHEN
12-0 x 12-8

UTIL.
6-6 x 8-0

GARAGE
21-2 x 20-0

bath

FOYER
11-8 x 5-8

DINING
13-0 x 13-2

storage

STUDY/ BED RM.
12-0 x 11-0

PORCH

DESIGN BY
Donald A. Gardner Architects, Inc.

Multi-pane windows, dormers, a covered porch and two projected windows with shed roofs offer a welcoming front exterior to this wonderful one-story home. The great room with a cathedral ceiling, paddle fan, built-in cabinets and bookshelves directly accesses the sun room through two sliding glass doors. Columns between the foyer and great room create a dramatic entrance to the great room. The kitchen and cooking island serve both the dining room and breakfast area as well as the great room via a pass-through. The owners suite has a double-door entrance and cathedral ceiling and overlooks the rear deck through a sliding glass door. Three family bedrooms are found at the other end of the house.

PLAN HPT100218

Square Footage: 2,413
Width: 77'-0" **Depth:** 60'-0"

PLAN HPT100219

Twin dormers and double gables adorn the exterior of this pleasing three-bedroom home. The foyer opens to the formal dining area and arches leading to the great room—which offers a warming corner fireplace. Add the optional greenhouse to the kitchen-sink window for a beautiful glass display or herb garden location. Keep household records and dry goods well organized with the desk and pantry room just off the galley kitchen. The vaulted breakfast room is brightened by three lovely windows. A lovely owners retreat features a whirlpool tub, separate shower and knee-space vanity. Two additional bedrooms share a full bath. Please specify crawlspace or slab foundation when ordering.

Square Footage: 1,725
Width: 56'-4"   Depth: 72'-8"

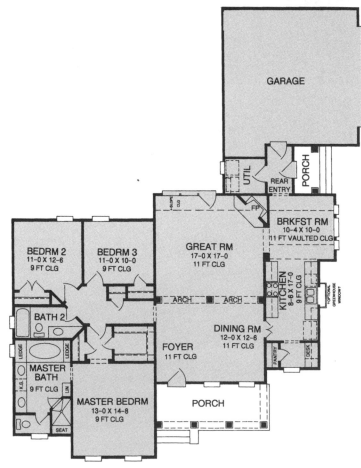

DESIGN BY
©**Larry E. Belk Designs**

FIRST FLOOR

KIT.
11'8" X 12'4"

NK.
9'8" X 14'2"

FAM.
VOLUME CEILING
18'2" X 14'2"

MBR.
14'0" X 16'0"

DIN.
12'0" X 12'0"

F.
2 STORY

SHELF

2 CAR GAR.
21'8" X 23'8"

SECOND FLOOR

BR.#3
12'4" X 14'2"

OPEN TO
FAM.

DN.

BR.#2
12'2" X 18'6"

PLANT
LEDGE

DESIGN BY
©**Ahmann Design, Inc.**

PLAN HPT100220

A covered porch and side-load garage are two of the many amazing amenities of this two-story home. When you enter this home, you are embraced by the beautiful two-story foyer and open staircase. The family room features a fireplace surrounded by large windows that extend upwards to the second level. There is an arched soffit that takes you into the efficient kitchen nook and then on to the kitchen. The well-organized kitchen provides a center island that allows for an eating area. A laundry room is conveniently located just off the kitchen, along with an additional powder room. This home also offers a formal dining room, perfect for family meals. The upper level holds two spare bedrooms, each with amazingly huge walk-in closets, and a full bath.

Total: 2,081 sq. ft.
First Floor: 1,435 sq. ft.
Second Floor: 646 sq. ft.
Width: 60'-4" **Depth:** 51'-4"

DESIGN BY
©Alan Mascord Design Associates, Inc.

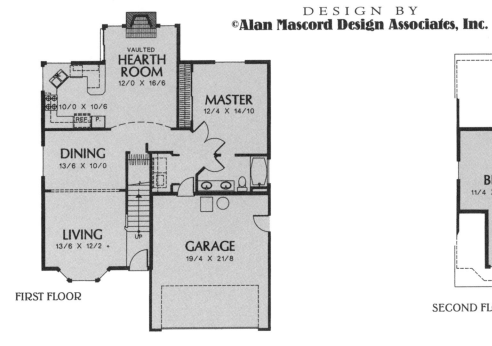

FIRST FLOOR

VAULTED
**HEARTH
ROOM**
12/0 X 16/6

10/0 X 10/6

REF. P.

MASTER
12/4 X 14/10

DINING
13/6 X 10/0

LIVING
13/6 X 12/2 +

UP

GARAGE
19/4 X 21/8

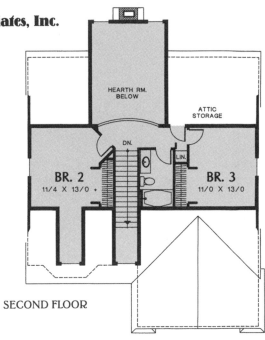

SECOND FLOOR

HEARTH RM.
BELOW

ATTIC
STORAGE

DN.

LIN.

BR. 2
11/4 X 13/0 +

BR. 3
11/0 X 13/0

PLAN HPT100221

Total: 1,693 sq. ft.
First Floor: 1,150 sq. ft.
Second Floor: 543 sq. ft.
Width: 38'-0" **Depth:** 50'-0"

Perfect for smaller lots, this functional cottage puts every inch of floor space to use with style. Enter into the formal living and dining room that's elegantly accented with a bay window. Casual living takes center stage in the fantastic hearth room with a dramatic two-story vaulted ceiling and windows flanking the fireplace. The adjoining kitchen furnishes a sunny corner sink and a snack bar. The first-floor owners suite features double-door access, an extra-long closet and a private owners bath. At the top of the stairs, a bowed balcony overlooks the hearth room while giving passage to the two secondary bedrooms and a full hall bath.

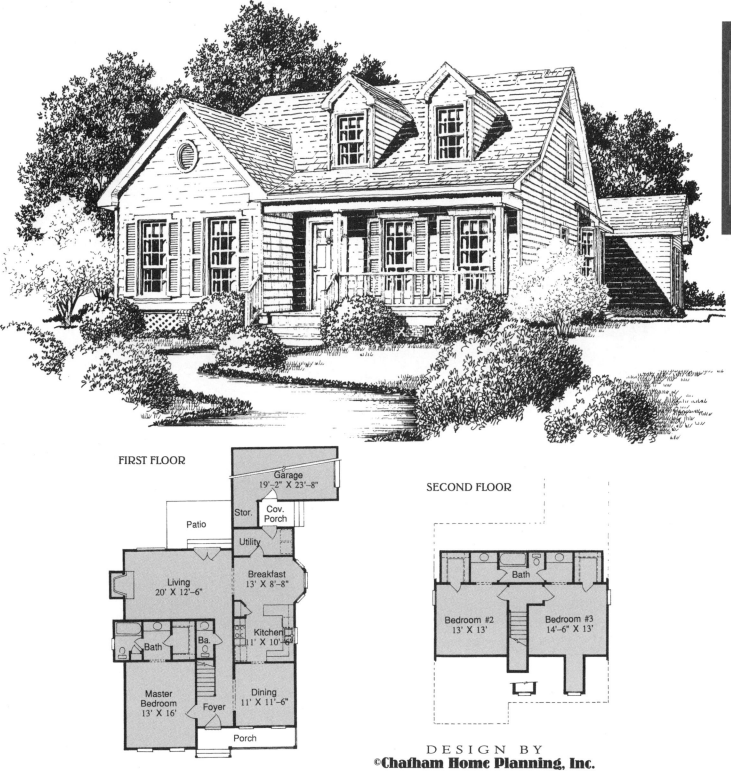

FIRST FLOOR

Garage
19'-2" X 23'-8"

Stor.

Cov. Porch

Patio

Utility

Breakfast
13' X 8'-8"

Living
20' X 12'-6"

Bath

Ba.

Kitchen
11' X 10'-6"

Master Bedroom
13' X 16'

Foyer

Dining
11' X 11'-6"

Porch

SECOND FLOOR

Bath

Bedroom #2
13' X 13'

Bedroom #3
14'-6" X 13'

D E S I G N   B Y
©**Chatham Home Planning, Inc.**

This perfectly charming country home features amenities to complement both quiet and active family lifestyles. The foyer opens to the warmth and hospitality of the expansive living area, complete with a fireplace and double doors leading to the rear patio. A convenient U-shaped kitchen easily serves both the formal dining room and the informal bay-windowed breakfast area. The main-floor owners suite sports a plush private bath and a great walk-in closet. Two large bedrooms upstairs each have their own access to a uniquely designed full bath with twin lavatories—separated by a compartmented toilet and tub. Please specify crawlspace or slab foundation when ordering.

PLAN HPT100222

Total: 1,802 sq. ft.
First Floor: 1,185 sq. ft.
Second Floor: 617 sq. ft.
Width: 36'-6" **Depth:** 69'-9"

PLAN HPT100223

A relaxing country image projects from the front and rear covered porches of this rustic three-bedroom home. Open planning extends to the great room, the dining room and the efficient kitchen. A shared cathedral ceiling creates an impressive space. Completing the first floor are two family bedrooms, a full bath and a handy utility area. The second floor contains the owners suite featuring a spacious walk-in closet and a private bath with a whirlpool tub and separate corner shower. A generous loft/study overlooks the great room below.

Total: 1,684 sq. ft.
First Floor: 1,100 sq. ft.
Second Floor: 584 sq. ft.
Width: 36'-8" **Depth:** 45'-0"

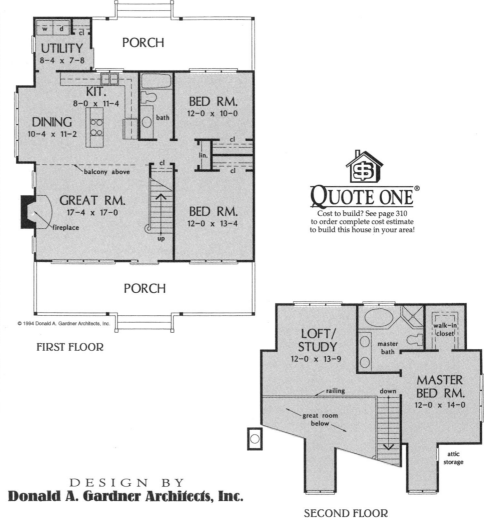

UTILITY
8-4 x 7-8

PORCH

KIT.
8-0 x 11-4

BED RM.
12-0 x 10-0

bath

DINING
10-4 x 11-2

balcony above

GREAT RM.
17-4 x 17-0

fireplace

BED RM.
12-0 x 13-4

up

PORCH

© 1994 Donald A. Gardner Architects, Inc.

FIRST FLOOR

Quote One®
Cost to build? See page 310 to order complete cost estimate to build this house in your area!

LOFT/
STUDY
12-0 x 13-9

master bath

walk-in closet

railing

down

great room below

MASTER
BED RM.
12-0 x 14-0

attic storage

SECOND FLOOR

DESIGN BY
Donald A. Gardner Architects, Inc.

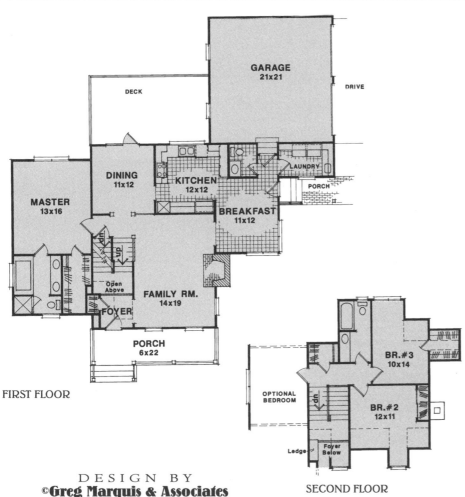

FIRST FLOOR

GARAGE
21x21

DECK

DRIVE

DINING
11x12

KITCHEN
12x12

LAUNDRY

PORCH

MASTER
13x16

BREAKFAST
11x12

Up

Open Abqve

FAMILY RM.
14x19

FOYER

PORCH
6x22

OPTIONAL
BEDROOM

BR.#3
10x14

BR.#2
12x11

dn

Ledge

Foyer
Below

SECOND FLOOR

DESIGN BY
©Greg Marquis & Associates

PLAN HPT100224

Looking like a picturesque vacation cottage, this home features an appealing facade complete with a covered front porch and dormers. A covered side entry ushers you into the breakfast room. The nearby laundry room offers extra work space and plenty of storage. A large, efficient U-shaped kitchen easily serves both the breakfast room and the formal dining room. The owners suite, featuring a roomy walk-in closet and a private bath with twin sinks, is separated from the living area and formal dining room. The second floor holds two additional bedrooms with plans for an optional fourth bedroom.

Total: 1,829 sq. ft.
First Floor: 1,339 sq. ft.
Second Floor: 490 sq. ft.
Bonus Room: 145 sq. ft.
Width: 57'-0" **Depth:** 60'-0"

© 1993 Donald A. Gardner Architects, Inc.

B. NATHAN

PLAN HPT100225

Quaint and cozy on the outside with porches at the front and back, this three-bedroom country home surprises with an open floor plan featuring a large great room with a cathedral ceiling. Nine-foot ceilings add volume throughout the home. A central kitchen with an angled counter opens to the breakfast and great rooms for easy entertaining. The privately located owners suite includes a cathedral ceiling and access to the deck. Operable skylights over the tub accent the luxurious bath. Two secondary bedrooms share a full hall bath. A bonus room makes expanding easy.

Square Footage: 1,864
Bonus Room: 420 sq. ft.
Width: 70'-4" **Depth:** 56'-4"

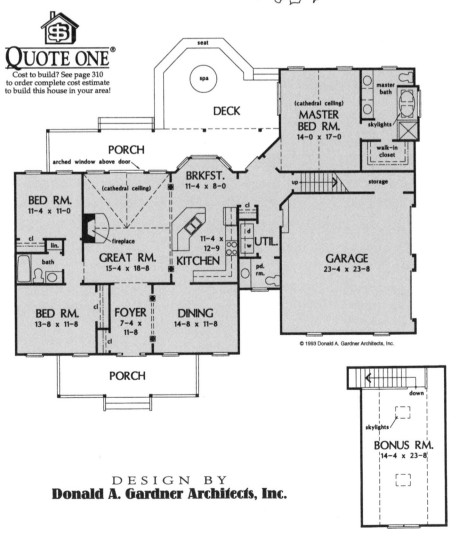

Quote One®
Cost to build? See page 310 to order complete cost estimate to build this house in your area!

© 1993 Donald A. Gardner Architects, Inc.

DESIGN BY
Donald A. Gardner Architects, Inc.

© 1992 Donald A. Gardner Architects, Inc.

B·NATHAN·

PLAN HPT100226

Charming and compact, this delightful two-story cabin is perfect for the small family or empty-nester. Designed with casual living in mind, the two-story great room is completely open to the dining area and the spacious island kitchen. The owners suite sits on the first floor for privacy and convenience. It features a roomy bath and a walk-in closet. Upstairs, two comfortable bedrooms—one includes a dormer window, the other features a balcony overlooking the great room—share a full hall bath.

PORCH
34-6 × 8-0

walk-in closet

w   d

KIT./ DINING
10-10 × 17-8

MASTER BED RM.
12-0 × 17-0

bedroom above

sto.

GREAT RM.
17-4 × 17-2

fireplace

up   cl

master bath

PORCH
34-6 × 8-0

© 1992 Donald A. Gardner Architects, Inc.

FIRST FLOOR

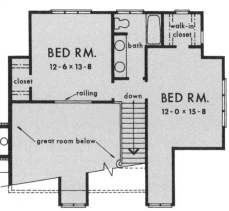

BED RM.
12-6 × 13-8

bath

walk-in closet

closet

railing

down

great room below

BED RM.
12-0 × 15-8

SECOND FLOOR

DESIGN BY
Donald A. Gardner Architects, Inc.

Total: 1,622 sq. ft.
First Floor: 1,039 sq. ft.
Second Floor: 583 sq. ft.
Width: 37'-9"   **Depth:** 44'-8"

229

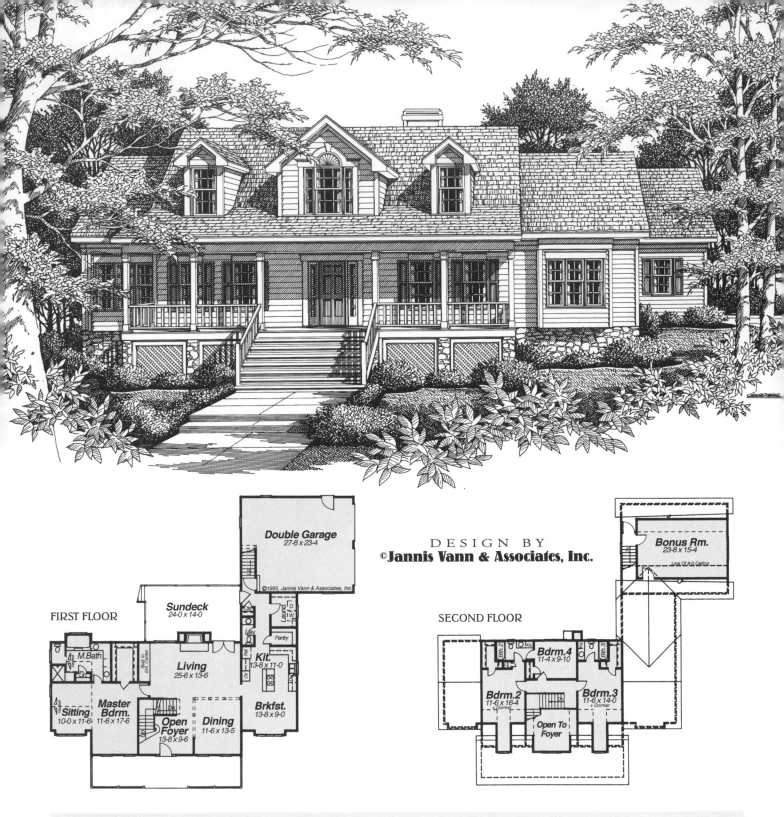

FIRST FLOOR

Double Garage
27-8 x 23-4

©1995, Jannis Vann & Associates, Inc

Sundeck
24-0 x 14-0

Laund.

Pantry

M.Bath

Built In Ent. Center

Living
25-6 x 13-6

Kit.
13-8 x 11-0

Sitting
10-0 x 11-6

Master Bdrm.
11-6 x 17-6

Open Foyer
13-8 x 9-6

Dining
11-6 x 13-5

Brkfst.
13-8 x 9-0

DESIGN BY
©**Jannis Vann & Associates, Inc.**

SECOND FLOOR

Bonus Rm.
23-8 x 15-4

Bdrm.4
11-4 x 9-10

Bth.2

Bth.3

Bdrm.2
11-6 x 16-4
+ Dormer

Bdrm.3
11-6 x 14-0
+ Dormer

Open To Foyer

PLAN HPT100227

Total: 2,636 sq. ft.
First Floor: 1,798 sq. ft.
Second Floor: 838 sq. ft.
Bonus Room: 389 sq. ft.
Width: 76'-0" **Depth:** 70'-0"

Two dormers frame a central, oversized dormer with a Palladian window over a raised porch on this comfortable four-bedroom home. Columns define the formal dining area, conveniently near the kitchen. The kitchen and breakfast nook feature a walk-in pantry, island workstation and a bumped out window. A built-in entertainment center and fireplace adorn the living room, which provides French-door access to the rear sun deck. The expansive owners suite features a light-filled sitting room, large walk-in closet and luxurious private bath. On the second level two family bedrooms share a bath, and a third bedroom features its own bath. Please specify basement or crawlspace foundation when ordering.

© 1990 Donald A. Gardner Architects, Inc.

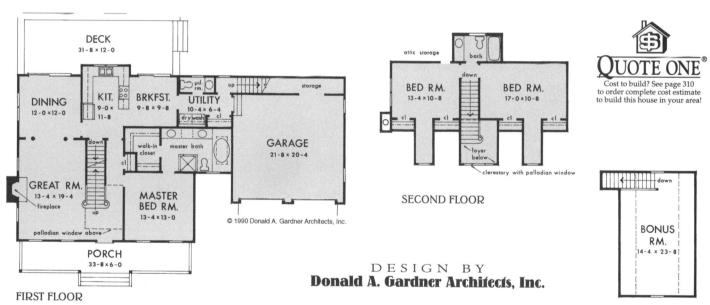

DECK
31-8 x 12-0

DINING
12-0 x 12-0

KIT.
9-0 x
11-8

BRKFST.
9-8 x 9-8

UTILITY
10-4 x 6-4

pd. rm.

dry wash

cl

up

storage

GARAGE
21-8 x 20-4

GREAT RM.
13-4 x 19-4

fireplace

down

up

walk-in closet

cl

master bath

MASTER
BED RM.
13-4 x 13-0

palladian window above

PORCH
33-8 x 6-0

FIRST FLOOR

© 1990 Donald A. Gardner Architects, Inc.

attic storage

bath

BED RM.
13-4 x 10-8

BED RM.
17-0 x 10-8

down

cl

cl

cl

cl

foyer below

clerestory with palladian window

SECOND FLOOR

QUOTE ONE®
Cost to build? See page 310
to order complete cost estimate
to build this house in your area!

down

BONUS
RM.
14-4 x 23-8

DESIGN BY
Donald A. Gardner Architects, Inc.

This cozy country cottage is perfect for the growing family—offering both an unfinished basement option and a bonus room. Enter through the two-story foyer with a Palladian window in a clerestory dormer above. The owners suite sits on the first floor for privacy and accessibility. Its accompanying bath boasts a whirlpool tub with a skylight above and a double-bowl vanity. The second floor contains two bedrooms, a full bath and plenty of storage. An optional bonus room over the garage allows for future expansion.

PLAN HPT100228

Total: 1,831 sq. ft.
First Floor: 1,289 sq. ft.
Second Floor: 542 sq. ft.
Bonus Room: 393 sq. ft.
Width: 66'-4" **Depth:** 50'-4"

PLAN HPT100229

The formal living and dining rooms flank the central foyer as you enter this home. The informal family room at the back of the home adjoins a cozy sun room that features skylights. A breakfast nook with a bay window separates the family room and the kitchen. All three bedrooms occupy the upper level, including an owners suite with two walk-in closets, a large oval tub, double-bowl vanity and separate shower.

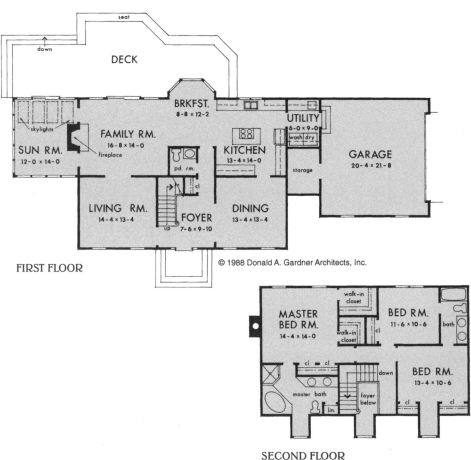

FIRST FLOOR

SECOND FLOOR

Total: 2,350 sq. ft.
First Floor: 1,401 sq. ft.
Second Floor: 949 sq. ft.
Width: 79'-4" **Depth:** 31'-10"

DESIGN BY
Donald A. Gardner Architects, Inc.

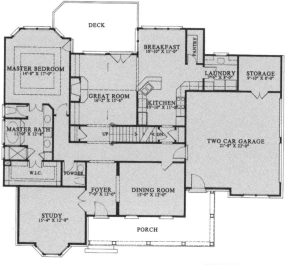

FIRST FLOOR

DESIGN BY
©**Stephen Fuller, Inc.**

DECK

MASTER BEDROOM
14'-8" X 17'-0"

BREAKFAST
10'-10" X 11'-0"

PANTRY

GREAT ROOM
16'-2" X 15'-6"

KITCHEN
10'-10" X 11'-0"

LAUNDRY
9'-6" X 8'-0"

STORAGE
9'-10" X 8'-0"

MASTER BATH
11'-0" X 12'-8"

TWO CAR GARAGE
21'-8" X 22'-0"

UP

DN

W.I.C.

POWDER

FOYER
7'-0" X 12'-0"

DINING ROOM
15'-0" X 12'-0"

STUDY
15'-4" X 12'-8"

PORCH

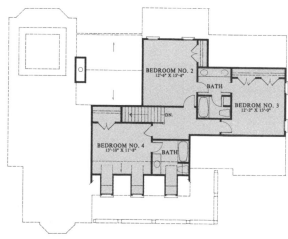

SECOND FLOOR

BEDROOM NO. 2
12'-6" X 15'-4"

BATH

BEDROOM NO. 3
12'-2" X 15'-0"

DN

BEDROOM NO. 4
13'-10" X 11'-8"

BATH

PLAN HPT100230

The facade of this charming home is Americana at its best, with a rocking-chair porch, bay window and dormers above. The main level features an easy flow, beginning with the dining room to the right of the foyer. The great room features a large hearth and French doors to the patio, and leads directly to the breakfast area and kitchen. Storage closets and a countertop desk area highlight the kitchen which, along with the laundry room, is conveniently located to the rear of the home. The owners suite, featuring a bay-windowed sitting area, large owners bath with double vanities and shower, and ample closet space, completes the main level. This home is designed with a walkout basement foundation.

Total: 2,925 sq. ft.
First Floor: 1,960 sq. ft.
Second Floor: 965 sq. ft.
Width: 64'-11" **Depth:** 51'-11"

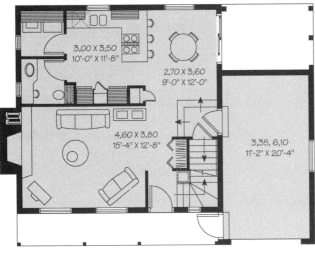

FIRST FLOOR

3,00 X 3,50
10'-0" X 11'-8"

2,70 X 3,60
9'-0" X 12'-0"

4,60 X 3,80
15'-4" X 12'-8"

3,35, 6,10
11'-2" X 20'-4"

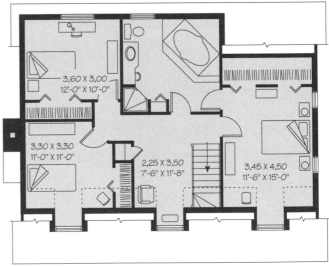

SECOND FLOOR

3,60 X 3,00
12'-0" X 10'-0"

3,30 X 3,30
11'-0" X 11'-0"

2,25 X 3,50
7'-6" X 11'-8"

3,45 X 4,50
11'-6" X 15'-0"

DESIGN BY
©Drummond Designs, Inc.

PLAN HPT100231

Total: 1,562 sq. ft.
First Floor: 676 sq. ft.
Second Floor: 886 sq. ft.
Width: 38'-0" **Depth:** 30'-0"

Three hipped dormers embellish the pitched gable roof of this lovely two-story house. This home design features a fireplace in the living room, a dining area that opens out to a back porch, and a snack bar in the kitchen. Three bedrooms occupy the second floor. An owners bath, which can be shared by all, includes a whirlpool tub and separate shower. The laundry room as well as a second bathroom are located off the kitchen. This home is designed with a basement foundation.

Brick or Stone Farmhouses

PLAN HPT100232

This amazing home is detailed with sloped roofs, a stone facade and muntin windows. Enjoy the stone fireplace whether relaxing in the great room or sipping a drink at the bar extended from the kitchen. Adjacent to the kitchen, a dining area includes sliding glass doors leading to a covered patio. A private patio area is available to the owners bedroom, as well as a spacious private bath, which includes a double-bowl sink and a vast walk-in closet. Two family bedrooms each have double-door closets and share a full bath. A three-car garage resides to the far right of the plan, with an entryway opening to the utility room.

Square Footage: 2,061
Width: 88'-0" **Depth:** 40'-9"

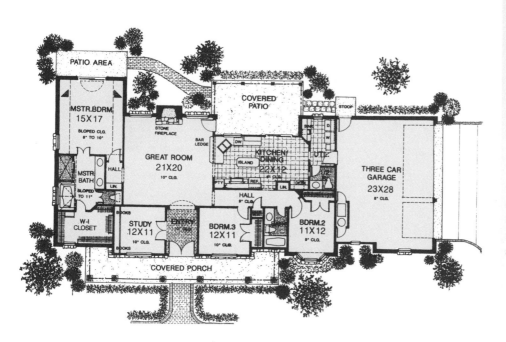

DESIGN BY
©Fillmore Design Group

235

PLAN HPT100233

This rural Colonial design calls up the charm of simpler times. Of course, we've made a few improvements to the classic American cabin—like plenty of square footage and amenities for easy living. Wraparound covered porches on both the main and second levels invite outdoor living and inspire a sense of shelter. An entry and foyer lead to a formal living room as well as to casual areas, designed with space to sprawl and relax. A through-hearth warms the living areas, while the den enjoys its own fireplace and built-in cabinetry. The second floor offers a spacious owners suite with a windowed garden tub, twin lavatories and a private hearth. Two additional bedrooms share a full bath.

Total: 2,240 sq. ft.
Main Level: 1,120 sq. ft.
Lower Level: 1,120 sq. ft.
Width: 52'-0" **Depth:** 40'-0"

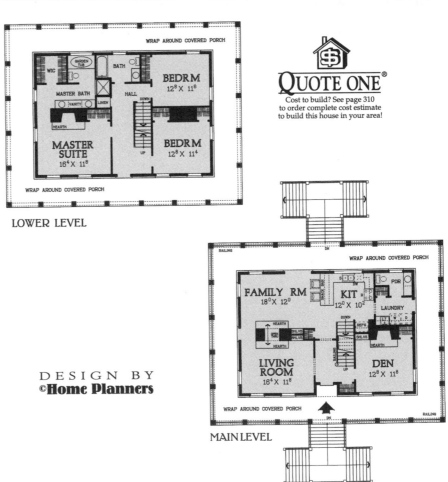

LOWER LEVEL

DESIGN BY
©**Home Planners**

MAIN LEVEL

QUOTE ONE®
Cost to build? See page 310
to order complete cost estimate
to build this house in your area!

236

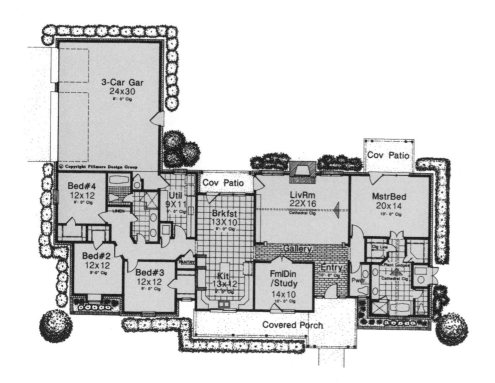

DESIGN BY
©**Fillmore Design Group**

PLAN HPT100234

Slight Victorian details added to the gabled roof and railed porch draw attention to this four-bedroom home. The tiled entryway becomes a gallery opening to a living room (with a fireplace) and a formal dining room/study. In the heart of the home, the U-shaped kitchen provides an island and a nearby breakfast room. This well-thought-out plan makes privacy a priority by separating the family bedrooms and owners suite from the living area. Each with walk-in closets, three family bedrooms occupy the far left side of the home and share a compartmented bath that includes a dual vanity. The owners bedroom resides to right of the design, pampered with a private covered patio, His and Hers closets and an extravagant owners bath.

Square Footage: 2,495
Width: 87'-10" **Depth:** 62'-7"

PLAN HPT100235

This attractive facade presents hipped roofs, muntin windows with shutters, and a wide porch—perfect for relaxing or welcoming guests. The fireplace and built-in media center adds to the great room. The kitchen and dining room connect by the peninsula with a sink and serving bar. The bay window of the dining area includes French doors that open to a large patio. Two family bedrooms occupy the right side of the plan, and share a full bath that includes a linen closet. Inside the owners bedroom, a private bath includes a garden tub, separate shower and immense walk-in closet. Don't miss the carport and storage space to the rear left of the plan. Please specify basement, crawlspace or slab foundation when ordering.

Square Footage: 1,689
Width: 67'-0" **Depth:** 43'-0"

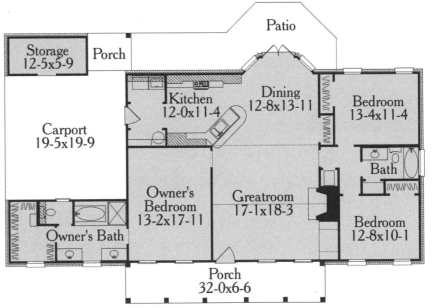

DESIGN BY
©**Larry James & Associates, Inc.**

Basement
Stair Location

Owner's
Bedroom
13-2x14-3

PLAN HPT100236

This three-bedroom traditional beauty possesses all of the features of a modern-day home but with the quaint look of an older home. The living room contains a fireplace, sloped ceilings and a large rear porch accessible via French doors. The kitchen is complete with all of the usual amenities, including a large pantry, and it is located directly between the eating area and the formal dining room. The garage contains a neat built-in workbench, built-in shelves and pelnty of storage. Please specify crawlspace or slab foundation when ordering.

Square Footage: 1,925
Width: 78'-0" **Depth:** 52'-0"

PORCH
20' X 8'

BEDROOM
12' x 12'

WIC

LIVING ROOM
24' X 16'
SLOPED CEILINGS

MASTER SUITE
16' X 16'

DRESS. RM.

BATH

WIC

STORAGE
9' X 9'

BOOKS

FIREPLACE

HEAT A/C

BATH

LINEN

STOR.

UTIL.
8' X 7'

SHWR.

LINEN

HALL

EATING AREA
10' X 10'

GARAGE
23' X 22'

BEDROOM
12' x 12'

LINEN

FOYER

DINING ROOM
12' x 12'

PANTRY

KITCHEN
12' x 12'

RANGE

REF.

SHVS.

SHVS.

BALCONY
10' X 6'

DW **SINK**

SHVS.

PORCH
44' X 8'

WORK BENCH **SHVS.**

DESIGN BY
©**Breland & Farmer Designers, Inc.**

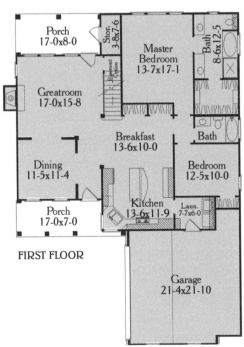

Porch
17-0x8-0

Stor.
3-8x7-6

Master
Bedroom
13-7x17-1

Bath
8-6x12-5

Greatroom
17-0x15-8

Bath

Breakfast
13-6x10-0

Dining
11-5x11-4

Bedroom
12-5x10-0

Porch
17-0x7-0

Kitchen
13-6x11-9

Laun.
7-7x6-0

FIRST FLOOR

Garage
21-4x21-10

Bedroom
16-4x15-4

Bath
9-0x6-0

SECOND FLOOR

DESIGN BY
©Larry James & Associates, Inc.

PLAN HPT100237

Total: 1,983 sq. ft.

First Floor: 1,596 sq. ft.

Second Floor: 387 sq. ft.

Width: 46'-6" **Depth:** 65'-0"

Front and rear covered porches add comfortable outdoor space to this fine three-bedroom home. A formal dining room resides near the entry. Nearby, a wall of windows and a warming fireplace characterize the comfortable great room. Just off the great room sits a covered porch, perfect for quiet reflection. When it's time to eat, the island work area in the kitchen will make food preparation a breeze. A luxurious owners suite features a private dual-vanity bath with a garden tub and separate shower. The other two bedrooms each have a full bath. Extra storage space is available off the rear porch. Please specify basement, crawlspace or slab foundation when ordering.

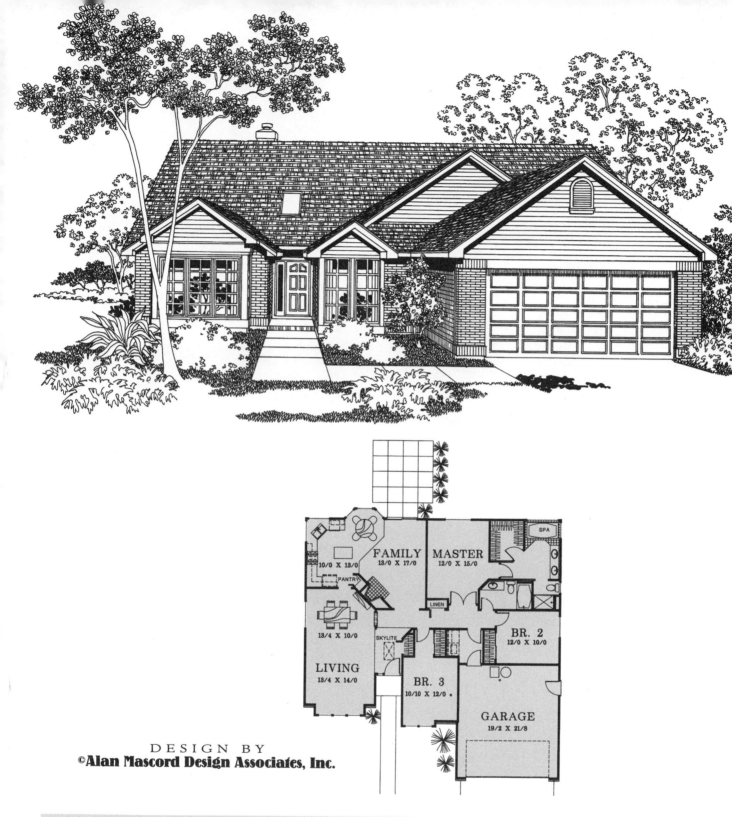

FAMILY
18/0 X 17/0

MASTER
12/0 X 15/0

SPA

10/0 X 13/0

PANTRY

LINEN

18/4 X 10/0

SKYLITE

BR. 2
12/0 X 10/0

LIVING
18/4 X 14/0

BR. 3
10/10 X 12/0 +

GARAGE
19/2 X 21/8

DESIGN BY
©Alan Mascord Design Associates, Inc.

Intriguing rooflines create a dynamic exterior for this home. The interior floor plan is equally attractive. Toward the rear, a wide archway forms the entrance to the spacious family living area with a fireplace and bay-windowed nook area. Inside the efficient kitchen, an island, mitered corner window and a walk-in pantry make food preparation a breeze. This home also boasts a terrific owners suite complete with a walk-in wardrobe, spa tub with corner windows, and a compartmented shower and toilet area. Bedrooms 2 and 3 share a full hall bath; Bedroom 3 also provides great views of the front yard through a muntin window in a hutch space.

PLAN HPT100238

Square Footage: 1,687
Width: 50'-0" **Depth:** 52'-0"

L

PLAN HPT100239

A covered porch welcomes both family and friends to this fine three-bedroom home. The vaulted great room gives this plan a much larger feel than the square footage would indicate, and the open feel of the dining bay and kitchen contributes to this airiness. The cathedral ceiling in the great room enhances the spaciousness, and the fireplace adds a touch of warmth to the atmosphere. Three bedrooms, including an indulgent owners suite with a private bath, are located down a short hall. Two front bedrooms share a full hall bath. The optional two-car garage will be perfect to shelter the family fleet.

Square Footage: 1,440
Width: 46'-11" **Depth:** 62'-9"

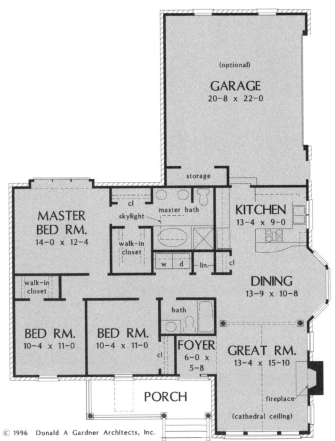

© 1996 Donald A Gardner Architects, Inc.

DESIGN BY
Donald A. Gardner Architects, Inc.

Sundeck
18-2 x 12-0

M.Bath

Master Bdrm.
15-6 x 13-4
Tray Ceil.

Living
17-10 x 17-2

Dining
8-4 x 13-0

Brkfst.
11-0 x 7-10

Tray Ceil.

Line Of Sloped Ceil.

Plantshelf Above

Kit.
11-0 x 9-6

Dw.

Ref.

Bdrm.2
12-0 x 10-0

Line Of Dormer

W.I.D.

P.

Cts.

Bth. 2

Linen

Bdrm.3
12-0 x 11-0

Double Garage
20-0 x 22-4

Bdrm.4
13-0 x 11-0

© 1995, Jannis Vann & Associates, Inc.

DESIGN BY
© Jannis Vann & Associates, Inc.

PLAN HPT100240

Gabled dormers, roofs and decorative keystone arches add to the stone facade of this European-style farmhouse. Upon entry, the living room greets family members and guests with a warming fireplace and a connecting dining area with a bay-window. Nearby, the kitchen and breakfast nook provide plenty of space for the entire family. To the left of the plan, three bedrooms share a full hall compartmented bath. Featured in the owners bedroom is a tray ceiling and a private bath that includes ample space for dressing, a double-bowl vanity and a vast walk-in closet. Don't miss the sun deck—perfect for relaxing on cool afternoons! Please specify crawlspace or slab foundation when ordering.

Square Footage: 1,817
Width: 58'-0" **Depth:** 55'-5"

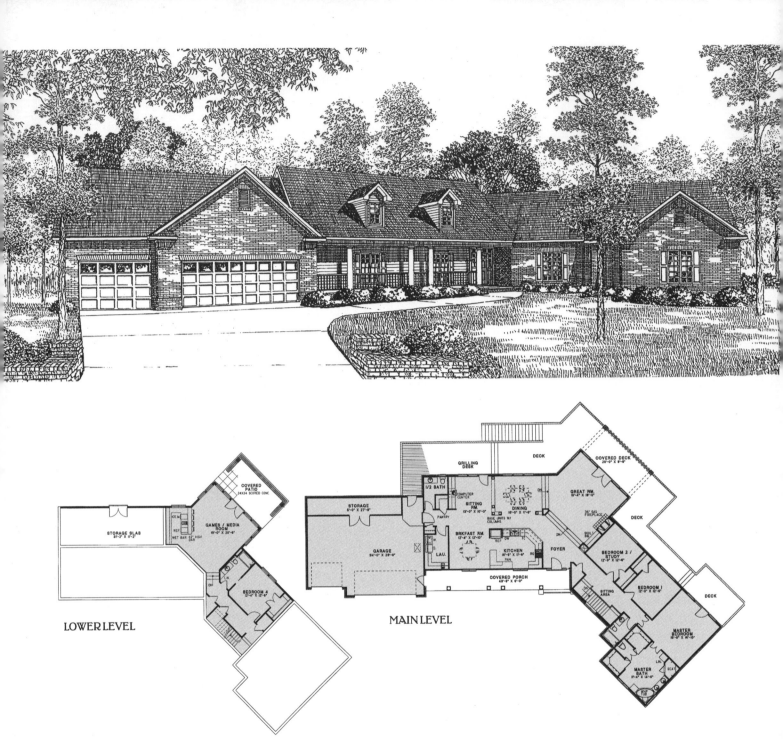

LOWER LEVEL

MAIN LEVEL

DESIGN BY
©**Michael E. Nelson, Nelson Design Group, LLC**

PLAN HPT100241

Total: 3,659 sq. ft.
Main Level: 2,711 sq. ft.
Lower Level: 948 sq. ft.
Width: 122'-10" **Depth:** 75'-5"

Spacious, attractive and perfect for lakeside living, this home is sure to please. A sunken great room features a warming fireplace and access to the rear covered deck. The efficient kitchen offers a breakfast room as well as easy access to the formal dining room. A sitting room nearby provides a built-in computer desk area. The lavish owners suite at the far right of the home includes two walk-in closets, a lavish bath and access to a rear deck. Two family bedrooms complete this level. Downstairs, a third family bedroom is perfect for a guest suite. This level is completed by a large games/media room, an extensive wet bar and outdoor access. Please specify crawlspace or slab foundation when ordering.

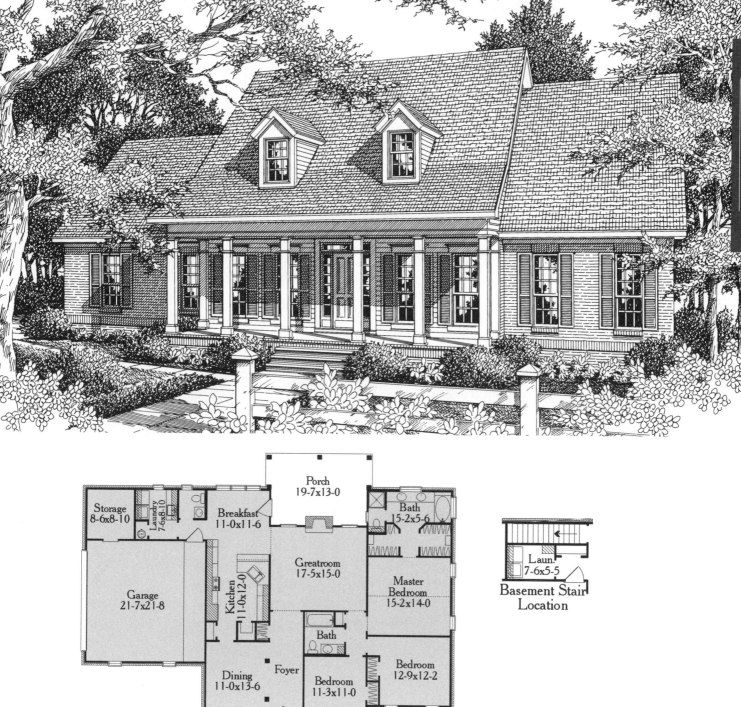

Porch
19-7x13-0

Storage
8-6x8-10

Laundry
7-6x8-10

Breakfast
11-0x11-6

Bath
15-2x5-6

Garage
21-7x21-8

Kitchen
11-0x12-0

Greatroom
17-5x15-0

Master
Bedroom
15-2x14-0

Laun.
7-6x5-5

Basement Stair
Location

Bath

Bedroom
12-9x12-2

Dining
11-0x13-6

Foyer

Bedroom
11-3x11-0

Porch
30-6x8-6

DESIGN BY
©Larry James & Associates, Inc.

Elegant pillars and multi-paned windows below two gabled dormers give this design classy curb appeal. Inside the foyer is connected to the dining room with columns. The convenient galley kitchen leads to a breakfast area with a ribbon of windows. The living room will draw people in to watch a crackling fire or look out the two windows framing the fireplace. Walk-in closets and extra storage space will fill the owners with relief, not to mention the privacy created by the split-bedroom floor plan. The two covered porches extend the living area outside. Please specify basement, crawlspace or slab foundation when ordering.

PLAN HPT100242

Square Footage: 1,894
Width: 68'-0" **Depth:** 56'-6"

PLAN HPT100243

The traditional style of this Cape Cod home creates a warm and friendly atmosphere. From the foyer you can easily access the fashionable library with built-in shelves and the formal dining room with columns and a dramatic view through the great room to the fireplace and rear windows. The spacious kitchen encourages family gatherings, offers an island with seating and opens into a roomy breakfast area surrounded by windows. An owners bedroom suite, with a deluxe bath and spacious walk-in closets, rounds out the first floor. The second-floor balcony overlooks the great room. Two additional bedrooms, each with a walk-in closet, the hall storage closet and a bonus room create a perfect home for today's family.

Total: 2,443 sq. ft.
First Floor: 1,710 sq. ft.
Second Floor: 733 sq. ft.
Bonus Room: 181 sq. ft.
Width: 78'-4" **Depth:** 47'-8"

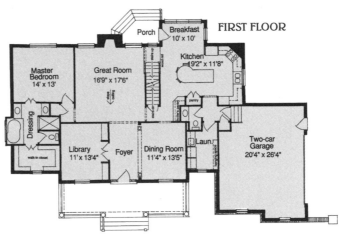

FIRST FLOOR

SECOND FLOOR

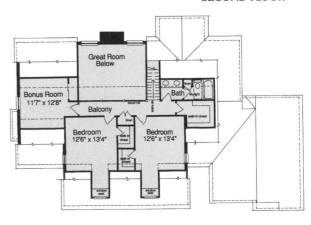

DESIGN BY
©Studer Residential Designs, Inc.

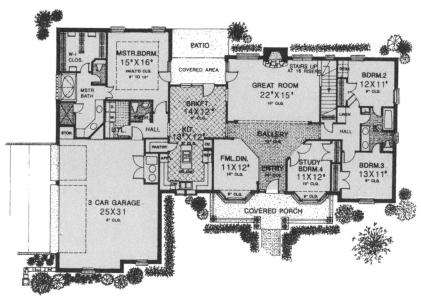

FUTURE UNFINISHED BONUS ROOM
23X21
NOT INCLUDED IN SQ. FT.

PLAN HPT100244

An array of arches are displayed above windows, twin dormers, and through the entryway to a covered porch. This home caters to any family, with three bedrooms, a study, a vast amount of living space and an immense kitchen. The U-shaped kitchen includes a cooktop island, walk-in pantry and a breakfast nook. The central gallery opens to the great room with a stone hearth, and accesses the formal dining area along with the bedroom/study. A secluded hallway holds two bedrooms which share a full bath. The superb owners bedroom provides an extensive owners bath and a private doorway to a covered patio.

Square Footage: 2,496
Bonus Room: 483 sq. ft.
Width: 83'-4" **Depth:** 57'-7"

DESIGN BY
©**Fillmore Design Group**

PLAN HPT100245

Making the most out of every square foot, this adorable farmhouse is bound to suit every need. This home begins with a covered porch and a great room featuring a fireplace. A spacious kitchen offers a snack bar and sits next to the hearth room, which accesses the grilling porch and the garage. The owners bedroom is complemented with a whirlpool tub, shower, linen closet, double-bowl vanity and an enormous walk-in closet. Bedrooms 2 and 3 share a full bath that includes a linen closet. The utility room is located near the kitchen. Please specify crawlspace or slab foundation when ordering.

Square Footage: 1,425
Width: 45'-0" **Depth:** 64'-10"

DESIGN BY
©**Michael E. Nelson, Nelson Design Group, LLC**

248

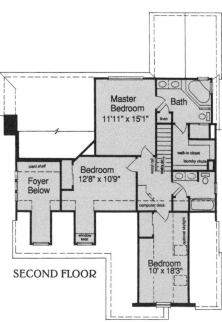

Screened-in
Porch
sloped ceiling

Dining Area
11'6" x 13'5"

Bath

Great Room
15'4" x 15'3"
11' ceiling height
sloped ceiling

Hobby
Area
8'2" x 6'6"

wood rail
9' ceiling height
wood rail

stairs dn

Laun.

Foyer

Kitchen
14'2" x 16'

pantry

Porch

Two-car Garage
20' x 25'6"

FIRST FLOOR

Master
Bedroom
11'11" x 15'1"

Bath

linen

plant shelf

Foyer
Below

Bedroom
12'8" x 10'9"

walk-in closet

wood rail
stairs dn

laundry chute

computer desk

*window
seat*

optional skylight

Bedroom
10' x 18'3"

SECOND FLOOR

DESIGN BY
©Studer Residential Designs, Inc.

PLAN HPT100246

This adorable home presents a set of twin dormers on its cross-gabled roof, double arches under the covered porch and sidelights complementing the four-panel door. On the first floor, columns define the great room from the kitchen and dining area. The columns are carefully placed—allowing the great room to be viewed from the workstation in the kitchen. Around the corner and up the stairs to the second floor reside an owners bedroom and two bedrooms. The owners bedroom includes a private bath with a walk-in closet and laundry chute. Each of the two family bedrooms have a different amenity, one with a window seat and the other with an optional skylight. In the hallway a computer desk and a full bath create convenience.

Total: 1,889 sq. ft.
First Floor: 964 sq. ft.
Second Floor: 925 sq. ft.
Width: 43'-0" **Depth:** 48'-0"

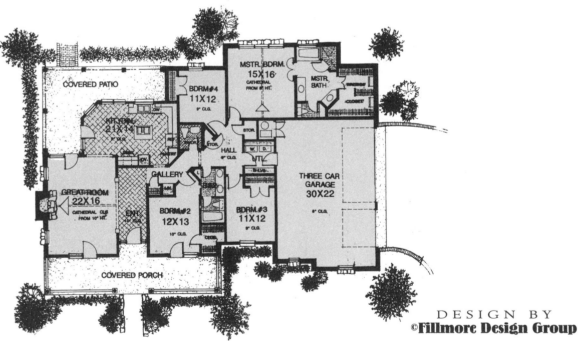

DESIGN BY
©Fillmore Design Group

PLAN HPT100247

Square Footage: 2,118
Width: 73'-4" **Depth:** 49'-1"

Welcome home, this four-bedroom European-style farmhouse is perfect for a growing family. The great room provides plenty of space for family gatherings—while enjoying the warming stone fireplace. The cooktop island is excellent for gourmet cooking in the efficient kitchen, which also leaves plenty of extended counter space for meal preparations. Nearby, the breakfast area accesses a covered patio. The owners bath presents a cathedral ceiling and a deluxe owners bath with an immense walk-in closet, two vanities, a garden tub, plus a separate shower. A full hall bath, a powder room, and two storage rooms are available to the three family bedrooms.

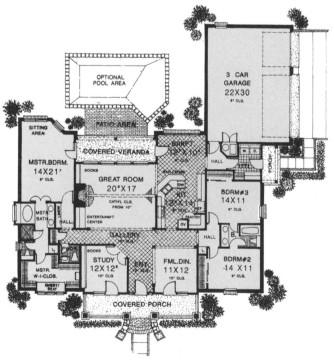

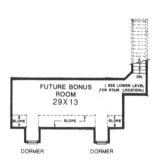

DESIGN BY
©Fillmore Design Group

Step up to a covered porch with sunburst windows and sidelights enhancing three separate entries—the three doorways enter the study, main entry and the formal dining room. The central area of the gallery opens to the great room (with fireplace) and extends to each side of the home. The owners bedroom possesses pampering amemites, which consist of a private hallway (with linen closet), sitting area, owners bath and a walk-in closet with a built-in seat/chest. Accessible solely from the two family bedrooms, a full bath furnishes a dual vanity. Nearby, the kitchen and breakfast area open to the veranda and optional pool area.

PLAN HPT100248

Square Footage: 2,387
Bonus Room: 377 sq. ft.
Width: 69'-6" **Depth:** 68'-11"

PLAN HPT100249

Dormer windows, a shingle-and-siding facade and a conveniently located garage are only a few of this pleasantly snug home's attractive features. Inside, the great room houses a fireplace and opens to a covered front porch. In the kitchen, a pantry gives added space and the serving bar and built-in desk are absolutely favorable. The breakfast nook leads to a grilling porch and accesses the garage. The owners suite includes a splendid bath, with a whirlpool tub, a compartmented toilet and His and Hers walk-in closets. Two bedrooms—located on the second floor—are perfect for family or guests. One bedroom comes with a walk-in closet, and both share a full hall bath. Please specify basement, crawlspace or slab foundation when ordering.

Total: 1,541 sq. ft.
First Floor: 980 sq. ft.
Second Floor: 561 sq. ft.
Width: 47'-0" **Depth:** 55'-2"

FIRST FLOOR

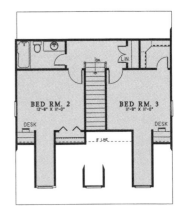

SECOND FLOOR

DESIGN BY
©Michael E. Nelson, Nelson Design Group, LLC

252

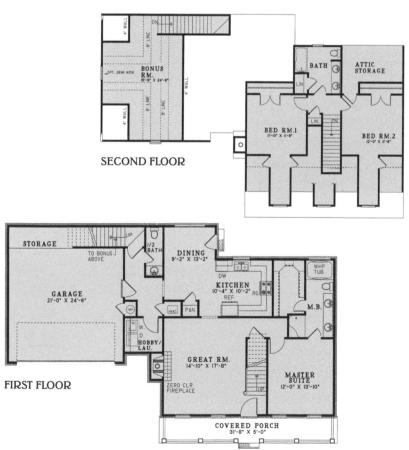

SECOND FLOOR

- BONUS RM. 15'-8" X 24'-6"
- OPT. 2850 WDW
- DN
- 4' WALL
- 8' LINE

- BATH
- ATTIC STORAGE
- LIN
- LIN
- DN
- BED RM.1 11'-10" X 11'-8"
- BED RM.2 12'-0" X 11'-8"

FIRST FLOOR

- STORAGE
- UP
- TO BONUS ABOVE
- 1/2 BATH
- DINING 9'-2" X 13'-2"
- DW
- KITCHEN 10'-4" X 10'-2"
- REF
- RG
- WHP TUB
- M.B.
- GARAGE 21'-0" X 24'-6"
- HVAC
- PAN.
- W
- D
- HOBBY/ LAU.
- GREAT RM. 14'-10" X 17'-8"
- ZERO CLR FIREPLACE
- MASTER SUITE 12'-0" X 13'-10"
- UP
- COVERED PORCH 31'-8" X 5'-0"

DESIGN BY
©Michael E. Nelson, Nelson Design Group, LLC

PLAN HPT100250

With a farmhouse facade that includes a covered front porch and three matching dormers, this home is full of family appeal. The entrance opens directly to the great room, where a fireplace waits to warm cool evenings. The U-shaped kitchen easily serves the nearby dining room and takes advantage of the access to the rear grounds. With the owners bedroom on the first floor, this home has the perfect setting for Mom and Dad to make the two bedrooms on the second floor their leisure area—when the kids have all grown and moved away. A bonus room over the garage is also available for future needs. Please specify crawlspace or slab foundation when ordering.

Total: 1,783 sq. ft.
First Floor: 1,124 sq. ft.
Second Floor: 659 sq. ft.
Bonus Room: 324 sq. ft.
Width: 60'-2" **Depth:** 39'-10"

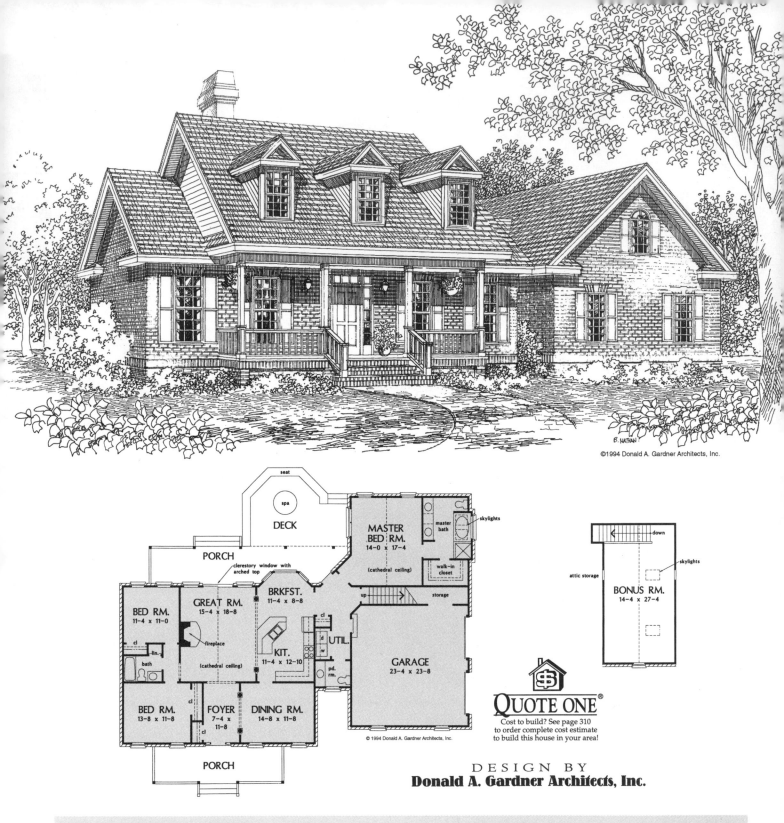

© 1994 Donald A. Gardner Architects, Inc.

DESIGN BY
Donald A. Gardner Architects, Inc.

PLAN HPT100251

Square Footage: 1,954
Bonus Room: 436 sq. ft.
Width: 71'-3" **Depth:** 62'-6"

This beautiful brick country home offers style and comfort for an active family. Two covered porches and a rear deck with a spa invite enjoyment of the outdoors, while a well-defined interior provides places to gather and entertain. A cathedral ceiling soars above the central great room, warmed by an extended-hearth fireplace and by sunlight through an arch-top clerestory window. A splendid owners suite enjoys its own secluded wing, and offers a skylit whirlpool bath, cathedral ceiling and private access to the deck. Two family bedrooms share a full bath on the opposite side of the plan. The two-car garage features a storage area and a service entrance. A skylit bonus room may be developed later.

© 1994 Donald A. Gardner Architects, Inc.

FIRST FLOOR

GARAGE
23-4 x 23-4

storage

seat

DECK

seat

covered breezeway

MASTER BED RM.
14-0 x 15-2

master bath

walk-in closet

bath

GREAT RM.
16-4 x 21-0

fireplace

balcony above

BRKFST.
11-8 x 10-4

UTIL
8-8 x 10-0

KITCHEN
15-10 x 10-10

pantry

BED RM./ STUDY
12-8 x 11-0

stor.

FOYER
15-4 x 5-5

DINING RM.
12-8 x 12-8

PORCH

© 1994 Donald A. Gardner Architects, Inc.

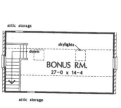

attic storage

skylights

BONUS RM.
27-0 x 14-4

attic storage

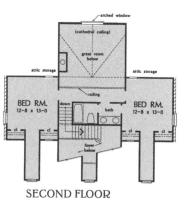

arched window

(cathedral ceiling)

great room below

attic storage   attic storage

BED RM.
12-8 x 13-0

railing

bath

down

foyer below

BED RM.
12-8 x 13-0

SECOND FLOOR

DESIGN BY
Donald A. Gardner Architects, Inc.

Three bay windows enhance the romance of this country home. Enter from the front porch to the great room with a cathedral ceiling and a fireplace. Enjoy a scenic dinner in the dining room, which is easily accessible from the kitchen. The kitchen provides an island cooktop, built-in pantry and sunny breakfast area with a view of the massive deck. The owners bedroom completes the picture with a bay window, deck access and a luxurious bath with a whirlpool tub. Two family bedrooms and a full hall bath occupy the second floor.

PLAN HPT100252

Total: 2,600 sq. ft.
First Floor: 1,966 sq. ft.
Second Floor: 634 sq. ft.
Bonus Room: 396 sq. ft.
Width: 80'-11" **Depth:** 79'-2"

© 1998 Donald A. Gardner, Inc.

PLAN HPT100253

Apleasing mixture of styles, this home combines a traditional brick veneer with an otherwise country home appearance. Built-ins flank the fireplace in the great room, while a soaring cathedral ceiling expands the room visually. The kitchen's angled counter opens the room to both the breakfast bay and the great room, while facing a large screened porch. In the owners room, a splendid private bath with a vast walk-in closet and a dual vanity provides true luxury. A family bedroom and a bedroom/study share a full hall bath. The two-car garage includes a storage area and a bonus room is available upstairs.

Square Footage: 2,042
Bonus Room: 475 sq. ft.
Width: 75'-11" **Depth:** 56'-7"

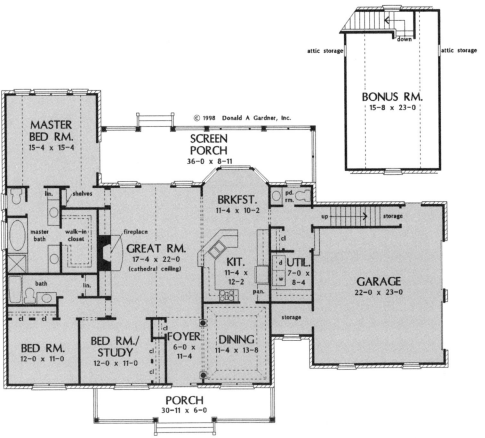

DESIGN BY
Donald A. Gardner Architects, Inc.

256

FIRST FLOOR

Covered Patio

Nook

Living Rm.
15⁶ • 16⁰

Kitchen

Laun.

Pwdr.

w.i.c.

storage

Foyer

Master Bath

Master Suite
12⁰ • 16⁰

Dining Rm.
11⁰ • 11⁰

Porch

DESIGN BY
©**Home Design Services, Inc.**

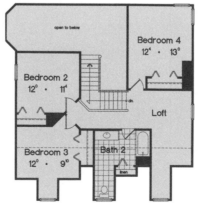

SECOND FLOOR

open to below

Bedroom 4
12⁴ • 13⁰

Bedroom 2
12⁰ • 11⁴

Loft

Bedroom 3
12⁰ • 9⁰

Bath 2

PLAN HPT100254

This is the perfect little home for a small lot. A lovely country porch trimmed in brick veneer welcomes you. From the foyer, the home offers many long vistas, especially one throughout the living room to the patio. A tiled or wood-planked hallway passes the dining room through to the country kitchen, which overlooks the bayed breakfast nook—large enough for the growing family. The owners suite occupies the front wing of the home, and boasts a lavishly appointed bath, with a corner tub and His and Her vanities. The living room features a media/fireplace wall, and the impressive staircase leads up to the three secondary bedrooms and a bonus loft space. The laundry/utility room leads to the detached garage.

Total: 2,271 sq. ft.
First Floor: 1,416 sq. ft.
Second Floor: 855 sq. ft.
Width: 50'-0" **Depth:** 48'-0"

257

PLAN HPT100255

The spunky character of this three-bedroom plan comes through in the four various-sized gables, the sloped roof and the use of brick and wood. The sunken family and living rooms share a double-hearth masonry fireplace. The living room features a bay window, and the family room, with access from the breakfast room, offers a sitting bay. Another bay window drenches the kitchen with natural light. The barrel-vaulted two-story foyer leads upstairs to an angled gallery. The owners suite boasts a barrel-vaulted sitting area and a skylit bath. Two additional bedrooms share a hall bath. A bonus room provides 390 extra square feet of living space.

Total: 2,170 sq. ft.
First Floor: 1,155 sq. ft.
Second Floor: 1,015 sq. ft.
Bonus Room: 390 sq. ft.
Width: 58'-0"   **Depth:** 36'-6"

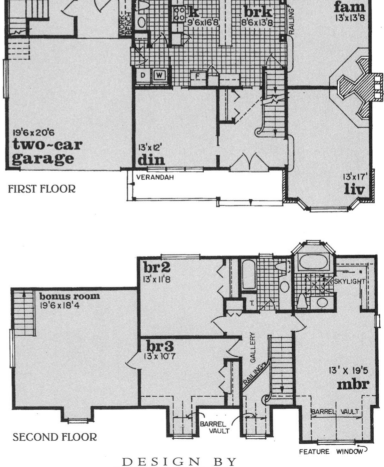

FIRST FLOOR

SECOND FLOOR

DESIGN BY
©Select Home Designs

PLAN HPT100256

3 Car Garage
30' • 21'

Pwdr

Laun

Wet Bar

Family Rm.
18' • 24'

Nook

Kitchen

Covered Patio

Master Suite
16' • 19'

Pwdr

w.i.c.

Living Rm.
19' • 16'

Solarium

w.i.c.

Master Bath

Dining Rm.
12' • 15'

Foyer

Study
12' • 14'

Entry

FIRST FLOOR

Bedroom 3
12' • 17'

Linen

Bedroom 2
12' • 17'

Bath 2

SECOND FLOOR

A lovely use of fieldstone, ship lap-siding and dormers creates the perfect country farmhouse elevation. Once in the foyer, a stately staircase ascends to the second floor. To the left is the formal dining room, while to the right the living room offers spectacular views of the covered patio through French doors. In the owners suite, angled walls create openness, as does the walls of glass that look out from the suite and onto the covered patio and pool area. The owners bath is lavish and well appointed with His and Her walk-in closets, a double vanity, spa tub, shower and private toilet/bidet chamber. The second floor leads to two well-sized bedrooms which share an oversized bath and loads of closet space. To the rear is the three-car garage.

Total: 3,485 sq. ft.
First Floor: 2,652 sq. ft.
Second Floor: 833 sq. ft.
Width: 62'-0" **Depth:** 90'-0"

DESIGN BY
©**Home Design Services, Inc.**

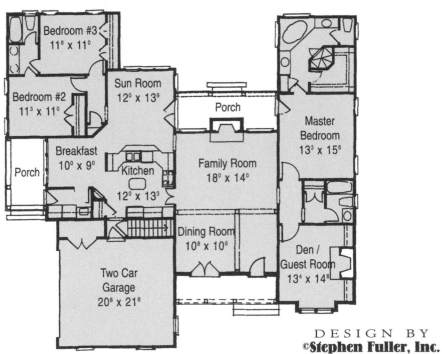

DESIGN BY
©Stephen Fuller, Inc.

PLAN HPT100257

Square Footage: 2,150
Width: 62'-0" **Depth:** 59'-8"

Sitting over a covered porch, twin dormers draw attention to an inviting terrace. Open, casual living space is offset by a quiet den or study with its own fireplace in this casual Colonial-style home. A bright sun room opens to the covered rear porch through French doors. The gourmet kitchen includes an island and bar ledge and enjoys a breakfast area convenient to the family bedrooms. Bedrooms 2 and 3 both share a full bath, each with a private entrance. A corner whirlpool tub highlights the owners suite, which also includes a walk-in closet and separate lavatories. This home is designed with a walkout basement foundation.

Quote One®

Cost to build? See page 310
to order complete cost estimate
to build this house in your area!

DESIGN BY
©Stephen Fuller, Inc.

This classic cottage features a stone and wooden exterior with an arch-detailed porch and a box-bay window. From the foyer, double doors open to the den with built-in bookcases and a fireplace. The family room's hearth is framed by windows overlooking the porch. The owners bedroom opens to the rear porch and the owners bath, with a large walk-in closet, double vanities, a corner tub and separate shower, completes this relaxing retreat. Left of the family room awaits a sun room with access to the covered porch. A breakfast area complements the attractive and efficiently designed kitchen. Two secondary bedrooms share a full bath featuring double vanities. This home is designed with a walkout basement foundation.

PLAN HPT100258

Square Footage: 2,170
Width: 62'-0" **Depth:** 61'-6"

PLAN HPT100259

Brick and stone go hand in hand to create a pleasing facade for this home. The appeal extends far beyond the exterior; the interior floor plan has many amenities and provides great traffic flow. An offset entry opens to a small hall and is distinguished by columns that separate it from the formal dining room. The great room features an eleven-foot ceiling and a corner fireplace. A spacious U-shaped kitchen and breakfast nook provide ample space and also include a snack bar. The first-floor owners bedroom features a private bath and a walk-in closet. The second floor entails two family bedrooms, a bonus room and a full hall bath. Bonus space and a loft area on the second floor expand its usefulness.

Total: 2,143 sq. ft.
First Floor: 1,457 sq. ft.
Second Floor: 686 sq. ft.
Width: 45'-4" **Depth:** 54'-0"

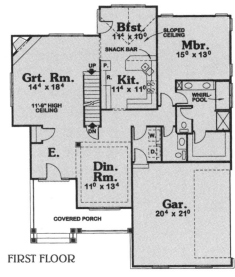

FIRST FLOOR

DESIGN BY
©**Design Basics, Inc.**

SECOND FLOOR

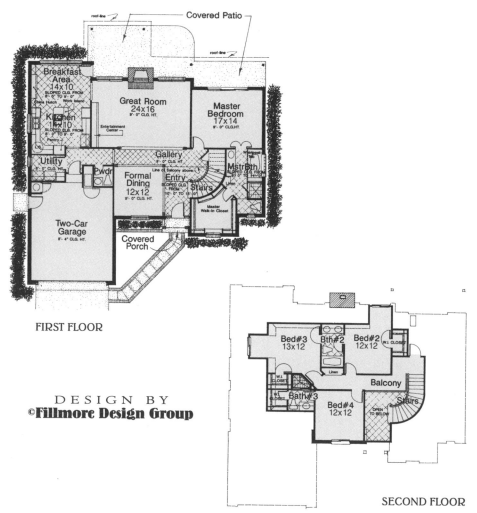

FIRST FLOOR

DESIGN BY
©Fillmore Design Group

SECOND FLOOR

PLAN HPT100260

This gracious French country home possesses an appealing stone-and-brick and rough-hewn cedar exterior. Inside, both the great room—with fireplace and built-in media center—along with the deluxe owners bedroom, face the covered patio that extends across the back of the house. Inside the owners bedroom resides a private bath with a whirlpool tub, separate shower and an enormous walk-in closet. The formal dining room is just a few steps from the island kitchen and the sunny breakfast area. Upstairs, Bedrooms 2 and 3 each access a full bath, and Bedroom 4 includes a full private bath. All of the upstairs bedrooms hold a generous amount of closet space.

Total: 2,538 sq. ft.
First Floor: 1,719 sq. ft.
Second Floor: 819 sq. ft.
Width: 56'-0" **Depth:** 51'-8"

FIRST FLOOR

Deck

Breakfast
11' x 12'2"

Kitchen
16'6" x 13'6"

pantry

Bath

Hall

Laun.

Great Room
20'6" x 18'6"

butler's pantry

Three-car Garage
20' x 34'1"

wood rail

Living Room
13'10" x 12'8"

Dining Room
13'4" x 16'2"
tray ceiling

Porch

SECOND FLOOR

walk-in closet

Dressing

Bedroom
11'3" x 11'

Bedroom
11'8" x 11'

Balcony
wood rail

Bath

Master Bedroom
13'10" x 16'4"
sloped ceiling

Foyer Below

stairs dn

Bedroom
13'4" x 11'11"

slope

DESIGN BY
©**Studer Residential Designs, Inc.**

PLAN HPT100261

Total: 2,725 sq. ft.

First Floor: 1,573 sq. ft.

Second Floor: 1,152 sq. ft.

Width: 59'-6"   **Depth:** 54'-0"

A covered front porch coupled with the stone and brick exterior provides warmth and a welcoming effect to this delightful home. Nine-foot ceilings and a two-story foyer add to the spaciousness of the first floor. For ease of serving formal gatherings, a butler's pantry is located between the kitchen and dining room. A tray ceiling tops the formal dining area, adding style and charm. The oversized kitchen offers an abundance of storage and a spacious walk-in pantry. The corner fireplace warms the great room while the openness of this family gathering area add enjoyment. An angled staircase leads to four bedrooms on the second floor. The sloped ceiling and luxurious dressing room/bath of the master suite are indulging.

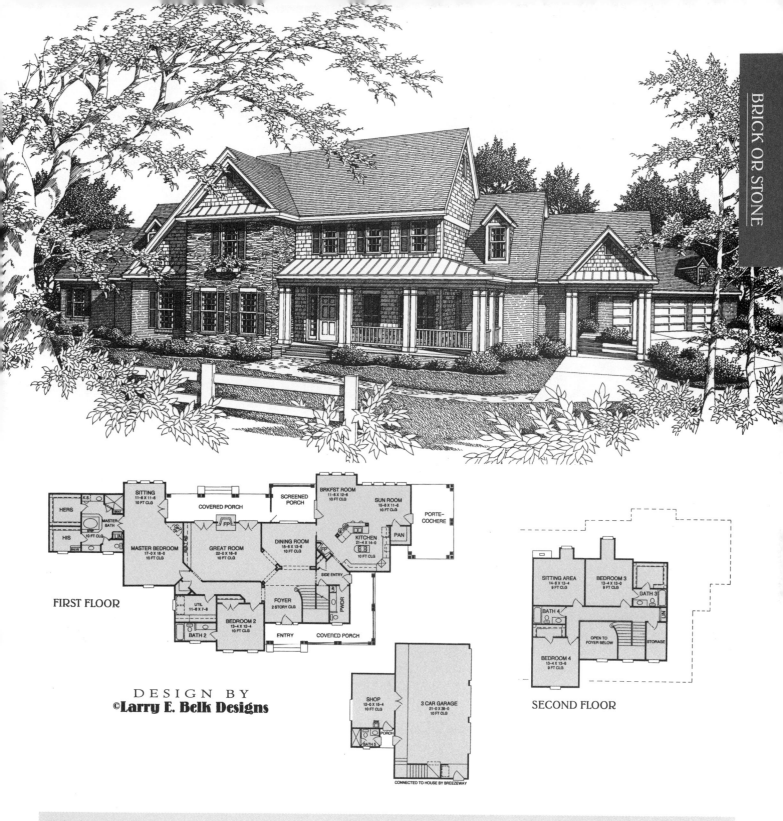

FIRST FLOOR

SITTING
11-6 X 11-6
10 FT CLG

HERS

K.S.

MASTER-
BATH
10 FT CLG

HIS

COVERED PORCH

SCREENED
PORCH

BRKFST ROOM
11-6 X 12-6
10 FT CLG

SUN ROOM
15-6 X 11-6
10 FT CLG

PORTE-
COCHERE

MASTER BEDROOM
17-0 X 18-0
10 FT CLG

GREAT ROOM
22-0 X 16-6
10 FT CLG

DINING ROOM
15-6 X 13-6
10 FT CLG

KITCHEN
21-4 X 14-0

10 FT CLG

PAN

FP

FP

SIDE ENTRY

UTIL
11-6 X 7-6

BEDROOM 2
13-4 X 12-4
10 FT CLG

FOYER
2 STORY CLG

PWDR

BATH 2

ENTRY

COVERED PORCH

DESIGN BY
©Larry E. Belk Designs

SHOP
12-0 X 15-4
10 FT CLG

3 CAR GARAGE
21-0 X 38-0
10 FT CLG

PORCH

BATH 5

CONNECTED TO HOUSE BY BREEZEWAY

SITTING AREA
14-6 X 13-4
9 FT CLG

BEDROOM 3
13-4 X 13-0
9 FT CLG

BATH 3

BATH 4

OPEN TO
FOYER BELOW

STORAGE

BEDROOM 4
13-4 X 13-6
9 FT CLG

SECOND FLOOR

The blending of natural materials and a nostalgic farmhouse look gives this home its unique character. Inside, a sophisticated floor plan includes all the amenities demanded by today's upscale family. Three large covered porches, one on the front and two on the rear, provide outdoor entertaining areas. The kitchen features a built-in stone fireplace visible from the breakfast and sun rooms. The owners suite includes a large sitting area and a luxurious bath. Upstairs, two additional bedrooms and a large game room will please family and guests. Please specify crawlspace or slab foundation when ordering.

PLAN HPT100262

Total: 4,203 sq. ft.
First Floor: 3,120 sq. ft.
Second Floor: 1,083 sq. ft.
Width: 118'-1" **Depth:** 52'-2"

PLAN HPT100263

This two-story home is made for the narrow lot and the family who revels in luxurious escapes. Plenty of built-ins and amenities allow for the ultimate in relaxation. Keep the kids entertained in their private nook while the adults fire up the barbecue on the grilling porch. One family member can work quietly in the computer center while another reads in the window-seat loft. A media center and a gas fireplace give the great room its name, while the whirlpool tub in the owners bath is always appreciated. Please specify basement, crawlspace, slab or block foundation when ordering.

Total: 1,987 sq. ft.
First Floor: 1,558 sq. ft.
Second Floor: 429 sq. ft.
Width: 36'-4" **Depth:** 73'-6"

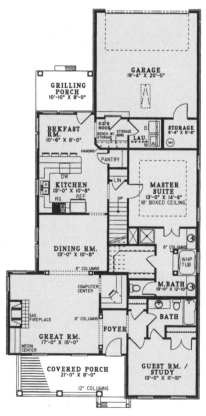

FIRST FLOOR

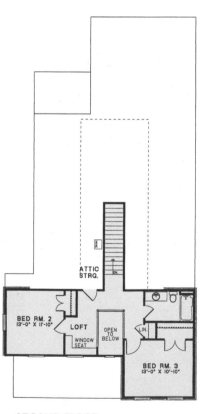

SECOND FLOOR

DESIGN BY
©Michael E. Nelson, Nelson Design Group, LLC

266

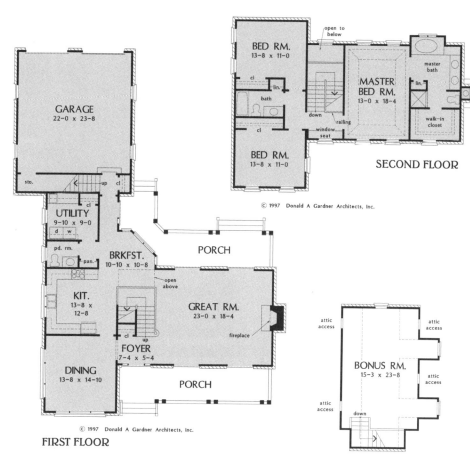

© 1997 Donald A Gardner Architects, Inc.

SECOND FLOOR

BED RM.
13-8 x 11-0

open to below

master bath

MASTER BED RM.
13-0 x 18-4

cl

lin.

bath

lin.

down

cl

walk-in closet

railing

window seat

BED RM.
13-8 x 11-0

GARAGE
22-0 x 23-8

sto.

up

cl

UTILITY
9-10 x 9-0

d | w

pd. rm.

pan.

BRKFST.
10-10 x 10-8

PORCH

open above

KIT.
13-8 x 12-8

GREAT RM.
23-0 x 18-4

fireplace

cl

up

FOYER
7-4 x 5-4

DINING
13-8 x 14-10

PORCH

© 1997 Donald A Gardner Architects, Inc.

FIRST FLOOR

attic access

attic access

BONUS RM.
15-3 x 23-8

attic access

attic access

down

DESIGN BY
Donald A. Gardner Architects, Inc.

PLAN HPT100264

A wide, covered front porch welcomes friends and family to this fine three-bedroom home. Inside, a spacious great room is anchored at one end by a warming fireplace and at the other by the staircase, and opens to both the front porch as well as the rear porch. The U-shaped kitchen serves the formal dining room and the sunny breakfast area with efficiency. Note the utility room nearby for convenience. Upstairs, two large secondary bedrooms share a full bath, while the owners suite is complete with a walk-in closet and a private bath.

Total: 2,401 sq. ft.
First Floor: 1,347 sq. ft.
Second Floor: 1,054 sq. ft.
Bonus Room: 475 sq. ft.
Width: 53'-11" **Depth:** 71'-9"

PLAN HPT100265

Multiple rooflines, charming stonework and a covered entryway all combine to give this home plenty of curb appeal. Inside, the two-story foyer leads to either the formal dining room or the spacious, vaulted great room. An efficient kitchen offers an abundance of counter and cabinet space, plus a vaulted breakfast room and a nearby keeping room. The owners suite is amazing; it displays a tray ceiling, while a vaulted owners bath with a large walk-in closet thoughtfully provides a separate space for linen. Upstairs, Bedrooms 2 and 3 share a compartmented bath, with two separate vanities. Please specify basement or crawlspace foundation when ordering.

Total: 2,155 sq. ft.
First Floor: 1,628 sq. ft.
Second Floor: 527 sq. ft.
Bonus Room: 207 sq. ft.
Width: 54'-0" **Depth:** 46'-10"

FIRST FLOOR

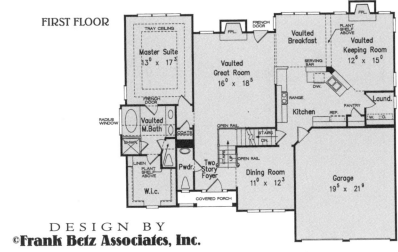

DESIGN BY
©**Frank Betz Associates, Inc.**

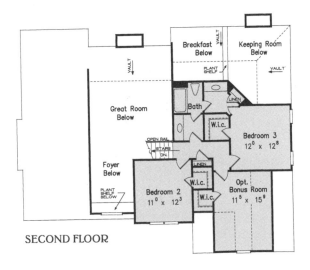

SECOND FLOOR

FIRST FLOOR

SECOND FLOOR

DESIGN BY
©Frank Betz Associates, Inc.

PLAN HPT100266

A perfect blend of stone and siding create just the right look for this stylish home. Comfort and beauty reside within, with a flexible floor plan that offers formal as well as casual space. The two-story foyer leads through arched openings to the living and dining rooms, well lit by lovely windows. A gourmet kitchen with a food-prep island features a breakfast area with a French door to a private covered porch. Upstairs, the sleeping quarters include an owners suite with a tray ceiling, two walk-in closets, a plant shelf and a box-bay window. Please specify basement or crawlspace foundation when ordering.

Total: 2,596 sq. ft.
First Floor: 1,204 sq. ft.
Second Floor: 1,392 sq. ft.
Width: 56'-0" **Depth:** 46'-6"

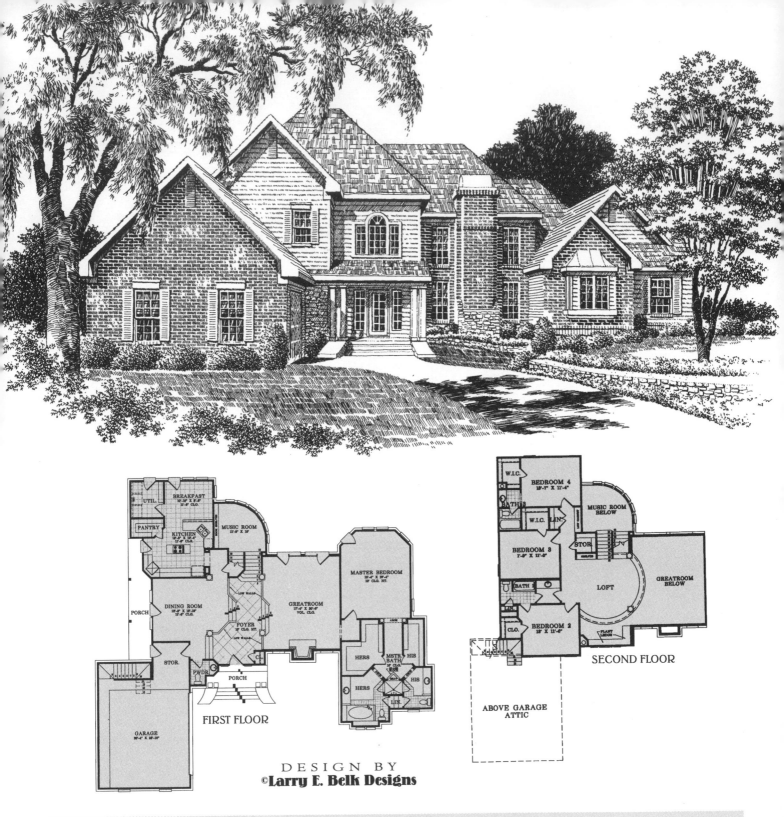

FIRST FLOOR

SECOND FLOOR

ABOVE GARAGE
ATTIC

DESIGN BY
©Larry E. Belk Designs

PLAN HPT100267

Total: 3,370 sq. ft.
First Floor: 2,270 sq. ft.
Second Floor: 1,100 sq. ft.
Width: 76'-6" **Depth:** 69'-4"

A combination of stacked stone, brick and wood siding makes this home a real beauty from the curb. The foyer steps up to a large great room with a view to the rear grounds. On the other side, steps lead down to the dining room with access to a side porch. The owners suite includes a fabulous owners bath—really two baths in one—with a His and Hers dressing area and a shared shower. At the half-landing, curved windows frame a traditional music room. Continuing up the stairs, a large circular loft overlooks the great room and leads to three bedrooms and two baths.

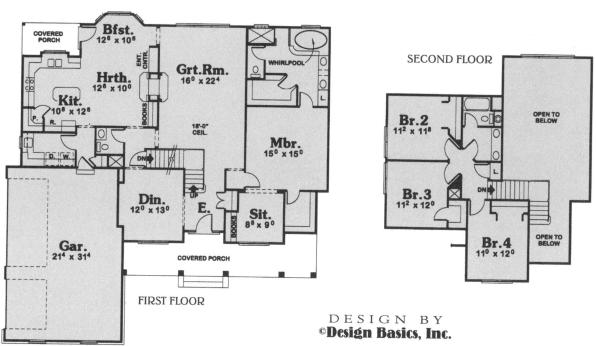

SECOND FLOOR

FIRST FLOOR

DESIGN BY
©**Design Basics, Inc.**

Hipped and gabled roofs draw your attention down to the covered porch, bringing you to a six-panel door with sidelights. Upon the entryway to this gorgeous farmhouse sit the formal dining area and the staircase. Straight ahead is great room with a see-through hearth to the kitchen and breakfast area. The kitchen includes an island and a walk-in pantry, while the breakfast room provides a doorway to the back porch. Providing extreme comfort is a deluxe owners bedroom with a sitting area and a whirlpool bath. Three bedrooms reside on the second floor and share a full hall bath that includes a dual vanity and compartmented lavatories. Please specify basement or block foundation when ordering.

PLAN HPT100268

Total: 2,615 sq. ft.
First Floor: 1,955 sq. ft.
Second Floor: 660 sq. ft.
Width: 60'-0" **Depth:** 60'-4"

PLAN HPT100269

Interesting window treatments—note the decorated Palladian window and transoms in a box-bay window—and varying rooflines give this home great curb appeal. A formal dining room is open to the front entry, and the kitchen is accessible through double doors to the right. Food preparation will be a breeze with the extra counter space of the snack bar and storage of the pantry in the L-shaped kitchen. A handy laundry room and a powder room reside between the breakfast nook and the two-car garage. Upstairs, the owners suite and two family bedrooms—with a shared bath—complete the plan.

Total: 1,701 sq. ft.
First Floor: 943 sq. ft.
Second Floor: 758 sq. ft.
Width: 50'-6" **Depth:** 56'-8"

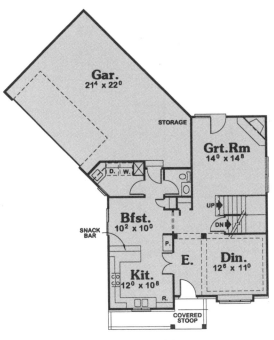

FIRST FLOOR

DESIGN BY
©Design Basics, Inc.

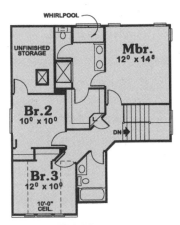

SECOND FLOOR

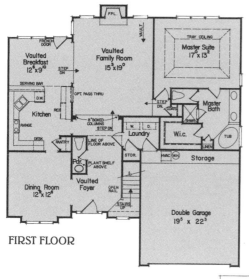

FIRST FLOOR

DESIGN BY
©**Frank Betz Associates, Inc.**

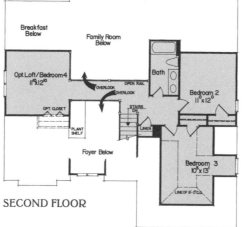

SECOND FLOOR

PLAN HPT100270

Arched windows set in two dormers and a hood over a box-bay window are only a few of the charming features on the exterior of this three-bedroom home. Amenities abound inside with plant shelves, interesting ceiling treatments and a loft. To the left of the entry is the dining room with a box-bay window. The U-shaped kitchen nearby includes a large pantry and sunny breakfast nook. Step down into the vaulted family room with its focal-point fireplace between two windows. An elegant owners bedroom is adorned with a tray ceiling and features a lavish bath with a garden tub. Upstairs, two bedrooms share a hall bath with the loft—or make this into a fourth bedroom. Please specify basement, crawlspace or slab foundation when ordering.

Total: 2,213 sq. ft.
First Floor: 1,488 sq. ft.
Second Floor: 725 sq. ft.
Width: 46'-0" **Depth:** 50'-10"

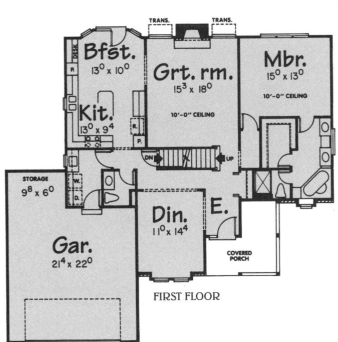

Bfst.
13⁰ x 10⁰

Grt. rm.
15³ x 18⁰
10'-0" CEILING

Mbr.
15⁰ x 13⁰
10'-0" CEILING

Kit.
13⁰ x 9⁴

STORAGE
9⁸ x 6⁰

Gar.
21⁴ x 22⁰

Din.
11⁰ x 14⁴

E.

COVERED PORCH

FIRST FLOOR

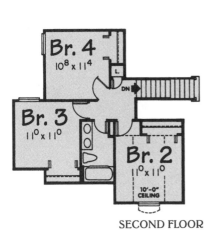

Br. 4
10⁸ x 11⁴

Br. 3
11⁰ x 11⁰

Br. 2
11⁰ x 11⁰
10'-0" CEILING

SECOND FLOOR

DESIGN BY
©Design Basics, Inc.

PLAN HPT100271

Total: 1,994 sq. ft.
First Floor: 1,426 sq. ft.
Second Floor: 568 sq. ft.
Width: 54'-8" **Depth:** 52'-0"

With brick, siding and a covered porch, this home presents plenty of curb appeal. Gatherings will be delightful in the spacious great room with its centered fireplace and transom windows. The L-shaped kitchen offers an island—perfect for gourmet cooking—a planning desk and bayed breakfast area. The first floor consists of a complete owners suite, which possesses a corner garden tub, separate shower and walk-in closet. Upstairs, three family bedrooms share a full bath and a linen closet. The two-car garage contains storage space and opens to the utility room.

Contemporary Farmhouses

QUOTE ONE®

Cost to build? See page 310
to order complete cost estimate
to build this house in your area!

SECOND FLOOR

BEDRM
11² x 12⁰

BEDRM
11² x 12⁰

BATH

OPEN TO BELOW

GARAGE
21⁰ x 22⁶

FIRST FLOOR

COVERED PORCH

GREAT RM
18² x 17⁴

MASTER SUITE
14⁰ x 15¹⁰

SITTING

LAUNDRY RM

BREAKFAST RM

KIT
11⁰ x 12⁶

FOYER
VOL. CLG.

WALK-IN CLOSET

DINING
11⁸ x 14⁸

MASTER BATH

COVERED PORCH

DESIGN BY
©Home Planners

PLAN HPT100272

An arched clerestory, multi-pane windows and a balustered porch splash this classic country exterior with an extraordinary new spirit. Inside, the two-story foyer is flanked by the sunny formal dining room and an elegant stairway. The great room offers a fireplace with a tiled hearth and a built-in media center. The L-shaped kitchen boasts a built-in desk, extra closet space and double ovens. The first floor owners suite is appointed with a sitting area and its bath boasts an angled whirlpool tub and twin lavatories. Upstairs, two secondary bedrooms—each with its own balcony—share a full bath that includes ample linen storage.

Total: 2,170 sq. ft.
First Floor: 1,655 sq. ft.
Second Floor: 515 sq. ft.
Width: 68'-6" **Depth:** 66'-5"

L·D

PLAN HPT100273

This compact one-story home has plenty of living in it. The owners suite features a sun-washed, vaulted sitting area with views to the rear of the home. A vaulted family room with a fireplace conveniently accesses the kitchen and vaulted breakfast area via a serving bar and pass-through window. For formal occasions, the dining area creates opulence with its decorative columns. Two family bedrooms located to the front of the home share a full bath. The owners suite is adorned with a tray ceiling and features a vaulted bay-windowed sitting area. Please specify basement or crawlspace foundation when ordering.

Square Footage: 1,712
Width: 55'-0" **Depth:** 55'-0"

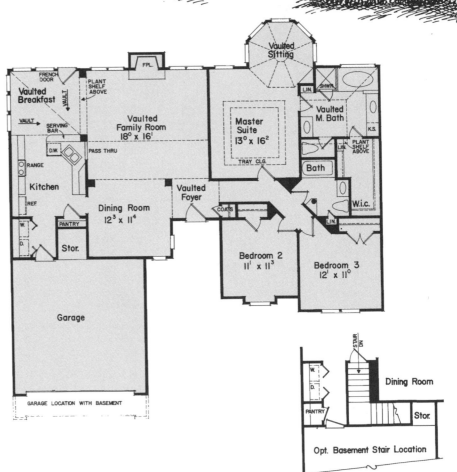

DESIGN BY
©**Frank Betz Associates, Inc.**

PLAN HPT100274

An impressive entrance embellished with a curved and multi-pane transom and sidelight at the entry door lends this three-bedroom home plenty of curb appeal. A roomy front porch welcomes guests, and the dining room with its bay window will captivate them. A light-filled breakfast nook joins the efficient kitchen over a serving bar. Nearby, the living room's sloped ceiling, large fireplace and windows will relax you. The sleeping zone to the right of the plan includes two family bedrooms, sharing a bath, and an opulent owners suite with a tray ceiling, private patio access, large walk-in closet and a bath with an oval corner tub, a separate shower and two vanity sinks.

Square Footage: 2,033
Width: 74'-0" **Depth:** 60'-0"

Floor plan labels:

M.Bath

Sundeck
21-6 x 12-0

Master Bdrm.
15-8 x 14-2

Tray.

Brkfst.
13-6 x 9-6

Living Area
21-6 x 15-6

Dn.

Lnd.

W.D.

Kit.
13-6 x 11-8

Bath 2

Double Garage
21-8 x 20-8

Pantry

Ref.

Cts.

Bdrm.3
12-0 x 11-6

© 1993, Jannis Vann & Associates, Inc.

Dining
13-6 x 11-6

Foyer

Bdrm.2
13-6 x 11-6

DESIGN BY
©**Jannis Vann & Associates, Inc.**

PLAN HPT100275

This country-style home is lovely to behold and economical to build. Front and back covered porches create a warm transition to the yard, where a charming porte cochere gives shelter to those disembarking from vehicles. From the dining room, steps lead down to the sunken family room with a warming fireplace. A second set of steps lead up to the main hallway, which connects the living room with the owners suite and two roomy bedrooms. The owners bedroom features private access to the rear porch, two walk-in closets and a well-appointed bathroom. Room to grow is available in the unfinished space on the second floor.

Square Footage: 2,842
Bonus Space: 1,172 sq. ft.
Width: 91'-0" **Depth:** 69'-4"

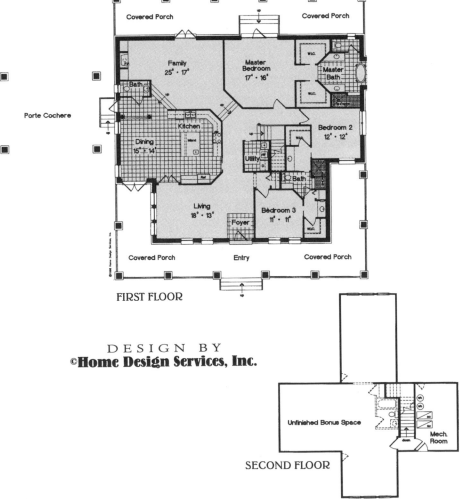

DESIGN BY
©**Home Design Services, Inc.**

278

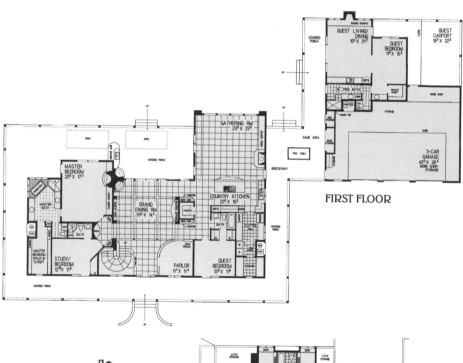

FIRST FLOOR

Quote One®

Cost to build? See page 310
to order complete cost estimate
to build this house in your area!

SECOND FLOOR

DESIGN BY
©**Home Planners**

PLAN HPT100276

A long, low-pitched roof distinguishes this Southwestern-style farmhouse design. The tiled entrance leads to a grand dining room and opens to a formal parlor secluded by half-walls. A country kitchen with a cooktop island overlooks the two-story gathering room with its full wall of glass, fireplace and built-in media shelves. The owners suite satisfies the most discerning tastes with a raised hearth, an adjacent study or exercise room, access to the wraparound porch, and a bath with a corner whirlpool tub. Rooms upstairs can serve as secondary bedrooms for family members, or can be converted to home office space or used as guest bedrooms.

Total: 4,116 sq. ft.
First Floor: 3,166 sq. ft.
Second Floor: 950 sq. ft.
Width: 154'-0" **Depth:** 94'-8"

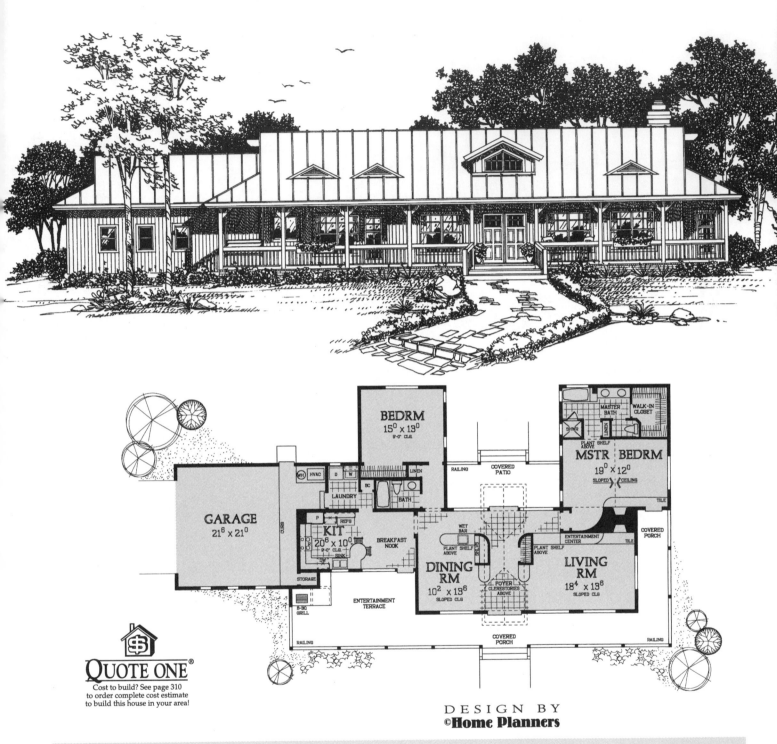

BEDRM
15⁰ x 13⁰
9'-0" CLG.

MASTER
BATH

WALK-IN
CLOSET

SHWR

LINEN

PLANT SHELF
ABOVE

MSTR BEDRM
19⁰ x 12⁰
SLOPED CEILING

TILE

COVERED
PATIO

RAILING

WH

HVAC

D

W

LINEN

LAUNDRY

BATH

GARAGE
21⁸ x 21⁰

P

REFG

KIT
20⁶ x 10⁰
9'-0" CLG.

SINK

BREAKFAST
NOOK

WET
BAR

PLANT SHELF
ABOVE

ENTERTAINMENT
CENTER

COVERED
PORCH

TILE

STORAGE

DINING
RM
10² x 13⁶
SLOPED CLG.

FOYER
CLERESTORIES
ABOVE

PLANT SHELF
ABOVE

LIVING
RM
18⁴ x 13⁶
SLOPED CLG.

B-BQ
GRILL

ENTERTAINMENT
TERRACE

RAILING

COVERED
PORCH

RAILING

DESIGN BY
©**Home Planners**

PLAN HPT100277

Square Footage: 1,800
Width: 89'-0" **Depth:** 46'-2"

L·D

Small but inviting, this ranch-style farmhouse is the perfect choice for a small family or empty-nesters. It's loaded with amenities even the most particular homeowner will appreciate. For example, the living room and dining room both have plant shelves, sloped ceilings and built-in cabinetry to enhance livability. The living room also sports a warming fireplace. The owners bedroom contains a well-appointed bath with dual vanities and a walk-in closet. The additional bedroom has its own bath with linen storage. The kitchen is separated from the breakfast nook by a clever bar area. Access to the two-car garage is through a laundry area with washer/dryer hook-up space.

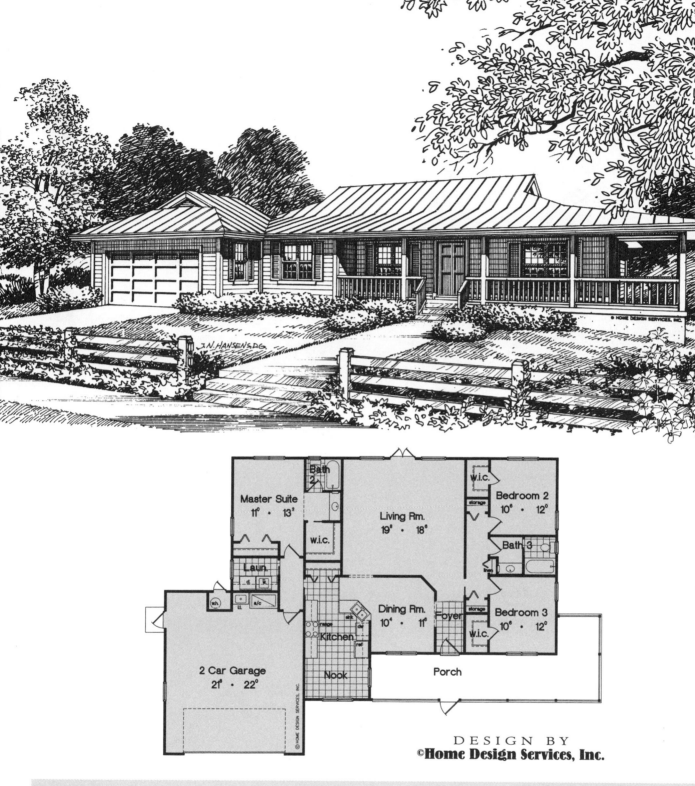

Master Suite
11⁰ · 13²

Bath 2

Living Rm.
19⁸ · 18⁶

w.i.c.

storage

Bedroom 2
10⁶ · 12⁰

w.i.c.

Bath 3

Laun.

2 Car Garage
21⁰ · 22⁰

Kitchen

Nook

Dining Rm.
10⁴ · 11⁰

Foyer

storage

w.i.c.

Bedroom 3
10⁶ · 12⁰

Porch

DESIGN BY
©Home Design Services, Inc.

The wraparound porch and standing-seam roof design makes this traditional style called "Cracker" a long-time favorite. The simplicity of the design is what gives it its charm and enduring quality. The living room is perfect for large family gatherings—as is the formal dining room with a view of the front porch. The split floor plan places the owners suite to the left of the plan, with a private entrance to the garage, walk-in closet and a private bath. Two family bedrooms—both with walk-in closets—share a roomy bath on the opposite end of the plan.

PLAN HPT100278

Square Footage: 1,668
Width: 70'-4" **Depth:** 47'-4"

PLAN HPT100279

This country-style ranch is the essence of excitement with its combination of exterior building materials and interesting shapes. Because it is angled, it allows for flexibility in design—the great room and/or the family room can be lengthened to meet family space requirements. Both the family room and great room possess cathedral ceilings. The great room is framed with a dramatic wall of windows and includes a cozy fireplace. The owners bedroom features a cathedral ceiling, walk-in closet, private deck and a spacious owners bath with a whirlpool tub. There are three family bedrooms—two that share a full bath and one that has a private bath. An expansive deck area with space for a hot tub wraps around interior family gathering areas.

Square Footage: 1,988
Width: 94'-8" **Depth:** 64'-4"

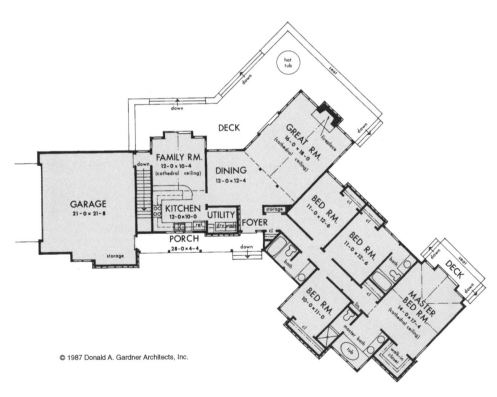

DESIGN BY
Donald A. Gardner Architects, Inc.

© 1987 Donald A. Gardner Architects, Inc.

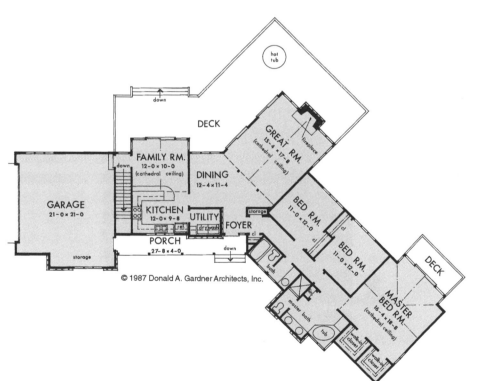

© 1987 Donald A. Gardner Architects, Inc.

DESIGN BY
Donald A. Gardner Architects, Inc.

PLAN HPT100280

What visual excitement is created in this country ranch with the use of a combination of exterior building materials and shapes! The angular nature of the plan allows for flexibility in design—lengthen the great room or family room, or both, to suit individual space needs. Cathedral ceilings grace both rooms and a fireplace embellishes the great room with warmth. An amenity-filled owners bedroom features a cathedral ceiling, a private deck and an owners bath with a whirlpool tub. Two family bedrooms share a full bath. An expansive deck area with a hot tub wraps around for enhanced outdoor living.

Square Footage: 1,842
Width: 92'-4" **Depth:** 61'-8"

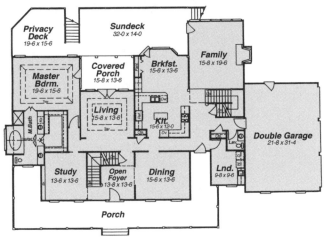

FIRST FLOOR

SECOND FLOOR

DESIGN BY
©Jannis Vann & Associates, Inc.

PLAN HPT100281

Total: 3,972 sq. ft.
First Floor: 2,708 sq. ft.
Second Floor: 1,264 sq. ft.
Bonus Room: 564 sq. ft.
Width: 90'-0" **Depth:** 64'-0"

Shed dormers decorate the roof, while the stone-and-wood-siding facade enhances the appeal of this lovely four-bedroom home. Settle into a chair on the porch to read a book or warm up by the family-room fireplace during inclement weather, and watch the storm pass via a wall of windows. The two-story foyer opens to a study on the left and a dining room to the right. The kitchen features an island workstation, pantry and breakfast nook with a bay window. The formal living room is elegant with a tray ceiling and French-door access to the rear covered porch. The second floor includes Bedrooms 2 and 4 sharing a bath, Bedroom 3 with a private bath, a loft overlooking the family room, and a bonus room.

DESIGN BY
©**Home Design Services, Inc.**

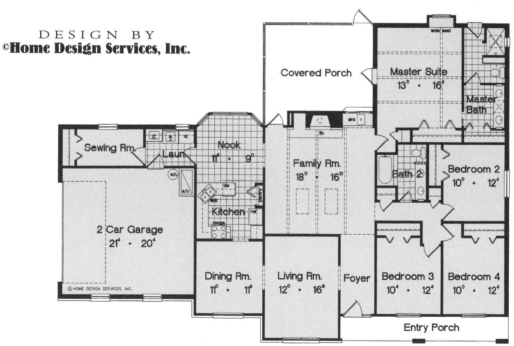

Covered Porch

Master Suite
13⁸ · 16⁴

Master Bath

Sewing Rm.

Laun.

Nook
11⁸ · 9⁰

Family Rm.
18⁰ · 16⁰

Bath 2

Bedroom 2
10⁰ · 12⁴

Kitchen

2 Car Garage
21' · 20⁴

©HOME DESIGN SERVICES, INC.

Dining Rm.
11⁰ · 11⁸

Living Rm.
12⁰ · 16⁶

Foyer

Bedroom 3
10⁴ · 12⁴

Bedroom 4
10⁰ · 12⁴

Entry Porch

This traditional design begins at the foyer, where an impressive view of the formal living and dining rooms is separated by archways. A beam ceiling with skylights draws attention to the fireplace with a built-in storage area for firewood and a wetbar. To the left is a U-shaped kitchen and a breakfast nook with a bay window. An unusual feature of the plan is a sewing room accessed from the laundry area. The sleeping zone to the right of the plan includes three family bedrooms sharing a full bath, and a luxurious owners suite. Beams line the ceiling of the owners suite, while the window provides a built-in seat. The owners bath features a door accessing the rear yard and a skylight over the shower.

PLAN HPT100282

Square Footage: 2,173
Width: 73'-4" **Depth:** 51'-4"

285

PLAN HPT100283

This traditional cottage combines an easy-care brick exterior with a planned-to-perfection interior design. A dream owners suite boasts amenities galore—two large walk-in closets with a double vanity, a garden tub and a separate shower. The corner kitchen with a sit-down bar is ideally positioned to serve the formal dining area as well as the roomy breakfast area. This eating area opens into a grand family room, complete with a fireplace and views to the rear patio. The two upstairs bedrooms feature dormers in each room along with attic access. Don't miss the double carport and extra storage area to the rear of the plan. Please specify crawlspace or slab foundation when ordering.

Total: 2,132 sq. ft.
First Floor: 1,576 sq. ft.
Second Floor: 556 sq. ft.
Width: 62'-11" **Depth:** 58'-0"

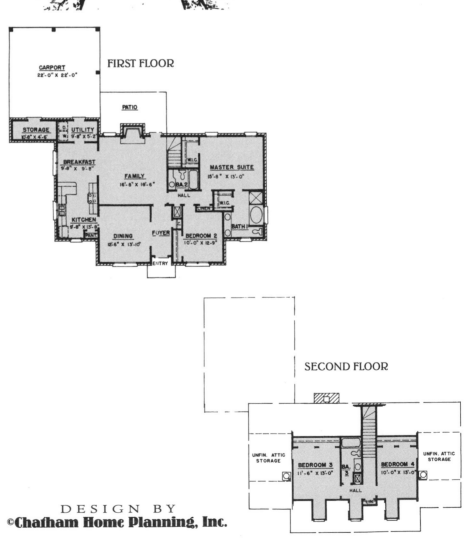

DESIGN BY
©Chatham Home Planning, Inc.

286

Covered Patio
44° · 11⁴

Master Bedroom
16° · 18°

w.i.c.

Family Room
15⁴ · 15⁴

Nook

Living Rm.
15⁴ · 13°

Mstr. Bath

w.i.c.

Kitchen

Dining Rm.
12° · 13°

Foyer

Laundry

pan.

Entry

Bath 2

FIRST FLOOR

Bedroom 2
11⁴ · 12⁴

2 Car Garage
21⁴ · 23⁴

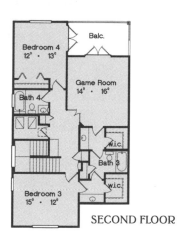

Bedroom 4
12° · 13°

Balc.

Game Room
14° · 16°

Bath 4

w.i.c.

Bath 3

w.i.c.

Bedroom 3
15° · 12°

SECOND FLOOR

DESIGN BY
©Home Design Services, Inc.

A two-story farmhouse with a wraparound front porch and plenty of natural light welcomes you to this graceful, four-bedroom country classic. The large kitchen featuring a center island with a counter and breakfast area opens to the large family room for easy entertaining. There are plenty of interior architectural effects, with columns, arches and niches to punctuate the interior spaces. A separate dining room provides formality. The owners suite, privately situated on the first floor, features separate double vanities, a garden whirlpool tub and separate walk-around shower. A second bedroom on the main level would be a great guest room or maid's quarters with a private bath and direct access to the garage. Bedrooms 3 and 4 are tucked upstairs with a game room and two full baths.

PLAN HPT100288

Total: 3,432 sq. ft.
First Floor: 2,390 sq. ft.
Second Floor: 1,042 sq. ft.
Width: 70'-0" **Depth:** 76'-4"

PLAN HPT100289

This modest-size home provides a quaint covered front porch that opens to a two-story foyer. The formal dining room features a boxed window that can be seen from the entry. A fireplace in the great room adds warmth and coziness to the attached breakfast room and the well-planned kitchen. Sliding glass doors lead from the breakfast room to the rear yard. A washer and dryer reside in a nearby utility room, and a closet provides ample storage. A powder room is provided nearby for guests. Three bedrooms occupy the second floor; one of these includes an arched window under a vaulted ceiling. The deluxe owners suite provides a large walk-in closet and a dressing area with a double vanity and a whirlpool tub.

Total: 1,650 sq. ft.
First Floor: 891 sq. ft.
Second Floor: 759 sq. ft.
Width: 44'-0" **Depth:** 40'-0"

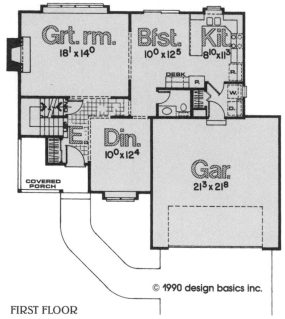

FIRST FLOOR

© 1990 design basics inc.

DESIGN BY
©Design Basics, Inc.

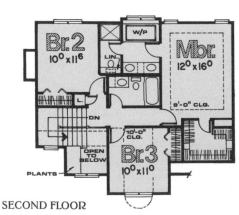

SECOND FLOOR

292

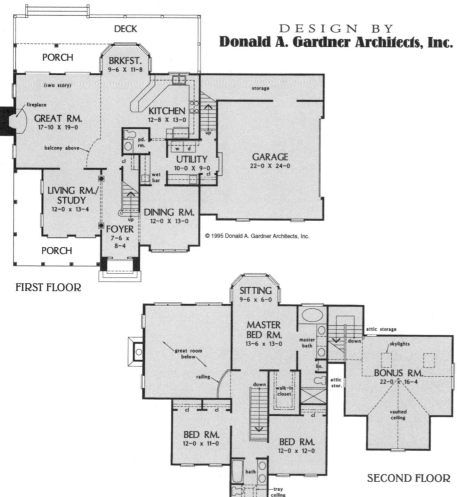

DECK

PORCH

BRKFST.
9-6 X 11-8

(two story)

fireplace

GREAT RM.
17-10 X 19-0

balcony above

storage

KITCHEN
12-8 X 13-0

pd.
rm.

cl

UTILITY
10-0 X 9-0

up

GARAGE
22-0 X 24-0

LIVING RM./
STUDY
12-0 x 13-4

wet
bar

cl

DINING RM.
12-0 X 13-0

FOYER
7-6 x
8-4

up

PORCH

FIRST FLOOR

DESIGN BY
Donald A. Gardner Architects, Inc.

© 1995 Donald A. Gardner Architects, Inc.

SITTING
9-6 x 6-0

MASTER
BED RM.
13-6 X 13-0

great room
below

railing

master
bath

ln.

down

walk-in
closet

attic
stor.

cl

attic storage

down

skylights

BONUS RM.
22-0 X 16-4

vaulted
ceiling

BED RM.
12-0 X 11-0

cl   cl

BED RM.
12-0 X 12-0

bath

tray
ceiling

SECOND FLOOR

PLAN HPT100290

In this traditional country home, a two-story great room accesses the porch and deck through French doors. Nine-foot ceilings throughout the first floor add extra volume and elegance. The great room is open to the kitchen. Here, a conveniently angled peninsula and a breakfast room with a bay window complement the work space. For added flexibility, a separate formal living room can double as a casual study. It features accent columns and French doors leading to the front porch. Upstairs, the roomy owners suite features a sitting area, a spacious walk-in closet and a bath with a garden tub. An ample bonus room is highlighted by skylights and a vaulted ceiling.

Total: 2,393 sq. ft.
First Floor: 1,385 sq. ft.
Second Floor: 1,008 sq. ft.
Width: 67'-10" **Depth:** 52'-4"

293

FIRST FLOOR

3,30 X 3,30
11'-0" X 11'-0"

2,40 X 3,70
8'-0" X 12'-4"

4,50 X 3,30
15'-0" X 11'-0"

4,60 X 5,10
15'-4" X 17'-0"

4,40 X 6,40
14'-8" X 21'-4"

SECOND FLOOR

3,60 X 3,30
12'-0" X 11'-0"

3,00 X 3,30
10'-0" X 11'-0"

4,80 X 2,20
16'-0" X 7'-4"

4,40 X 4,00
14'-8" X 13'-4"

DESIGN BY
©**Drummond Designs, Inc.**

PLAN HPT100291

Total: 2,129 sq. ft.
First Floor: 1,162 sq. ft.
Second Floor: 967 sq. ft.
Width: 40'-0" **Depth:** 42'-0"

This exterior is a standout with interesting rooflines and a variety of window treatments. Inside, a large corner fireplace and a cathedral ceiling highlight the living room. The kitchen easily serves the formal dining room and is open to the family room. The owners bedroom—one of three bedrooms on the second floor—boasts French doors, a walk-in closet and its own entrance to the shared bath featuring a garden tub and separate shower. This home is designed with a basement foundation.

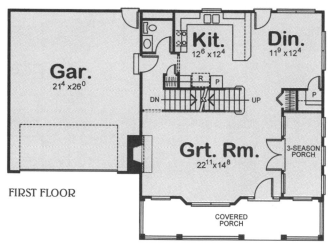

Gar.
21⁴ x 26⁰

Kit.
12⁶ x 12⁴

Din.
11⁹ x 12⁴

DN   R   P   UP   P

Grt. Rm.
22¹¹ x 14⁸

3-SEASON
PORCH

FIRST FLOOR

COVERED
PORCH

DESIGN BY
©**Design Basics, Inc.**

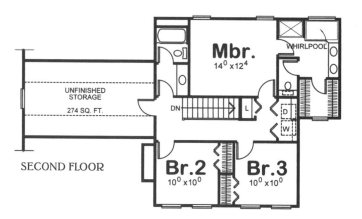

Mbr.
14⁰ x 12⁴

WHIRLPOOL

UNFINISHED
STORAGE
274 SQ. FT.

DN   L   D   W

SECOND FLOOR

Br. 2
10⁰ x 10⁰

Br. 3
10⁰ x 10⁰

L arge multi-pane windows and steeply sloping rooflines lend a calming elegance to this two-story farmhouse. Inside, the great room features a warming fireplace and a bumped-out window. French doors access the three-season porch, a great place to escape to after a busy day. The U-shaped kitchen conveniently accesses a powder room to the left and the dining area to the right. Three bedrooms are nestled on the second floor—two family bedrooms sharing a full bath and an owners suite with an oversized whirlpool tub, separate shower and twin vanity sinks. Laundry facilities sit on the second level for convenience. An unfinished storage area will protect all the family heirlooms.

PLAN HPT100292

Total: 1,650 sq. ft.
First Floor: 846 sq. ft.
Second Floor: 804 sq. ft.
Bonus Room: 274 sq. ft.
Width: 50'-0"   **Depth:** 37'-0"

PLAN HPT102003

Designed for lovers of the outdoors, this country home crafts a native creek stone and rugged lap-siding exterior. Massive stone fireplaces and rustic, high-beam ceilings set a casually elegant scene in the great room and the formal living room. An island kitchen provides comfortable work space while the wide rear porch invites outside entertaining. A separate vestibule leads to the elegant master suite with a luxurious bath and sizable walk-in closet. Upstairs, three family bedrooms share a hall that offers a balcony overlook. This home is designed with a walkout basement foundation.

Total: 3,398 sq. ft.
First Floor: 2,270 sq. ft.
Second Floor: 1,128 sq. ft.
Width: 62'-3" **Depth:** 59'-9"

FIRST FLOOR

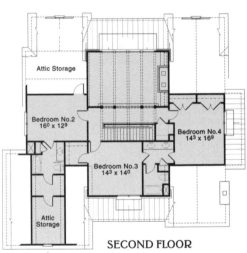

SECOND FLOOR

BASEMENT

DESIGN BY
©**Stephen Fuller, Inc.**

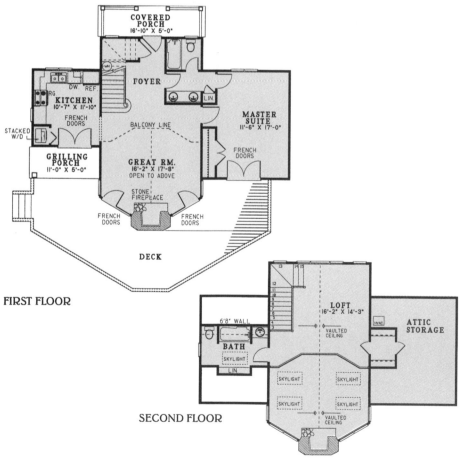

FIRST FLOOR

COVERED PORCH
16'-10" X 5'-0"

FOYER

KITCHEN
10'-7" X 11'-10"

DW. REF.

RG

FRENCH DOORS

STACKED W/D

GRILLING PORCH
11'-0" X 5'-0"

BALCONY LINE

GREAT RM.
16'-2" X 17'-8"
OPEN TO ABOVE

STONE FIREPLACE

FRENCH DOORS

FRENCH DOORS

LIN

MASTER SUITE
11'-6" X 17'-0"

FRENCH DOORS

DECK

SECOND FLOOR

6'8" WALL

BATH
SKYLIGHT

LIN

LOFT
16'-2" X 14'-3"
VAULTED CEILING

HVAC

ATTIC STORAGE

SKYLIGHT

SKYLIGHT

SKYLIGHT

SKYLIGHT

VAULTED CEILING

DESIGN BY
©**Michael E. Nelson, Nelson Design Group, LLC**

PLAN HPT100294

The front of this two-bedroom home is sweet and simple, while the rear is dedicated to fun and sun. Inside, the foyer opens to the two-story great room, where sunlight pours into the room not only from the wall of windows but also from four skylights. A large stone fireplace dominates the window wall and offers warmth on cool spring evenings. The L-shaped kitchen features French doors out to the grilling porch, perfect for numerous cookouts. On the opposite side of the home, a large owners suite awaits to pamper the homeowner. Here, a second set of French doors leads out to the deck. Upstairs, a loft offers a walk-in closet and a full bath with a skylight. Please specify crawlspace or slab foundation when ordering.

Total: 1,194 sq. ft.
First Floor: 862 sq. ft.
Second Floor: 332 sq. ft.
Width: 42'-0" **Depth:** 36'-2"

PLAN HPT100295

Special attention to exterior details and interior nuances gives this relaxed farmhouse fine distinction on any street. From the large covered porch, enter to find a roomy, well-zoned plan. A striking, central staircase separates the first-floor living area, which boasts a home office and a cathedral-ceilinged living room. The second floor includes the owners suite, two bedrooms that share a full bath, and a flexible upstairs sitting area. The owners suite contains a bath with double-bowl vanities and a walk-in closet. This home is designed with a basement foundation.

Total: 2,257 sq. ft.
First Floor: 1,274 sq. ft.
Second Floor: 983 sq. ft.
Width: 50'-0" **Depth:** 46'-0"

FIRST FLOOR

DESIGN BY
©**Drummond Designs, Inc.**

SECOND FLOOR

4,50 X 3,60
15'-0" X 12'-0"

6,20 X 7,00
20'-8" X 23'-4"

7,30 X 3,70
24'-4" X 12'-4"

3,20 X 3,60
10'-8" X 12'-0"

3,60 X 4,20
12'-0" X 14'-0"

2,60 X 3,00
8'-8" X 10'-0"

FIRST FLOOR

DESIGN BY
©**Drummond Designs, Inc.**

3,30 X 2,70
11'-0" X 9'-0"

3,60 X 5,70
12'-0" X 19'-0"

3,60 X 3,60
12'-0" X 12'-0"

3,60 X 4,20
12'-0" X 14'-0"

SECOND FLOOR

PLAN HPT100296

This charming country-traditional home provides a well-lit home office, harbored in a beautiful bay with three windows. The second-floor bay brightens the owners bath, which has a double-bowl vanity, step-up tub and dressing area. The living and dining rooms share a two-sided fireplace. The nearby kitchen contains a cooktop island and outdoor views through sliding glass doors in the breakfast area. A sizable bonus room above the garage can be developed into hobby space or a recreation room. This home is designed with a basement foundation.

Total: 1,938 sq. ft.
First Floor: 1,044 sq. ft.
Second Floor: 894 sq. ft.
Bonus Room: 228 sq. ft.
Width: 58'-0" **Depth:** 43'-6"

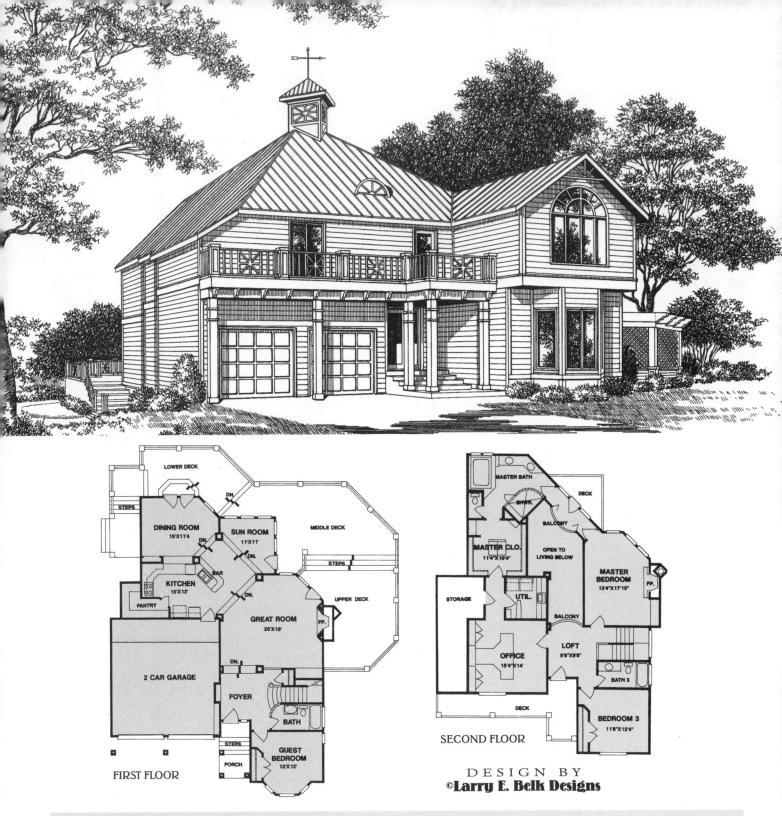

LOWER DECK

DINING ROOM
15'X11'4

SUN ROOM
11'X11'

MIDDLE DECK

DN.

DN.

STEPS

KITCHEN
15'X12'

BAR

DN.

STEPS

PANTRY

DN.

UPPER DECK

GREAT ROOM
20'X18'

FP.

2 CAR GARAGE

DN.

FOYER

BATH

FIRST FLOOR

STEPS

PORCH

GUEST
BEDROOM
12'X12'

MASTER BATH

DECK

SHWR.

BALCONY

MASTER CLO.
11'4"X10'4"

OPEN TO
LIVING BELOW

MASTER
BEDROOM
13'4"X17'10"

FP.

STORAGE

UTIL.

BALCONY

OFFICE
15'4"X14'

LOFT
9'8"X9'8"

BATH 3

DECK

BEDROOM 3
11'8"X12'4"

SECOND FLOOR

DESIGN BY
©Larry E. Belk Designs

PLAN HPT100297

Total: 2,652 sq. ft.
First Floor: 1,309 sq. ft.
Second Floor: 1,343 sq. ft.
Width: 44'-4" **Depth:** 58'-2"

— L —

Clean, contemporary lines, a unique floor plan and a metal roof with a cupola set this farmhouse apart. Remote-control transoms in the cupola open to create an airy and decidedly unique foyer. The great room, sun room, dining room and kitchen flow from one to another for casual entertaining with flair. The rear of the home is fashioned with plenty of windows overlooking the multi-level deck. A front bedroom and a bath would make a comfortable guest suite. The owners bedroom and bath upstairs are bridged by a pipe-rail balcony that also gives access to a rear deck. An additional bedroom, home office and bath complete this very special plan.

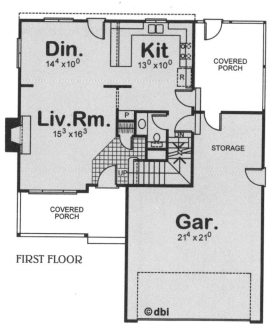

Din.
14⁴ x 10⁰

Kit
13⁰ x10⁰

COVERED PORCH

R

Liv.Rm.
15³ x16³

P

STORAGE

DN

UP

COVERED PORCH

Gar.
21⁴ x 21⁰

©dbi

FIRST FLOOR

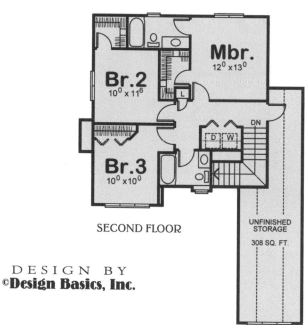

Br.2
10⁰ x 11⁶

Mbr.
12⁰ x13⁰

L

D   W

DN

Br.3
10⁰ x10⁰

SECOND FLOOR

UNFINISHED STORAGE
308 SQ. FT.

DESIGN BY
©Design Basics, Inc.

Multi-pane windows and gables set in a hipped roof lend beauty and charm to this three-bedroom home. A warming fireplace greets visitors who enter the living room from the relaxing covered porch. The adjoining dining room accesses the rear yard. A powder room is available for guests between the kitchen and the access doors to the rear covered porch and the two-car garage. Three bedrooms tucked upstairs include two family bedrooms sharing a bath, and an owners bedroom with a walk-in closet and private bath. Keep all the family treasures in the unfinished storage area.

PLAN HPT100298

Total: 1,491 sq. ft.
First Floor: 749 sq. ft.
Second Floor: 742 sq. ft.
Bonus Room: 308 sq. ft.
Width: 39'-4"   **Depth:** 48'-8"

PLAN HPT102004

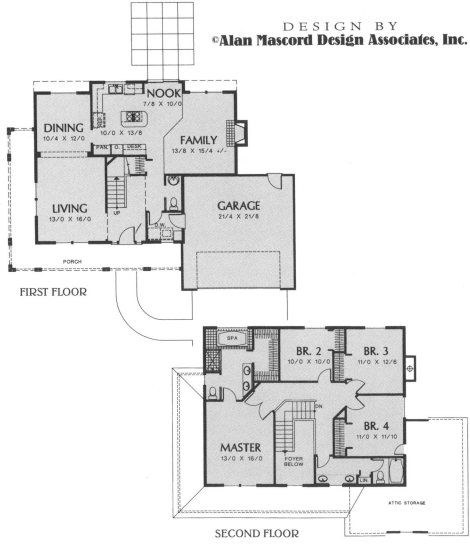

D E S I G N   B Y
©Alan Mascord Design Associates, Inc.

Cedar siding makes a beautiful difference in this two-story country plan. Its symmetrical floor plan serves the needs of family living. Main living areas radiate from the entry hall: the formal living room is to the left and connects directly to the dining room; the family room is to the right and behind the garage. An L-shaped kitchen includes an island cooktop and a casual eating area that contains sliding glass doors to a rear terrace. The bedrooms on the second floor center around the open-railed staircase. The master suite enjoys a whirlpool spa, twin lavatories and a generous walk-in closet. Family bedrooms share a full bath with double-sink vanity.

Total: 2,127 sq. ft.
First Floor: 1,037 sq. ft.
Second Floor: 1,090 sq. ft.
Width: 50'-0"   **Depth:** 40'-0"

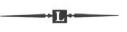

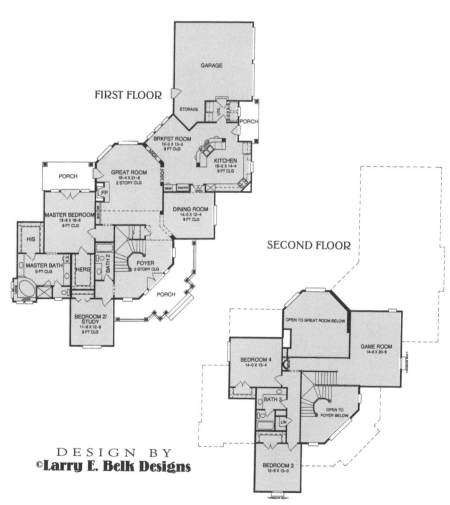

FIRST FLOOR

GARAGE

STORAGE

PORCH

UTIL.

BRKFST ROOM
12-0 X 13-0
9 FT CLG

KITCHEN
15-0 X 14-4
9 FT CLG

PORCH

GREAT ROOM
18-4 X 21-6
2 STORY CLG

FP

PANTRY
DESK

DINING ROOM
14-0 X 12-4
9 FT CLG

MASTER BEDROOM
13-8 X 16-6
9 FT CLG

HIS

MASTER BATH
9 FT CLG

HERS

BATH 2

FOYER
2 STORY CLG

PORCH

BEDROOM 2/
STUDY
11-6 X 12-6
9 FT CLG

SECOND FLOOR

OPEN TO GREAT ROOM BELOW

GAME ROOM
14-6 X 20-6

BEDROOM 4
14-0 X 13-4

BATH 3

OPEN TO
FOYER BELOW

LIN

BEDROOM 3
12-6 X 13-0

DESIGN BY
©Larry E. Belk Designs

PLAN HPT100300

Elegant angles and an abundance of space make this a most appealing design. A grand two-story foyer greets you and displays a graceful staircase. Columns define the parameters of the formal dining room and are echoed to separate the well-proportioned great room from the kitchen/breakfast room. The sumptuous owners suite is replete with luxuries ranging from His and Hers walk-in closets to a pampering bath and is secluded for privacy on the first floor. Upstairs, two family bedrooms—each with walk-in closets—share a full hall bath and access to a large game room. Plenty of storage can be found in the two-car garage. Please specify crawlspace or slab foundation when ordering.

Total: 3,325 sq. ft.
First Floor: 2,276 sq. ft.
Second Floor: 1,049 sq. ft.
Width: 66'-9" **Depth:** 89'-6"

FIRST FLOOR

BRKFST RM
13-0 X 9-0
10 FT CLG

COVERED PORCH

MASTER BEDROOM
15-4 X 15-4
10 FT CLG

FP

FAMILY ROOM
13-4 X 16-6
10 FT CLG

42" LEDGE

KITCHEN
12-6 X 13-0
10 FT CLG

PAN

LIVING ROOM
13-8 X 13-6
10 FT CLG

HERS

STOR

LIN

MASTER BATH
10 FT CLG

BATH 2

ARCH

FOYER
2 STORY
CLG

HIS

ARCH

BEDROOM 2
12-4 X 12-0
10 FT CLG

UTIL
9-0 X 7-0

DINING ROOM
13-4 X 13-0
10 FT CLG

PORCH

GARAGE

SECOND FLOOR

BEDROOM 4
13-8 X 11-6

K.S.

DRESSING

BATH 3

DRESSING

GAME ROOM
14-4 X 17-4

ATTIC

BEDROOM 3
12-4 X 12-6

OPEN TO FOYER BELOW

ATTIC/ EXPANDABLE AREA
375 FT

DESIGN BY
©Larry E. Belk Designs

PLAN HPT102005

Total: 3,041 sq. ft.
First Floor: 2,121 sq. ft.
Second Floor: 920 sq. ft.
Width: 63'-0" **Depth:** 63'-0"

A striking combination of brick and siding complements multi-pane windows and a columned entry to create a fresh face on this classic design. The two-story foyer opens to the formal living and dining rooms, set off by columned archways. Casual living space includes a spacious family area, open to the sunny breakfast room and the kitchen. The main-level master suite boasts two walk-in closets, an angled whirlpool tub, a separate shower and additional linen storage. A guest suite or family bedroom with a full bath is positioned for privacy on the opposite side of the plan. Please specify crawlspace or slab foundation when ordering.

FIRST FLOOR

Kit.
12⁰ x 11⁰

Bfst.
10⁰ x 14⁰

Hrth.
10⁰ x 14⁰

ENTERTAINMENT
CENTER

TRANSOMS

SNACK BAR

DESK

Grt. rm.
15⁸ x 17³

10'-0" CEILING

Gar.
22⁷ x 28⁰

Din.
12⁰ x 14⁰

UP

DN

Den
11³ x 13⁸

10'-0"
CLG.

COVERED
PORCH

TRANSOMS

SECOND FLOOR

Br 4
11⁸ x 12⁰

Br 2
11⁰ x 14⁰

DESK

WHIRLPOOL

10'-0"
CEILING

DN

LIN.

TRANSOMS

LINEN

Mbr.
16⁰ x 15⁴

9'-0" CEILING

Br 3
12⁰ x 12⁰

DESK

SEAT

DESIGN BY
©**Design Basics, Inc.**

Country living is evident from the covered porch and charming boxed window on this elevation. A private den with French doors and a spider-beam boxed ceiling is viewed from the entry, as well as the dining room with hutch space. An open kitchen/dinette is complete with a planning desk, pantry and snack bar. The hearth room is accented by a bayed window, entertainment center and through-fireplace. Home buyers will consider the volume great room a dynamic living space due to its comfort, bright windows and French-door access to the hearth room. Sunny windows, a boxed ceiling, two closets, a whirlpool tub, and His and Hers vanities exude luxury in the owners suite.

PLAN HPT100302

Total: 2,720 sq. ft.
First Floor: 1,426 sq. ft.
Second Floor: 1,294 sq. ft.
Width: 54'-0" **Depth:** 54'-0"

PLAN HPT100303

This great-looking traditional design features all the amenities sought after in today's home! Ceilings throughout the first floor are nine feet high except in the family room, where a thirteen-foot tray ceiling features clerestory glass. A large den opens off the foyer with a pair of French doors. Matching French doors lead to the family room and the kitchen/nook. The kitchen features a stove-top island, built-in desk and pantry. Upstairs, the owners bedroom is enhanced with a spa tub, a tiled shower and a walk-in closet. Two other generous bedrooms and a bonus room round out the second floor.

Total: 2,867 sq. ft.
First Floor: 1,665 sq. ft.
Second Floor: 1,202 sq. ft.
Bonus Room: 290 sq. ft.
Width: 60'-0" **Depth:** 45'-0"

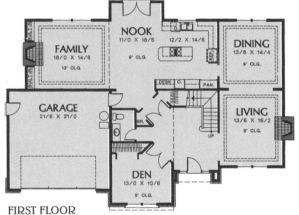

FIRST FLOOR

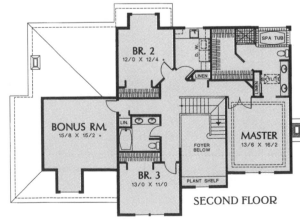

SECOND FLOOR

DESIGN BY
©Alan Mascord Design Associates, Inc.

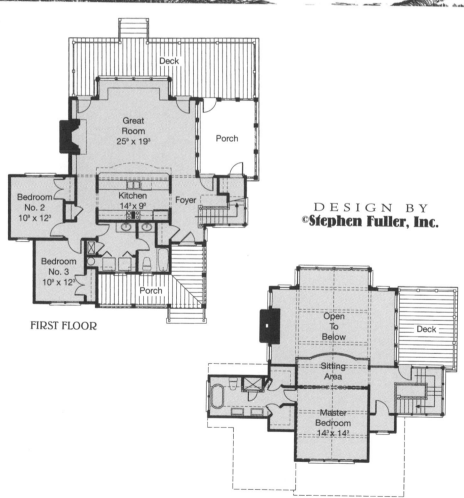

Deck

Great
Room
25⁹ x 19³

Porch

Bedroom
No. 2
10⁹ x 12³

Kitchen
14³ x 9⁹

Foyer

Bedroom
No. 3
10⁹ x 12³

Porch

FIRST FLOOR

D E S I G N   B Y
©**Stephen Fuller, Inc.**

Open
To
Below

Deck

Sitting
Area

Master
Bedroom
14³ x 14³

SECOND FLOOR

PLAN HPT100304

With horizontal siding, plentiful windows and a wraparound porch, this home is designed for comfort as well as presenting a pleasant facade. The great room is aptly named, with a fireplace, built-in seating and access to the rear deck. Make meal preparation a breeze with a galley kitchen designed for efficiency. A screened porch is available for sipping lemonade on warm summer afternoons. The first floor contains two bedrooms and a unique bath to serve family and guests. The second floor offers a private getaway with an owners suite that supplies panoramic views from its adjoining sitting area. An owners bath with His and Hers walk-in closets and a private deck complete the upstairs. This home is designed with a basement foundation.

Total: 1,939 sq. ft.
First Floor: 1,341 sq. ft.
Second Floor: 598 sq. ft.
Width: 50'-3" **Depth:** 46'-3"

PLAN HPT102006

Graceful arches and columns make a delicate complement to the brick facade of this country house. An extended foyer introduces an exciting interior plan—ten-foot ceilings throughout give a spacious feeling. A cozy fireplace will be appreciated in the great room, as will the nearby screened porch. An efficient kitchen, with cooktop-island counter and an angled sink, serves both the breakfast room and the formal dining room. The master suite, located at the rear of the plan for privacy, offers many amenities. Two family bedrooms are clustered nearby and share a full bath. Please specify crawlspace or slab foundation when ordering.

Square Footage: 2,439
Width: 81'-2" **Depth:** 67'-10"

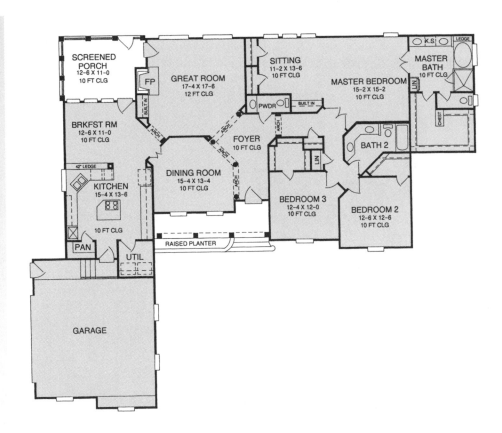

LET US SHOW YOU OUR HOME BLUEPRINT PACKAGE.

BUILDING A HOME? PLANNING A HOME?

OUR BLUEPRINT PACKAGE HAS NEARLY EVERYTHING YOU NEED TO GET THE JOB DONE RIGHT,

whether you're working on your own or with help from an architect, designer, builder or subcontractors. Each Blueprint Package is the result of many hours of work by licensed architects or professional designers.

QUALITY

Hundreds of hours of painstaking effort have gone into the development of your blueprint set. Each home has been quality-checked by professionals to insure accuracy and buildability.

VALUE

Because we sell in volume, you can buy professional quality blueprints at a fraction of their development cost. With our plans, your dream home design costs substantially less than the fees charged by architects.

SERVICE

Once you've chosen your favorite home plan, you'll receive fast, efficient service whether you choose to mail or fax your order to us or call us toll free at 1-800-521-6797. For customer service, call toll free 1-888-690-1116.

SATISFACTION

Over 50 years of service to satisfied home plan buyers provide us unparalleled experience and knowledge in producing quality blueprints.

ORDER TOLL FREE 1-800-521-6797

After you've looked over our Blueprint Package and Important Extras, call toll free on our Blueprint Hotline: 1-800-521-6797, for current pricing and availability prior to mailing the order form on page 317. We're ready and eager to serve you. For customer service, call toll free 1-888-690-1116.

Each set of blueprints is an interrelated collection of detail sheets which includes components such as floor plans, interior and exterior elevations, dimensions, cross-sections, diagrams and notations. These sheets show exactly how your house is to be built.

SETS MAY INCLUDE:

FRONTAL SHEET
This artist's sketch of the exterior of the house gives you an idea of how the house will look when built and landscaped. Large floor plans show all levels of the house and provide an overview of your new home's livability, as well as a handy reference for deciding on furniture placement.

FOUNDATION PLANS
This sheet shows the foundation layout including support walls, excavated and unexcavated areas, if any, and foundation notes. If slab construction rather than basement, the plan shows footings and details for a monolithic slab. This page, or another in the set, may include a sample plot plan for locating your house on a building site.

DETAILED FLOOR PLANS
These plans show the layout of each floor of the house. Rooms and interior spaces are carefully dimensioned and keys are given for cross-section details provided later in the plans. The positions of electrical outlets and switches are shown.

HOUSE CROSS-SECTIONS
Large-scale views show sections or cut-aways of the foundation, interior walls, exterior walls, floors, stairways and roof details. Additional cross-sections may show important changes in floor, ceiling or roof heights or the relationship of one level to another. Extremely valuable for construction, these sections show exactly how the various parts of the house fit together.

INTERIOR ELEVATIONS
Many of our drawings show the design and placement of kitchen and bathroom cabinets, laundry areas, fireplaces, bookcases and other built-ins. Little "extras," such as mantelpiece and wainscoting drawings, plus molding sections, provide details that give your home that custom touch.

EXTERIOR ELEVATIONS
These drawings show the front, rear and sides of your house and give necessary notes on exterior materials and finishes. Particular attention is given to cornice detail, brick and stone accents or other finish items that make your home unique.

IMPORTANT EXTRAS TO DO THE JOB RIGHT!

INTRODUCING EIGHT IMPORTANT

PLANNING AND CONSTRUCTION AIDS DEVELOPED BY

OUR PROFESSIONALS TO HELP YOU SUCCEED IN YOUR HOME-BUILDING PROJECT

MATERIALS LIST

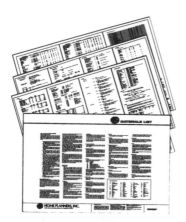

(Note: Because of the diversity of local building codes, our Materials List does not include mechanical materials.)

For many of the designs in our portfolio, we offer a customized materials take-off that is invaluable in planning and estimating the cost of your new home. This Materials List outlines the quantity, type and size of materials needed to build your house (with the exception of mechanical system items). Included are framing lumber, windows and doors, kitchen and bath cabinetry, rough and finish hardware, and much more. This handy list helps you or your builder cost out materials and serves as a reference sheet when you're compiling bids. A Materials List cannot be ordered before blueprints are ordered.

SPECIFICATION OUTLINE

This valuable 16-page document is critical to building your house correctly. Designed to be filled in by you or your builder, this book lists 166 stages or items crucial to the building process. It provides a comprehensive review of the construction process and helps in choosing materials. When combined with the blueprints, a signed contract, and a schedule, it becomes a legal document and record for the building of your home.

QUOTE ONE®

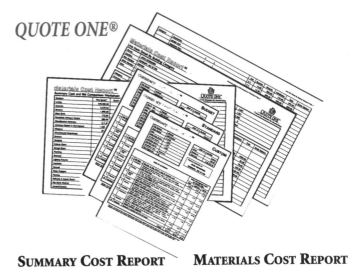

SUMMARY COST REPORT   **MATERIALS COST REPORT**

A product for estimating the cost of building select designs, the Quote One® system is available in two separate stages: The Summary Cost Report and the Materials Cost Report.

The **Summary Cost Report** is the first stage in the package and shows the total cost per square foot for your chosen home in your zip-code area and then breaks that cost down into various categories showing the costs for building materials, labor and installation. The report includes three grades: Budget, Standard and Custom. These reports allow you to evaluate your building budget and compare the costs of building a variety of homes in your area.

Make even more informed decisions about your home-building project with the second phase of our package, our **Materials Cost Report.** This tool is invaluable in planning and estimating the cost of your new home. The material and installation (labor and equipment) cost is shown for each of over 1,000 line items provided in the Materials List (Standard grade), which is included when you purchase this estimating tool. It allows you to determine building costs for your specific zip-code area and for your chosen home design. Space is allowed for additional estimates from contractors and subcontractors, such as for mechanical materials, which are not included in our packages. This invaluable tool includes a Materials List. A Materials Cost Report cannot be ordered before blueprints are ordered. Call for details. In addition, ask about our Home Planners Estimating Package.

If you are interested in a plan that is not indicated as Quote One®, please call and ask our sales reps. They will be happy to verify the status for you. To order these invaluable reports, use the order form on page 317 or call 1-800-521-6797 for availability.

CONSTRUCTION INFORMATION

IF YOU WANT TO KNOW MORE ABOUT TECHNIQUES— and deal more confidently with subcontractors — we offer these useful sheets. Each set is an excellent tool that will add to your understanding of these technical subjects. These helpful details provide general construction information and are not specific to any single plan.

PLUMBING

The Blueprint Package includes locations for all the plumbing fixtures, including sinks, lavatories, tubs, showers, toilets, laundry trays and water heaters. However, if you want to know more about the complete plumbing system, these Plumbing Details will prove very useful. Prepared to meet requirements of the National Plumbing Code, these fact-filled sheets give general information on pipe schedules, fittings, sump-pump details, water-softener hookups, septic system details and much more. Sheets also include a glossary of terms.

ELECTRICAL

The locations for every electrical switch, plug and outlet are shown in your Blueprint Package. However, these Electrical Details go further to take the mystery out of household electrical systems. Prepared to meet requirements of the National Electrical Code, these comprehensive drawings come packed with helpful information, including wire sizing, switch-installation schematics, cable-routing details, appliance wattage, doorbell hook-ups, typical service panel circuitry and much more. A glossary of terms is also included.

CONSTRUCTION

The Blueprint Package contains information an experienced builder needs to construct a particular house. However, it doesn't show all the ways that houses can be built, nor does it explain alternate construction methods. To help you understand how your house will be built—and offer additional techniques—this set of Construction Details depicts the materials and methods used to build foundations, fireplaces, walls, floors and roofs. Where appropriate, the drawings show acceptable alternatives.

MECHANICAL

These Mechanical Details contain fundamental principles and useful data that will help you make informed decisions and communicate with subcontractors about heating and cooling systems. Drawings contain instructions and samples that allow you to make simple load calculations, and preliminary sizing and costing analysis. Covered are the most commonly used systems from heat pumps to solar fuel systems. The package is filled with illustrations and diagrams to help you visualize components and how they relate to one another.

PLAN-A-HOME®

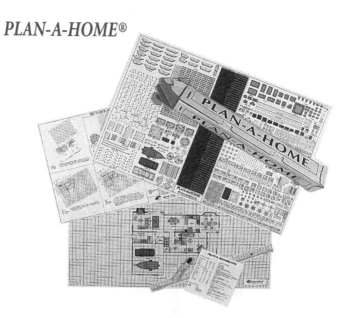

PLAN-A-HOME® is an easy-to-use tool that helps you design a new home, arrange furniture in a new or existing home, or plan a remodeling project. Each package contains:

✓ **More than 700 reusable peel-off planning symbols** on a self-stick vinyl sheet, including walls, windows, doors, all types of furniture, kitchen components, bath fixtures and many more.

✓ **A reusable, transparent, ¼" scale planning grid** that matches the scale of actual working drawings (¼" equals one foot). This grid provides the basis for house layouts of up to 140' x 92'.

✓ **Tracing paper** and a protective sheet for copying or transferring your completed plan.

✓ **A felt-tip pen**, with water-soluble ink that wipes away quickly.

PLAN-A-HOME® lets you lay out areas as large as a 7,500 square foot, six-bedroom, seven-bath house.

To Order, Call Toll Free
1-800-521-6797

After you've looked over our Blueprint Package and Important Extras on these pages, call toll free on our Blueprint Hotline: 1-800-521-6797 for current pricing and availability prior to mailing the order form on page 317. We're ready and eager to serve you. For customer service, call toll free 1-888-690-1116.

THE DECK BLUEPRINT PACKAGE

Many of the homes in this book can be enhanced with a professionally designed Home Planners Deck Plan. Those home plans highlighted with a **D** have a matching Deck Plan, sold separately, which includes a Deck Plan Frontal Sheet, Deck Framing and Floor Plans, Deck Elevations and a Deck Materials List. A Standard Deck Details Package, also available, provides all the how-to information necessary for building *any* deck. Our Complete Deck Building Package contains one set of Custom Deck Plans of your choice, plus one set of Standard Deck Building Details, all for one low price. Our plans and details are carefully prepared in an easy-to-understand format that will guide you through every stage of your deck-building project. This page shows a sample of Deck layouts to match your favorite house. See page 313 for prices and ordering information.

THE LANDSCAPE BLUEPRINT PACKAGE

For the homes marked with an **L** in this book, Home Planners has created a front-yard Landscape Plan that matches or is complementary in design to the house plan. These comprehensive blueprint packages include a Frontal Sheet, Plan View, Regionalized Plant & Materials List, a sheet on Planting and Maintaining Your Landscape, Zone Maps and Plant Size and Description Guide. These plans will help you achieve professional results, adding value and enjoyment to your property for years to come. Each set of blueprints is a full 18" x 24" in size with clear, complete instructions and easy-to-read type. A sample Landscape Plan is shown below.

CONTEMPORARY LEISURE DECK
Deck ODA021

CAPE COD COTTAGE
Landscape OLA003

Regional Order Map

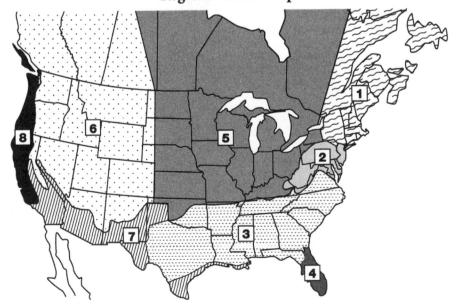

Most Landscape Plans are available with a Plant & Materials List adapted by horticultural experts to 8 different regions of the country. Please specify the Geographic Region when ordering your plan. See pages 313–315 for prices, ordering information and regional availability.

Region	1	Northeast
Region	2	Mid-Atlantic
Region	3	Deep South
Region	4	Florida & Gulf Coast
Region	5	Midwest
Region	6	Rocky Mountains
Region	7	Southern California & Desert Southwest
Region	8	Northern California & Pacific Northwest

HOUSE BLUEPRINT PRICE SCHEDULE

Prices guaranteed through December 31, 2002

TIERS	1-SET STUDY PACKAGE	4-SET BUILDING PACKAGE	8-SET BUILDING PACKAGE	1-SET REPRODUCIBLE
P1	$20	$50	$90	$140
P2	$40	$70	$110	$160
P3	$70	$100	$140	$190
P4	$100	$130	$170	$220
P5	$140	$170	$210	$270
P6	$180	$210	$250	$310
A1	$440	$480	$520	$660
A2	$480	$520	$560	$720
A3	$520	$560	$600	$780
A4	$565	$605	$645	$850
C1	$610	$655	$700	$915
C2	$655	$700	$745	$980
C3	$700	$745	$790	$1050
C4	$750	$795	$840	$1125
L1	$825	$875	$925	$1240
L2	$900	$950	$1000	$1350
L3	$1000	$1095	$1100	$1500
L4	$1100	$1150	$1200	$1650

OPTIONS FOR PLANS IN TIERS A1–L4

Additional Identical Blueprints
in same order for "A1–L4" price plans ....$50 per set
Reverse Blueprints (mirror image)
with 4- or 8-set order for "A1–L4" plans ....$50 fee per order
Specification Outlines ....$10 each
Materials Lists for "A1–C3" plans ....$60 each
Materials Lists for "C4–L4" plans...$70 each

OPTIONS FOR PLANS IN TIERS P1–P6

Additional Identical Blueprints
in same order for "P1–P6" price plans..$10 per set
Reverse Blueprints (mirror image) for "P1–P6" price plans ....$10 per set
1 Set of Deck Construction Details ....$14.95 each
Deck Construction Package ....**add $10 to Building Package price**
(includes 1 set of "P1–P6" plans, plus 1 set Standard Deck Construction Details)
1 Set of Gazebo Construction Details ....$14.95 each
Gazebo Construction Package ....**add $10 to Building Package price**
(includes 1 set of "P1–P6" plans, plus 1 set Standard Gazebo Construction Details)

IMPORTANT NOTES

• The 1-set study package is marked "not for construction."
• Prices for 4- or 8-set Building Packages honored only at time of original order.
• Some foundations carry a $225 surcharge.
• Right-reading reverse blueprints, if available, will incur a $165 surcharge.
• Additional identical blueprints may be purchased within 60 days of original order.

TO USE THE INDEX, refer to the design number listed in numerical order (a helpful page reference is also given). Note the price tier and refer to the House Blueprint Price Schedule above for the cost of one, four or eight sets of blueprints or the cost of a reproducible drawing. Additional prices are shown for identical and reverse blueprint sets, as well as a very useful Materials List for some of the plans. Also note in the Plan Index, those plans that have Deck Plans or Landscape Plans. Refer to the schedules above for prices of these plans. The letter "Y" identifies plans that are part of our Quote One® estimating service and those that offer Materials Lists. See page 310 for more information.

TO ORDER, Call toll free 1-800-521-6797 or 520-297-8200 for current pricing and availability prior to mailing the order form on page 317. FAX: 1-800-224-6699 or 520-544-3086.

PLAN INDEX

DESIGN	PRICE	PAGE	MATERIALS LIST	QUOTE ONE®	DECK	DECK PRICE	LANDSCAPE	LANDSCAPE PRICE	REGIONS
HPT100001	C2	4	Y	Y	ODA015	P2	OLA008	P4	1234568
HPT100002	C1	5	Y	Y	ODA001	P2	OLA001	P3	123568
HPT100003	C1	6	Y						
HPT100004	A4	7	Y	Y					
HPT100005	C1	8	Y						
HPT100006	C4	9							
HPT100007	A4	10	Y	Y					
HPT100008	C2	11	Y						
HPT100009	C1	12	Y						
HPT100010	C3	13	Y						
HPT100011	A4	14	Y						
HPT100012	C4	15	Y	Y					
HPT100013	C4	16							
HPT100014	C4	17							
HPT100015	C3	18	Y	Y					
HPT100016	C3	19	Y	Y					
HPT100017	A3	20	Y	Y					
HPT100018	A4	21							
HPT100019	C1	22							
HPT100020	A3	23	Y	Y					
HPT100021	A3	24	Y	Y					
HPT100022	A3	25							
HPT100023	A3	26	Y						
HPT100024	C3	27							
HPT100025	C1	28							
HPT100026	A3	29	Y	Y					
HPT100027	A3	30							
HPT100028	A4	31	Y	Y	ODA016	P2	OLA093	P3	12345678
HPT100029	A4	32	Y	Y	ODA013	P2	OLA001	P3	123568
HPT100030	C1	33							
HPT100031	C2	34	Y	Y	ODA018	P3	OLA006	P3	123568
HPT100032	C2	35	Y	Y					
HPT100033	A3	36	Y						
HPT100034	A4	37	Y						
HPT100035	C1	38	Y						
HPT100036	C2	39	Y	Y	ODA001	P2	OLA039	P3	3478
HPT100037	C2	40	Y	Y					
HPT100038	C3	41	Y	Y			OLA010	P3	1234568
HPT100039	A3	42	Y						
HPT100040	L1	43							
HPT100041	C3	44							
HPT100042	C1	45	Y	Y					
HPT100043	C4	46							
HPT100044	C3	47	Y						
HPT100045	A4	48	Y						
HPT100046	A4	49	Y				OLA004	P3	123568
HPT100047	A4	50	Y						
HPT100048	A3	51	Y						
HPT100049	A4	52							
HPT100050	A4	53	Y	Y			OLA008	P4	1234568
HPT100051	C1	54							
HPT100052	A4	55	Y						
HPT100053	A4	56	Y						
HPT100054	C2	57	Y						
HPT100055	A3	58	Y	Y					
HPT100056	C1	59	Y						
HPT100057	A4	60	Y						
HPT100058	A3	61	Y						
HPT100059	C1	62	Y						
HPT100060	A4	63	Y						
HPT100061	C3	64							

BEFORE FILLING OUT THE ORDER FORM, PLEASE CALL US ON OUR TOLL-FREE BLUEPRINT HOTLINE, YOU MAY WANT TO LEARN MORE ABOUT OUR SERVICES AND PRODUCTS. HERE'S SOME INFORMATION YOU WILL FIND HELPFUL.

OUR EXCHANGE POLICY

With the exception of reproducible plan orders, we will exchange your entire first order for an equal or greater number of blueprints within our plan collection within 90 days of the original order. The entire content of your original order must be returned before an exchange will be processed. Please call our customer service department for your return authorization number and shipping instructions. If the returned blueprints look used, redlined or copied, we will not honor your exchange. Fees for exchanging your blueprints are as follows: 20% of the amount of the original order...plus the difference in cost if exchanging for a design in a higher price bracket or less the difference in cost if exchanging for a design in a lower price bracket. **(Reproducible blueprints are not exchangeable or refundable.)** Please call for current postage and handling prices. Shipping and handling charges are not refundable.

ABOUT REVERSE BLUEPRINTS

Although lettering and dimensions will appear backward, reverses will be a useful aid if you decide to flop the plan. See Price Schedule and Plans Index for pricing.

REVISING, MODIFYING AND CUSTOMIZING PLANS

Like many homeowners who buy these plans, you and your builder, architect or engineer may want to make changes to them. We recommend purchase of a reproducible plan for any changes made by your builder, licensed architect or engineer. As set forth below, we cannot assume any responsibility for blueprints which have been changed, whether by you, your builder or by professionals selected by you or referred to you by us, because such individuals are outside our supervision and control.

ARCHITECTURAL AND ENGINEERING SEALS

Some cities and states are now requiring that a licensed architect or engineer review and "seal" a blueprint, or officially approve it, prior to construction due to concerns over energy costs, safety and other factors. Prior to application for a building permit or the start of actual construction, we strongly advise that you consult your local building official who can tell you if such a review is required.

ABOUT THE DESIGNS

The architects and designers whose work appears in this publication are among America's leading residential designers. Each plan was designed to meet the requirements of a nationally recognized model building code in effect at the time and place the plan was drawn. Because national building codes change from time to time, plans may not comply with any such code at the time they are sold to a customer. In addition, building officials may not accept these plans as final construction documents of record as the plans may need to be modified and additional drawings and details added to suit local conditions and requirements. We strongly advise that purchasers consult a licensed architect or engineer, and their local building official, before starting any construction related to these plans.

LOCAL BUILDING CODES AND ZONING REQUIREMENTS

At the time of creation, our plans are drawn to specifications published by the Building Officials and Code Administrators (BOCA) International, Inc.; the Southern Building Code Congress (SBCCI) International, Inc.; the International Conference of Building Officials (ICBO); or the Council of American Building Officials (CABO). Our plans are designed to meet or exceed national building standards. Because of the great differences in geography and climate throughout the United States and Canada, each state, county and municipality has its own building codes, zone requirements, ordinances and building regulations. Your plan may need to be modified to comply with local requirements regarding snow loads, energy codes, soil and seismic conditions and a wide range of other matters. In addition, you may need to obtain permits or inspections from local governments before and in the course of construction. Prior to using blueprints ordered from us, we strongly advise that you consult a licensed architect or engineer—and speak with your local building official—before applying for any permit or beginning construction. We authorize the use of our blueprints on the express condition that you strictly comply with all local building codes, zoning requirements and other applicable laws, regulations, ordinances and requirements. Notice: Plans for homes to be built in Nevada must be re-drawn by a Nevada-registered professional. Consult your building official for more information on this subject.

Have You Seen Our Newest Designs?

At least 50 of our latest creations are featured in each edition of our New Design Portfolio. You may have received a copy with your latest purchase by mail. If not, or if you purchased this book from a local retailer, just return the coupon below for your FREE copy. Make sure you consider the very latest of what Home Planners has to offer.

Yes! Please send my FREE copy of your latest New Design Portfolio.

Offer good to U.S. shipping address only.

Name _____

Address_____

City _____ State_____ Zip _____

HOME PLANNERS, LLC
Wholly owned by Hanley-Wood, LLC
3275 WEST INA ROAD, SUITE 110 • TUCSON, ARIZONA 85741

Order Form Key
HPT102

DISCLAIMER

The designers we work with have put substantial care and effort into the creation of their blueprints. However, because they cannot provide on-site consultation, supervision and control over actual construction, and because of the great variance in local building requirements, building practices and soil, seismic, weather and other conditions, WE CANNOT MAKE ANY WARRANTY, EXPRESS OR IMPLIED, WITH RESPECT TO THE CONTENT OR USE OF THE BLUEPRINTS, INCLUDING BUT NOT LIMITED TO ANY WARRANTY OF MERCHANTABILITY OR OF FITNESS FOR A PARTICULAR PURPOSE. ITEMS, PRICES, TERMS AND CONDITIONS ARE SUBJECT TO CHANGE WITHOUT NOTICE. REPRODUCIBLE PLAN ORDERS MAY REQUIRE A CUSTOMER'S SIGNED RELEASE BEFORE SHIPPING.

TERMS AND CONDITIONS

These designs are protected under the terms of United States Copyright Law and may not be copied or reproduced in any way, by any means, unless you have purchased Reproducibles which clearly indicate your right to copy or reproduce. We authorize the use of your chosen design as an aid in the construction of one single family home only. You may not use this design to build a second or multiple dwellings without purchasing another blueprint or blueprints or paying additional design fees.

HOW MANY BLUEPRINTS DO YOU NEED?

Although a standard building package may satisfy many states, cities and counties, some plans may require certain changes. For your convenience, we have developed a Reproducible plan which allows a local professional to modify and make up to 10 copies of your revised plan. As our plans are all copyright protected, with your purchase of the Reproducible, we will supply you with a Copyright release letter. The number of copies you may need, 1 for owner; 3 for builder; 2 for local building department and 1-3 sets for your mortgage lender.

ORDER TOLL FREE!
For information about any of our services or to order call

1-800-521-6797
OR **520-297-8200**
Browse our website:
www.eplans.com

BLUEPRINTS ARE NOT REFUNDABLE EXCHANGES ONLY

For Customer Service,
CALL TOLL FREE **1-888-690-1116.**

HOME PLANNERS, LLC wholly owned by Hanley-Wood, LLC
3275 WEST INA ROAD, SUITE 110 • TUCSON, ARIZONA • 85741

THE BASIC BLUEPRINT PACKAGE

Rush me the following (please refer to the Plans Index and Price Schedule in this section):

____ Set(s) of blueprints, plan number(s) _____ indicate foundation type _____ $_____
____ Set(s) of reproducibles, plan number(s) _____ indicate foundation type _____ $_____
____ Additional identical blueprints (standard or reverse) in same order @ $50 per set. $_____
____ Reverse blueprints @ $50 fee per order. Right-reading reverse @ $165 surcharge $_____

IMPORTANT EXTRAS

Rush me the following:

____ Materials List: $60 (Must be purchased with Blueprint set.) Add $10 for Schedule C4–L4 plans. $_____
____ **Quote One®** Summary Cost Report @ $29.95 for one, $14.95 for each additional,
for plans _____ $_____
Building location: City _____ Zip Code _____
____ **Quote One®** Materials Cost Report @ $120 Schedules P1–C3; $130 Schedules C4–L4,
for plan _____ (Must be purchased with Blueprints set.) $_____
Building location: City _____ Zip Code _____
____ Specification Outlines @ $10 each. $_____
____ Detail Sets @ $14.95 each; any two $22.95; any three $29.95; all four for $39.95 (save $19.85). $_____
____ ❑ Plumbing ❑ Electrical ❑ Construction ❑ Mechanical
____ Plan-A-Home® @ $29.95 each. $_____

DECK BLUEPRINTS

(Please refer to the Plans Index and Price Schedule in this section)

____ Set(s) of Deck Plan _____.
____ Additional identical blueprints in same order @ $10 per set. $_____
____ Reverse blueprints @ $10 fee per order. $_____
____ Set of Standard Deck Details @ $14.95 per set. $_____
____ Set of Complete Deck Construction Package (Best Buy!) Add $10 to Building Package
Includes Custom Deck Plan _____ Plus Standard Deck Details

LANDSCAPE BLUEPRINTS

(Please refer to the Plans Index and Price Schedule in this section)

____ Set(s) of Landscape Plan _____.
____ Additional identical blueprints in same order @ $10 per set. $_____
Reverse blueprints @ $10 fee per order. $_____

Please indicate the appropriate region of the country for Plant & Material List.
(See map on page 312): Region _____

POSTAGE AND HANDLING	1–3 sets	4+ sets
Signature is required for all deliveries. **DELIVERY** No COD's (Requires street address—No P.O. Boxes)		
•Regular Service (Allow 7–10 business days delivery)	❑ $20.00	❑ $25.00
•Priority (Allow 4–5 business days delivery)	❑ $25.00	❑ $35.00
•Express (Allow 3 business days delivery)	❑ $35.00	❑ $45.00
OVERSEAS DELIVERY	fax, phone or mail for quote	

Note: All delivery times are from date Blueprint Package is shipped.

POSTAGE (From box above) $_____
SUBTOTAL $_____
SALES TAX (AZ & MI residents, please add appropriate state and local sales tax.) $_____
TOTAL (Subtotal and tax) $_____

YOUR ADDRESS (please print legibly)

Name _____
Street _____
City _____ State _____ Zip _____
Daytime telephone number (required) (_____) _____

FOR CREDIT CARD ORDERS ONLY

Credit card number _____ Exp. Date: (M/Y) _____
Check one ❑ Visa ❑ MasterCard ❑ Discover Card ❑ American Express

Order Form Key

Signature (required) _____

| HPT102 |

Please check appropriate box: ❑ Licensed Builder-Contractor ❑ Homeowner

ORDER TOLL FREE!
1-800-521-6797 or 520-297-8200

BY FAX: Copy the order form above and send it on our FAXLINE: 1-800-224-6699 OR 1-520-544-3086

HOME PLANNERS WANTS YOUR BUILDING EXPERIENCE TO BE AS PLEASANT AND TROUBLE-FREE AS POSSIBLE.

That's why we've expanded our library of Do-It-Yourself titles to help you along. In addition to our beautiful plans books, we've added books to guide you through specific projects as well as the construction process. In fact, these are titles that will be as useful after your dream home is built as they are right now.

BIGGEST & BEST

1001 of our best-selling plans in one volume. 1,074 to 7,275 square feet. 704 pgs $12.95 1K1

ONE-STORY

450 designs for all lifestyles. 800 to 4,900 square feet. 384 pgs $9.95 OS

MORE ONE-STORY

475 superb one-level plans from 800 to 5,000 square feet. 448 pgs $9.95 MOS

TWO-STORY

443 designs for one-and-a-half and two stories. 1,500 to 6,000 square feet. 448 pgs $9.95 TS

VACATION

465 designs for recreation, retirement and leisure. 448 pgs $9.95 VSH

HILLSIDE

208 designs for split-levels, bi-levels, multi-levels and walkouts. 224 pgs $9.95 HH

FARMHOUSE

200 country designs from classic to contemporary by 7 winning designers. 224 pgs $8.95 FH

COUNTRY HOUSES

208 unique home plans that combine traditional style and modern livability. 224 pgs $9.95 CN

BUDGET-SMART

200 efficient plans from 7 top designers, that you can really afford to build! 224 pgs $8.95 BS

BARRIER FREE

Over 1,700 products and 51 plans for accessible living. 128 pgs $15.95 UH

ENCYCLOPEDIA

500 exceptional plans for all styles and budgets—the best book of its kind! 528 pgs $9.95 ENC

ENCYCLOPEDIA II

500 completely new plans. Spacious and stylish designs for every budget and taste. 352 pgs $9.95 E2

AFFORDABLE

Completely revised and updated, featuring 300 designs for modest budgets. 256 pgs $9.95 AF

VICTORIAN

NEW! 210 striking Victorian and Farmhouse designs from today's top designers. 224 pgs $15.95 VDH2

ESTATE

Dream big! Twenty-one designers showcase their biggest and best plans. 208 pgs $15.95 EDH

LUXURY

170 lavish designs, over 50% brand-new plans added to a most elegant collection. 192 pgs $14.95 LD2

EUROPEAN STYLES

200 homes with a unique flair of the Old World. 224 pgs $15.95 EURO

COUNTRY CLASSICS

Donald Gardner's 101 best Country and Traditional home plans. 192 pgs $17.95 DAG

WILLIAM POOLE

70 romantic house plans that capture the classic tradition of home design. 160 pgs $17.95 WEP

TRADITIONAL

85 timeless designs from the Design Traditions Library. 160 pgs $17.95 TRA

COTTAGES

25 fresh new designs that are as warm as a tropical breeze. A blend of the best aspects of many coastal styles. 64 pgs. $19.95 CTG

CLASSIC

Timeless, elegant designs that always feel like home. Gorgeous plans that are flexible and up-to-date as their occupants. 240 pgs. $9.95 CS

CONTEMPORARY

The most complete and imaginative collection of contemporary designs available anywhere. 240 pgs. $9.95 CM

EASY-LIVING

200 efficient and sophisticated plans that are small in size, but big on livability. 224 pgs $8.95 EL

SOUTHERN

207 homes rich in Southern styling and comfort. 240 pgs $8.95 SH

SOUTHWESTERN

138 designs that capture the spirit of the Southwest. 144 pgs $10.95 SW

WESTERN

215 designs that capture the spirit and diversity of the Western lifestyle. 208 pgs $9.95 WH

NEIGHBORHOOD

170 designs with the feel of main street America. 192 pgs $12.95 TND

CRAFTSMAN

170 Home plans in the Craftsman and Bungalow style. 192 pgs $12.95 CC

COLONIAL HOUSES

181 Classic early American designs. 208 pgs $9.95 COL

DUPLEX & TOWNHOMES

Over 50 designs for multi-family living. 64 pgs $9.95 DTP

WATERFRONT

200 designs perfect for your waterside wonderland. 208 pgs $10.95 WF

WINDOWS

33 Discover the power of windows with over 160 designs featuring Pella's best. 192 pgs $9.95 WIN

STREET OF DREAMS

34 Over 300 photos showcase 54 prestigious homes. 256 pgs $19.95 SOD

MOVE-UP

35 200 stylish designs for today's growing families from 9 hot designers. 224 pgs $8.95 MU

OUTDOOR

36 74 easy-to-build designs, lets you create and build your own backyard oasis. 128 pgs $7.95 YG

GARAGES

37 101 multi-use garages and outdoor structures to enhance any home. 96 pgs $7.95 GG

DECKS

38 25 outstanding single-, double- and multi-level decks you can build. 112 pgs $7.95 DP

HOME BUILDING

39 Everything you need to know to work with contractors and subcontractors. 212 pgs $14.95 HBP

BOOK & CD-ROM

40 Both the Home Planners Gold book and matching Windows™ CD-ROM with 3D floorplans. $24.95 HPGC Book only $12.95 HPG

LANDSCAPE DESIGNS

SOFTWARE

41 Home design made easy! View designs in 3D, take a virtual reality tour, add decorating details and more. $59.95 PLANSUITE

EASY-CARE

42 41 special landscapes designed for beauty and low maintenance. 160 pgs $14.95 ECL

FRONT & BACK

43 The first book of do-it-yourself landscapes. 40 front, 15 backyards. 208 pgs $14.95 HL

BACKYARDS

44 40 designs focused solely on creating your own specially themed backyard oasis. 160 pgs $14.95 BYL

BUYER'S GUIDE

45 A comprehensive look at 2700 products for all aspects of landscaping & gardening. 128 pgs $19.95 LPBG

FRAMING

46 For those who want to take a more hands-on approach to their dream. 319 pgs $21.95 SRF

BASIC WIRING

47 A straightforward guide to one of the most misunderstood systems in the home. 160 pgs $12.95 CBW

TILE

48 Every kind of tile for every kind of application. Includes tips on use, installation and repair. 176 pgs $12.95 CWT

BATHROOMS

49 An innovative guide to organizing, remodeling and decorating your bathroom. 96 pgs $10.95 CDB

KITCHENS

50 An imaginative guide to designing the perfect kitchen. Chock full of bright ideas to make your job easier. 176 pgs $16.95 CKI

HOUSE CONTRACTING

51 Everything you need to know to act as your own general contractor, and save up to 25% off building costs. 134 pgs $14.95 SBC

VISUAL HANDBOOK

52 A plain-talk guide to the construction process; financing to final walk-through, this book covers it all. 498 pgs $19.95 RVH

ROOFING

53 Information on the latest tools, materials and techniques for roof installation or repair. 80 pgs $7.95 CGR

WINDOWS & DOORS

54 Installation techniques and tips that make your project easier and more professional looking. 80 pgs $7.95 CGD

PATIOS & WALKS
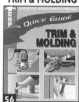
55 Clear step-by-step instructions take you from the basic design stages to the finished project. 80 pgs $7.95 CGW

TRIM & MOLDING

56 Step-by-step instructions for installing baseboards, window and door casings and more. 80 pgs $7.95 CGT

Additional Books Order Form

To order your books, just check the box of the book numbered below and complete the coupon. We will process your order and ship it from our office within two business days. Send coupon and check (in U.S. funds).

YES! Please send me the books I've indicated:

❑ 1:IKI $12.95	❑ 20:TRA $17.95	❑ 39:HBP $14.95
❑ 2:OS $9.95	❑ 21:CTG $19.95	❑ 40:HPG $12.95
❑ 3:MOS $9.95	❑ 22:CS $9.95	❑ 40:HPGC $24.95
❑ 4:TS $9.95	❑ 23:CM $9.95	❑ 41:PLANSUITE ..$59.95
❑ 5:VSH $9.95	❑ 24:EL $8.95	❑ 42:ECL $14.95
❑ 6:HH $9.95	❑ 25:SH $8.95	❑ 43:HL $14.95
❑ 7:FH $8.95	❑ 26:SW $10.95	❑ 44:BYL $14.95
❑ 8:CN $9.95	❑ 27:WH $9.95	❑ 45:LPBG $19.95
❑ 9:BS $8.95	❑ 28:TND $12.95	❑ 46:SRF $21.95
❑ 10:UH $15.95	❑ 29:CC $12.95	❑ 47:CBW $12.95
❑ 11:ENC $9.95	❑ 30:COL $9.95	❑ 48:CWT $12.95
❑ 12:E2 ....$9.95	❑ 31:DTP $9.95	❑ 49:CDB $10.95
❑ 13:AF $9.95	❑ 32:WF $10.95	❑ 50:CKI $16.95
❑ 14:VDH2 ....$15.95	❑ 33:WIN $9.95	❑ 51:SBC $14.95
❑ 15:EDH $15.95	❑ 34:SOD $19.95	❑ 52:RVH $19.95
❑ 16:LD2 ....$14.95	❑ 35:MU $8.95	❑ 53:CGR $7.95
❑ 17:EURO $15.95	❑ 36:YG $7.95	❑ 54:CGD $7.95
❑ 18:DAG $17.95	❑ 37:GG $7.95	❑ 55:CGW $7.95
❑ 19:WEP $17.95	❑ 38:DP $7.95	❑ 56:CGT $7.95

Canadian Customers Order Toll Free 1-877-223-6389

(Please print)

Additional Books Subtotal	$_____
ADD Postage and Handling (allow 4–6 weeks for delivery)	$ 4.00
Sales Tax: (AZ & MI residents, add state and local sales tax.)	$_____
YOUR TOTAL (Subtotal, Postage/Handling, Tax)	$_____

YOUR ADDRESS (PLEASE PRINT)

Name _____

Street _____

City _____ State _____ Zip _____

Phone (_____) _____—_____

YOUR PAYMENT

Check one: ❑ Check ❑ Visa ❑ MasterCard ❑ Discover ❑ American Express
Required credit card information:

Credit Card Number _____

Expiration Date (Month/Year) _____ / _____

Signature Required _____

Home Planners, LLC
Wholly owned by Hanley-Wood, LLC
® 3275 W. Ina Road, Suite 110, Dept. BK, Tucson, AZ 85741

HPT102

About the Designers

AHMANN DESIGN, INC.
Ahmann Design is a residential design firm specializing in custom residential, stock plan sales, and color rendering. Recognized several times as a finalist in Professional Builder Magazine's "Best of American Living" contest, Ahmann Design, Inc. continues to grow as a leader in the residential design market.

ALAN MASCORD DESIGN ASSOCIATES, INC.
Founded in 1983 as a local supplier to the building community, Mascord Design Associates of Portland, Oregon began to successfully publish plans nationally in 1985. The company's trademark is creating floor plans that work well and exhibit excellent traffic patterns.

STEPHEN FULLER, INC.
Stephen Fuller, Inc. was established by Stephen S. Fuller with the tenets of innovation, quality, originality and uncompromising architectural techniques in traditional and European homes. Especially popular throughout the Southeast, Stephen Fuller's plans are known for their extensive detail and thoughtful design.

BRELAND & FARMER
Designers Edsel Breland is owner and President of Breland & Farmer Designers, Inc., which he founded in 1973. The homes designed by Breland have a definite Southern signature, but fit perfectly in any region.

CHATHAM HOME PLANNING, INC.
Chatham Home Planning, Inc., founded over 15 years ago, is a professional member of the AIBD and the National Association of Home Builders. The company specializes in designs that have a strong historical look: Early American Southern cottages, Georgian classics, French Colonials, Southern Louisiana design and traditionals.

DESIGN BASICS, INC.
For nearly a decade, Design Basics, a nationally recognized home design service located in Omaha, has been developing plans for custom home builders. Since 1987, the firm has consistently appeared in Builder magazine, the official magazine of the National Association of Home Builders, as one of the top-selling designers.

DONALD A. GARDNER ARCHITECTS, INC.
The South Carolina firm of Donald A. Gardner was established in response to a growing demand for residential designs that reflect constantly changing lifestyles. The company's specialty is providing homes with refined, custom-style details and unique features such as passive-solar designs and open floor plans.

DRUMMOND DESIGNS
Drummond Designs has been involved in the business of residential architecture since 1973, with over 70,000 satisfied customers. Their primary goal is to offer consumers top-quality homes that meet or exceed most of the world's building code requirements.

FILLMORE DESIGN GROUP
Fillmore Design Group was formed in 1960 in Oklahoma City by Robert L. Fillmore, president and founder. "Our designs are often characterized by their European influence, by massive brick gables and by high-flowing, graceful rooflines," comments Fillmore.

FRANK BETZ ASSOCIATES, INC.
Frank Betz Associates, Inc. located in Smyrna, Georgia, is one of the nation's leaders in the design of stock plans. FBA, Inc. has provided builders and developers with home plans since 1977.

GREG MARQUIS & ASSOCIATES
The designs of Greg Marquis have proven to be popular not only across the United States, but internationally as well. He is a native of New Orleans, and many of his designs incorporate various features of the architectural style of South Louisiana.

HOME DESIGN SERVICES
Home Design Services is a full-service design firm that has specialized in residential and multi-family design for thirty years. The firm offers a full complement of services, taking a project from concept through completed construction documents.

HOME PLANNERS
Headquartered in Tucson, Arizona, with additional offices in Detroit, Home Planners is one of the longest-running and most successful home design firms in the United States. With over 2,500 designs in its portfolio, the company provides a wide range of styles, sizes and types of homes for the residential builder.

JANNIS VANN & ASSOCIATES
Jannis Vann is the President and principle designer of Jannis Vann & Associates, In. in Woodstock, Georgia. She has been in business since 1982 and has been publishing since 1987. Her collection showcases traditional, country and European exteriors with contemporary, open, flowing interiors.

LARRY E. BELK DESIGNS
Through the years, Larry E. Belk has worked with individuals and builders alike to provide a quality product. Flowing, open spaces and interesting angles define his interiors. Great emphasis is placed on providing views that showcase the natural environment.

LARRY JAMES & ASSOCIATES
Larry James has been designing classic homes since 1972. His goal is to create a collection of timeless designs. He likes to design new homes that trigger pleasant memories of times-gone-by. "Twenty-first Century living wrapped in a turn-of-the-Century package." He strives to design beautiful homes that will never fade.

NELSON DESIGN GROUP
Michael E. Nelson is a certified member of the American Institute of Building Designers, providing both custom and stock residential home plans. He designs homes that families enjoy now and which also bring maximum appraisal value at resale.

SELECT HOME DESIGNS
Select Home Designs has 50 years of experience delivering top-quality and affordable residential designs to the North American housing market. Since the company's inception in 1948, more than 350,000 new homes throughout North America and overseas have been built from Select's plans.

STUDER RESIDENTIAL DESIGNS, INC.
Studer Residential Designs, Inc. was founded in 1971. Brothers Mike and Paul Studer base their design strategy on the idea that families desire serviceable floor plans with skillfully detailed interiors and exteriors that reflect the homeowner's excellent taste, as well as providing lasting value to their homes.

THE HOUSING ASSOCIATES
Rodney L. Pfotenhauer opened the doors of The Housing Associates in 1987 as a design consultant and illustrator for the manufactured housing industry. Pfotenhauer's designs are characterized by carefully composed traditional exteriors with up-to-date interiors.

THE SATER DESIGN COLLECTION
The Sater Design Collection has a long established tradition of providing South Florida's most diverse and extraordinary custom designed homes. This is exemplified by over 50 national design awards, numerous magazine features and, most important, satisfied clients.